A Godward Life

JOHN PIPER

CLAUDD
£300

KINGSWAY PUBLICATIONS
EASTBOURNE

ISBN 0 85476 786 X

Designed and produced by Bookprint Creative Services
P.O. Box 827, BN21 3YJ, England for
KINGSWAY PUBLICATIONS
Lottbridge Drove, Eastbourne, E. Sussex BN23 6NT.
Printed in Great Britain.

Reproduced from the original text by arrangement with
Multnomah Publishers, Inc.

To
David and Karin Livingston
David and Sally Michael
Brad and Cindy Nelson

Precious partners in the Godward life
who have loved and labored for over ten years with me
at Bethlehem Baptist Church

OTHER BOOKS BY THE AUTHOR

LOVE YOUR ENEMIES
*Jesus' Love Command in the Synoptic Gospels
and the Early Christian Paraenesis*

THE JUSTIFICATION OF GOD
An Exegetical and Theological Study of Romans 9:1–23

DESIRING GOD
Meditations of a Christian Hedonist

THE SUPREMACY OF GOD IN PREACHING

THE PLEASURES OF GOD
Meditations on God's Delight in Being God

RECOVERING BIBLICAL MANHOOD AND WOMANHOOD
A Response to Evangelical Feminism
(edited with Wayne Grudem)

LET THE NATIONS BE GLAD
The Supremacy of God in Missions

A HUNGER FOR GOD
Desiring God through Fasting and Prayer

FUTURE GRACE
The Purifying Power of Living by Faith in...

CONTENTS

B ooks don't change people; paragraphs do. Sometimes even sentences. I can still remember an afternoon in the fall of 1968 in a bookstore on Colorado Avenue in Pasadena, California, as I read the first page of *The Weight of Glory* by C. S. Lewis. Even if I had not read another page, my life would have been changed forever. I can probably boil it down to two sentences: "We are halfhearted creatures, fooling about with drink and sex and ambition when infinite joy is offered us, like an ignorant child who wants to go on making mud pies in a slum because he cannot imagine what is meant by the offer of a holiday at the sea. We are far too easily pleased."[1] Almost thirty years later I still feel the shudder of discovery and the rush of light that passed through me. Nothing would ever be the same again. Just one paragraph and the decisive work was done.

This is not new. Sixteen hundred years earlier in August of 386, Saint Augustine was in spiritual turmoil. In a garden in Milan, Italy, he flung himself down beneath a fig tree and gave way to the tears which streamed from his eyes. "I tore my hair and hammered my forehead with my fists; I locked my fingers and hugged my knees." Then he heard "the sing-song voice of a boy or a girl, I cannot say, but again and again it repeated the refrain, 'Take it and read, take it and read.'" Augustine took this as a "divine command to open my book of Scripture and read the first passage on which my eyes should fall." He opened and read, "Not in reveling and drunkenness, not in lust and wantonness, not in quarrels and rivalries. Rather, arm yourselves with the Lord Jesus Christ, spend no more thought on nature and nature's appetites." In two sentences the knot was cut. "I had no wish to read more and no need to do so. For in an instant, as I came to the end of the sentence, it was as though the light of confidence flooded into my heart and all the darkness of doubt was dispelled."[2]

For Luther it was another one of Saint Paul's great sentences, Romans 1:16–17. For Jonathan Edwards it was 1 Timothy 1:17. For John Wesley it was the Preface to Luther's *Commentary on Romans*. And the list could go on. The point is that much reading of many books may be like the gathering of wood, but the fire blazes forth from a sentence. The mark is left on the mind not by the kindling of many pages, but by the red-hot iron of a sentence set on fire by God.

My prayer is that God might be pleased to take the short readings of this book and set a sentence or a paragraph on fire in your mind. The readings are only two or three pages long. They are not arranged in any topical order. What holds them together is a quest to savor the supremacy of God in all of life. Awakening and feeding that hunger is my aim.

ACKNOWLEDGMENTS

Thanks to Noël for reading and rereading these pages. I love being married to an editor who sees the flaw but savors the vision. Thanks to Steve Halliday for nursing my ten-year pregnancy with this idea and for your final midwifery. Thanks to Carol Steinbach who could, I think, do indexes in her sleep but still stays up late and meets merciless deadlines.

As I complete this book, David and Karin Livingston and Brad and Cindy Nelson complete ten years with me on the pastoral team at Bethlehem Baptist Church. Last year David and Sally Michael passed the same milestone. With overflowing gratitude to God, I dedicate *A Godward Life* to these patient partners in the Great Work.

David and Karin, thank you for twenty-three years of unwavering friendship, countless acts of Godward hospitality, relentless love for lost people, and ten years of ungrudging flexibility in burden-bearing love for all the saints. David and Sally, thank you for giving yourselves to the inner city before any of us dreamed that dream, and for bleeding Bible when you are pricked, and for knowing the difference between man-centered moralizing and God-centered meaning in the ministry of the Word to our children. Brad and Cindy, thank you for one of the rarest triumphs—ten years of faithful God-exalting ministry to teenagers—and for standing strong when the thanks were few, for weaving world missions into all your dreams, for building Bible and worship and witness into the lives of our youth, and for shepherding my four sons toward a passion for the supremacy of God.

I love you and the church we joyfully serve.

THE TEACHER, THE BIBLE, AND A GODWARD LIFE

I admit that it seems like a contradiction. I am tempting you to read something other than the Bible, namely, the book in your hands. Yet the point of this book is that reading the Bible itself is what really counts. I love the words of John Wesley: "I am a creature of a day. I am a spirit come from God, and returning to God. I want to know one thing: the way to heaven. God himself has condescended to teach me the way. He has written it down in a book. Oh, give me that book! At any price give me the book of God. Let me be a man of one book."[1] That book is the Bible, the precious Word of God. Only there do we find the way to heaven. Only there do we learn a Godward life.

But is it a contradiction? It would be but for one thing: The Bible itself tells us that God calls human teachers to explain and apply his Book. Barnabas, Simeon, Lucius, Manaen, and Saul were called "teachers" in the church of Antioch (Acts 13:1). Paul says in 1 Corinthians 12:28, "God has appointed in the church...teachers." In Ephesians 4:11 he says, "[Christ's] gifts were that some should be...teachers" (RSV). We also know from 1 Timothy 3:2 that overseers of the church are to be "able to teach." Therefore, human teachers are God's design for his people. Their job is to explain and apply the Bible so that people can understand it, believe it, and live it.

Some of these teachers write. I cannot speak for others, but for myself it is simply a matter of necessity. I cannot get clear what I think until I try to write it down. It is a fruitful infirmity. I am no John Calvin or Saint

Augustine, but I do say with them, "I count myself one of the number of those who write as they learn and learn as they write."[2]

But no matter how much we learn or say, teachers are not the Bible. We all see "through a glass, darkly" (1 Corinthians 13:12, KJV). "Let not many of you become teachers," James warns, "...For we all stumble in many ways" (James 3:1–2). It is sad but true that many ordinary Christians can say with the psalmist, "I have more insight than all my teachers, for Your testimonies are my meditation" (Psalm 119:99). It is the testimony of the Lord, not the teaching of man, that makes "wise the simple" (Psalm 19:7). Lots of teachers speak little Bible, but their words are like grass. "The grass withers, and the flower falls off, but the word of the LORD abides forever" (1 Peter 1:24–25).

Teaching that lasts—and books that last—will be the kind that "bleed Bible." C. H. Spurgeon said of John Bunyan, "Prick him anywhere; and you will find that his blood is Bibline, the very essence of the Bible flows from him. He cannot speak without quoting a text, for his soul is full of the Word of God."[3] God wills that there be human teachers of his divine Word, but he wills that teachers be "full of the Word of God." The Bible should "flow from them." Their blood—and their books—should be "Bibline."

Teaching is not the only gift in the church. The teaching mouth cannot say to the touching hand or the running foot, "I have no need of you" (1 Corinthians 12:21). There is a reciprocity: "Let him who is taught the word share all good things with him who teaches" (Galatians 6:6, RSV). That doesn't just mean "pay your preacher." It also means that the ones teaching need all the "good things" that the ones being taught are and do. I could not survive without the echo of truth in the love of my people.

This book is the overflow of my calling as a teacher in the church. For more than seventeen years I have preached to the flock at Bethlehem Baptist Church. But there is so much more to say than a preacher can say on Sundays and Wednesdays. The Bible is an inexhaustible spring of insight into God and his ways. So for those same seventeen years, I have written a letter to my people about once a week in what we affectionately call the *Star*. What you have in your hands is a collection of some of those meditations.

They are, by design, almost entirely meditations on Scripture. Some focus on personal or social application. Others focus on biblical explanation. In both cases the aim is to be implicitly and explicitly biblical. That is their only claim to abiding usefulness in life. Many of the weekly letters have vanished in the merciful forgetfulness of history. Others are too limited in focus to be of interest beyond our church. (Who would want to hear about our budget shortfall every December?) Yet I believe some of them have enough abiding relevance and biblical rootedness to magnify Christ beyond one church and one decade. Whether that is true, time will tell.

One of the great things about being at a church for seventeen years is that the mission of the church and the mission of the preacher tend to become one. This is true at Bethlehem. We exist to spread a passion for the supremacy of God in all things for the joy of all peoples. That is our church mission. It is also my life's mission. I try to measure all my speaking and writing and living by this standard: Does it spread a passion for the supremacy of God?

So, if there is a thread that holds these meditations together, it is the relentless aim of my life to savor the supremacy of God in all things. Hence the subtitle of this book. "Savoring" is the right word. The supremacy of God is not a mere idea. It is not even a mere magnificent fact. It is a sweet reality. God means not only to be seen as supreme, but also savored. "O taste and see that the LORD is good!" (Psalm 34:8, RSV). The supremacy of God's goodness and holiness and power and knowledge and justice and wisdom are honey for the heart's tongue and gold for the treasury of our soul. God means for us to know them with our minds and relish them with our hearts.

I feel about the supremacy of God the way Jonathan Edwards felt about the sovereignty of God: "God's absolute sovereignty...is what my mind seems to rest assured of, as much as of any thing that I see with my eyes....

The doctrine has very often appeared exceeding pleasant, bright, and sweet. Absolute sovereignty is what I love to ascribe to God.... God's sovereignty has ever appeared to me, [a] great part of his glory. It has often been my delight to approach God, and adore him as a sovereign God."[4]

This savoring is a deep and delightful duty. The Bible says, "Let all who seek You rejoice and be glad in You; and let those who love Your salvation say continually, 'Let God be magnified'" (Psalm 70:4). In fact, these two things—being glad in God and magnifying God—are not separate things. The banner over every meditation in this book is the conviction that God is most magnified in us when we are most satisfied in him.

When the psalmist says, "I will go to the altar of God, to God my exceeding joy; and I will praise thee with the lyre, O God, my God" (Psalm 43:4, RSV), he means that the extent of his joy is part of what makes his praise authentic. The supremacy of God's beauty and all-satisfying value is the final food for the savoring of our souls, not his gifts. There is no other way to account for words like these:

> *Though the fig tree do not blossom,*
> *nor fruit be on the vines,*
> *the produce of the olive fail*
> *and the fields yield no food,*
> *the flock be cut off from the fold*
> *and there be no herd in the stalls,*
> *yet I will rejoice in the LORD,*
> *I will joy in the God of my salvation.*
> (Habakkuk 3:17–18, RSV)

Only one thing accounts for the words of Paul when he said, "I count everything as loss because of the surpassing worth of knowing Christ Jesus my Lord" (Philippians 3:8)—Christ, the essence and image of God, is more to be desired than all his gifts. He is the end of our soul's savoring, not the means.

The gifts of God are good. They are to be received with thanks and joy, but they are not God, nor are they the soul's final food. They point away from themselves to God. "The heavens are telling the glory of God" (Psalm 19:1, RSV), and so is every other gift that we enjoy. Again and again I go back to Augustine's prayer to get my bearings: "He loves Thee too little, who loves anything together with Thee, which he loves not for Thy sake."[5] In these meditations I rejoice in many gifts of God, but I will have failed in my aim if the overall impact of this book does not move us from seeking his gifts to savoring himself.

A Godward life is a life lived for the sake of seeing and savoring and showing God in all things. "Whether you eat or drink, or whatever you do, do all to the glory of God" (1 Corinthians 10:31, RSV), and the glory is most fully manifest when its all-satisfying sweetness frees us to suffer—even joyfully—for the sake of his name. "They went on their way from the presence of the Council, rejoicing that they had been considered worthy to suffer shame for His name" (Acts 5:41).

A Godward life is lived with a constant view to the reward of eternal fellowship with God. This Godward hope is the power that unleashes sacrificial love (Colossians 1:4–5) in a restless world that wants it all now. "When you give a reception, invite the poor, the crippled, the lame, the blind, and you will be blessed, since they do not have the means to repay you; for you will be repaid at the resurrection of the righteous" (Luke 14:13–14). They look to the reward of God's fellowship and they love. This is a Godward life. "You showed sympathy to the prisoners and accepted joyfully the seizure of your property, knowing that you have for yourselves a better possession and a lasting one" (Hebrews 10:34). They looked to the reward of God's fellowship and loved. This is a Godward life.

The only hope that such a reward could be inherited by sinners like us is the death of Christ in our place. "Christ also died for sins once for all, the just for the unjust, in order that He might bring us to God" (1 Peter 3:18). Christ died in our place so that sinners might feast on the holiness of God without being destroyed. This is our only hope. The just died for the unjust. Without this, a Godward life would be impossible and, if possible, suicidal. Until the wrath of God is averted from my sinful soul by the death of Christ, God is a consuming fire. Afterward, by faith, he is the light of life and the end of all my desires. This is the final testimony of a Godward life:

> *Whom have I in heaven but thee?*
> *And there is nothing upon earth that I desire besides thee.*
> *My flesh and my heart may fail,*
> *but God is the strength of my heart and my portion for ever.*
> (Psalm 73:25–26, RSV)

I

Loving God
for Who He Is

◆◈◆

A Pastor's Perspective

O ne of the most important discoveries I have ever made is this
truth: God is most glorified in me when I am most satisfied in
him. This is the motor that drives my ministry as a pastor. It
affects everything I do.

Whether I eat or drink or preach or counsel or whatever I do, my aim
is to glorify God by the way I do it (1 Corinthians 10:31). This means my
aim is to do it in a way that shows how the glory of God has satisfied the
longings of my heart. If my preaching betrayed that God had not even met
my own needs, it would be fraudulent. If Christ were not the satisfaction of
my heart, would people really believe me when I herald his words, "I am
the bread of life; he who comes to me shall not hunger, and he who believes
in me shall never thirst" (John 6:35, RSV)?

The glory of bread is that it satisfies. The glory of living water is
that it quenches thirst. We do not honor the refreshing, self-replenishing,
pure water of a mountain spring by lugging buckets of water up the
path to make our contributions from the ponds below. We honor the
spring by feeling thirsty, getting down on our knees, and drinking with
joy. Then we say, "Ahhhh!" (that's worship!), and we go on our journey
in the strength of the fountain (that's service). The mountain spring is
glorified most when we are most satisfied with its water.

Tragically, most of us have been taught that duty, not delight, is the way to glorify God. We have not been taught that delight in God is our duty! Being satisfied in God is not an optional add-on to the real stuff of Christian duty. It is the most basic demand of all. "Delight yourself in the LORD" (Psalm 37:4) is not a suggestion, but a command. So are: "Serve the LORD with gladness" (Psalm 100:2), and, "Rejoice in the Lord always" (Philippians 4:4).

The burden of my ministry is to make plain to others that the "steadfast love [of the Lord] is better than life" (Psalm 63:3, RSV). If it is better than life, it is better than all that life in this world offers. This means that what satisfies are not the gifts of God, but the glory of God—the glory of his love, the glory of his power, the glory of his wisdom, holiness, justice, goodness, and truth.

This is why the psalmist Asaph cried out, "Whom have I in heaven but you? Besides you I desire nothing on earth. My flesh and my heart may fail, but God is the strength of my heart and my portion for ever" (Psalm 73:25–26). Nothing on the earth—none of God's good gifts of creation— could satisfy Asaph's heart. Only God could. This is what David meant when he said to the Lord, "You are my Lord; I have no good besides you" (Psalm 16:2).

David and Asaph teach us by their own God-centered longings that God's gifts of health, wealth, and prosperity do not satisfy. Only God does. It would be presumptuous not to thank him for his gifts ("Forget not all his benefits" [Psalm 103:2, RSV]), but it would be idolatry to call the gladness we get from them, love for God. When David said to the Lord, "In your presence is fullness of joy, in your right hand there are pleasures forever" (Psalm 16:11), he meant that nearness to God himself is the only all-satisfying experience of the universe.

It is not for God's gifts that David yearns like a heartsick lover. "As a deer pants for the water brooks, so my soul pants for you, O God. My soul thirsts for God, for the living God" (Psalm 42:1–2). What David wants to experience is a revelation of the power and the glory of God: "O God, you are my God, I seek you, my soul thirsts for you; my flesh faints for you, as in a dry and weary land where there is no water. So I have looked upon you in the sanctuary, beholding your power and glory" (Psalm 63:1–2, NRSV). Only God will satisfy a heart like David's, and David was a man after God's own heart. That's the way we were created to be.

This is the essence of what it means to love God—to be satisfied in him. In him! Loving God may include obeying all his commands; it may include believing all his Word; it may include thanking him for all his gifts; but the essence of loving God is enjoying all he is. It is this enjoyment of God that glorifies his worth most fully, especially when all around our soul gives way.

We all know this intuitively as well as from Scripture. Do we feel most honored by the love of those who serve us from the constraints of duty, or from the delights of fellowship? My wife is most honored when I say, "It makes me happy to spend time with you." My happiness is the echo of her excellence. So it is with God. He is most glorified in us when we are most satisfied in him.

None of us has arrived at perfect satisfaction in God. I grieve often over the murmuring of my heart at the loss of worldly comforts, but I have tasted that the Lord is good. By God's grace I now know the fountain of everlasting joy, and so I love to spend my days luring people into joy until they say with me, "One thing have I asked of the LORD, that will I seek after; that I may dwell in the house of the LORD all the days of my life, to behold the beauty of the LORD, and to inquire in his temple" (Psalm 27:4, RSV). ❧

2

TODAY'S MERCIES
FOR TODAY'S TROUBLES

——◆◆◆——

Meditation on Matthew 6:34

*Do not be anxious about tomorrow, for tomorrow will be anxious for itself.
Sufficient for the day is its own trouble.* (author's translation)

P art of saving faith is the assurance that you will have faith tomorrow.
Trusting Christ today includes trusting him to give you tomorrow's
trust when tomorrow comes. Often we feel today like our reservoir
of strength is not going to last for another day. The fact is, it won't. Today's
resources are for today, and part of those resources is the confidence that
new resources will be given tomorrow.

The basis of this assurance is the wonderful teaching of the Bible that
God assigns only as much trouble to each day as that day can bear. God will
not let his children be tested in any given day beyond what his mercy for that
day will sustain. That's what Paul means when he says, "No test has over-
taken you but such as is common to man; and God is faithful, who will not
allow you to be tested beyond what you are able, but with the test will provide the way of escape also, that you may be able to endure it" (1 Corinthians
10:13, author's translation).

The old Swedish hymn "Day by Day" is based on Deuteronomy
33:25: "As your days, so shall your strength be." It gives us the same
assurance:

Day by day, and with each passing moment,
strength I find to meet my trials here;
Trusting in my Father's wise bestowment,
I've no cause for worry or for fear.

The "Father's wise bestowment" is the amount of trouble that we can bear each day—and no more:

He whose heart is kind beyond all measure
Gives unto each day what he deems best
Lovingly its part of pain and pleasure,
Mingling toil with peace and rest.

With every day's measure of pain, he gives new mercies. This is the point of Lamentations 3:22–23, "The LORD's lovingkindnesses indeed never cease, for His compassions never fail. They are new every morning; great is Your faithfulness."

God's mercies are new every morning because each day has enough mercy in it only for that day. This is why we tend to despair when we think that we may have to bear tomorrow's load on today's resources. God wants us to know that we won't. Today's mercies are for today's troubles. Tomorrow's mercies are for tomorrow's troubles.

Sometimes we wonder if we will have the mercy to stand in terrible testing. Yes, we will. Peter says, "If you are reviled for the name of Christ, you are blessed, because the Spirit of glory and of God rests on you" (1 Peter 4:14). When the reviling comes, the Spirit of glory comes. It happened for Stephen as he was being stoned (Acts 7:55–60). It will happen for you. When the Spirit and the glory are needed, they will come.

The manna in the wilderness was given one day at a time. There was no storing up. That is the way we must depend on God's mercy. You do not receive today the strength to bear tomorrow's burdens. You are given mercies today for today's troubles. Tomorrow the mercies will be new. "God is faithful, by whom you were called into the fellowship of his Son, Jesus Christ our Lord" (1 Corinthians 1:9, RSV). "Faithful is He who calls you, and He also will act!" (1 Thessalonians 5:24, author's translation). ➴

3

GOD WAS UP ALL NIGHT

Meditation on Psalm 121:3

He will not let your foot be moved,
he who keeps you will not slumber. (RSV)

The worship team and prayer teams gathered around me and prayed for me before I preached. Our worship leader remarked that God was up all night working on this service and the people who would be there—including me. He thanked the Lord for this and praised him for his unwearying work on our behalf.

O what a truth this is! For every Christian. Let me encourage you with it. Psalm 121:2–3 says it plainly: "My help comes from the LORD, who made heaven and earth. He will not let your foot be moved, he who keeps you will not slumber." The one who helps you never sleeps. He stays up all night, every night.

Do you need help? I do. Where do you look for help? When the psalmist lifted up his eyes to the hills and asked, "From where does my help come?" he answered, "My help comes from the Lord"—not from the hills, but from the God who made the hills. So he reminded himself of two great truths: One is that God is a mighty Creator over all the problems of life; the other is that God never sleeps.

God is a tireless worker. Think of God as a worker in your life. Yes, it is amazing. We are prone to think of ourselves as workers in God's life. But the Bible wants us first to be amazed that God is a worker in our lives: "From of old no one has heard or perceived by the ear, no eye has seen a

God besides thee, who works for those who wait for him" (Isaiah 64:4, RSV).

God is working for us around the clock. He does not take days off, and he does not sleep. In fact, he is so eager to work for us that he goes around looking for more work to do for people who will trust him: "The eyes of the LORD run to and fro throughout the whole earth, to show his might in behalf of those whose heart is whole toward him" (2 Chronicles 16:9, RSV).

God loves to show his tireless power and wisdom and goodness by working for people who trust him. Jesus himself is the clearest revelation of this truth: "The Son of man also came not to be served but to serve" (Mark 10:45, RSV). Jesus works for his followers. He serves them. This is a revelation of the way God is.

He worked for us when he was on the earth, and he keeps on working now that he is risen and reigning with the Father in heaven. Paul experienced this in a powerful way: "I will not venture to speak of anything except what Christ has wrought through me to win obedience from the Gentiles, by word and deed" (Romans 15:18, RSV). Christ worked for Paul all his life. At the very end of his life, in his last letter, he said, "The Lord stood by me and gave me strength to proclaim the message fully" (2 Timothy 4:17, RSV). Through all his life Paul could say, "I can do all things in him who strengthens me" (Philippians 4:13, RSV). Jesus is the great worker, the great strength-giver.

The eagerness of God to work for us is astonishing. His eyes are running to and fro, looking for opportunities to work for people who trust him (2 Chronicles 16:9). He is pursuing us with goodness and mercy all our days (Psalm 23:6, literally "pursue" not just "follow"). He is not just waiting for us to get his help; he is seeking ways to give us help. He is doing this with overflowing eagerness. "I will not turn away from doing good to them; and I will put the fear of me in their hearts, that they may not turn from me. I will rejoice in doing them good...with all my heart and all my soul" (Jeremiah 32:40–41, RSV).

No wonder he stays up all night! With all his heart and with all his soul he works for those who wait for him and trust him. This is what we must believe—really believe—in order to rejoice always (Philippians 4:4) and give thanks for everything (Ephesians 5:20) and have the peace that passes understanding (Philippians 4:7) and be anxious for nothing (Philippians 4:6) and hate our lives in this world (John 12:25) and love our neighbor as we love ourselves (Matthew 22:39).

What a truth! What a reality! God is up all night and all day to work for those who wait for him. ✒

4

WHEN WORDS ARE WIND

Meditation on Job 6:26

Do you think that you can reprove words,
when the speech of a despairing man is wind? (RSV)

W hen in grief and pain and despair, people often say things they would not otherwise say. They paint reality with darker strokes than they will paint it tomorrow, when the sun comes up. They sing in minor keys and talk as though that were the only music. They see only clouds and speak as if there were no sky.

They say, "Where is God?" Or, "There is no use in going on." Or, "Nothing makes any sense." Or, "There's no hope for me." Or, "If God were good, this couldn't have happened."

What shall we do with these words?

Job says that we do not need to reprove them. These words are wind, or literally, "for the wind." They will be quickly blown away. There will come a turn in circumstances, and the despairing person will waken from the dark night and regret the hasty words.

Therefore, let us not spend our time and energy reproving such words. They will be blown away of themselves, on the wind. One need not clip the leaves in autumn; it is a wasted effort. They will soon scatter to the four winds.

How quickly we are given to defending God—or sometimes the truth—from words that are for the wind alone. There are enough words, premeditated and studied, that need our rebuttal, but not every despairing heresy blurted out in the hour of agony needs to be answered. If we had discernment, we could tell the difference between the words with roots and the words blowing in the wind.

There are words with roots in deep error and deep evil. But not all gray words get their color from a black heart. Some are colored mainly by the pain, the despair. What you hear is not the deepest thing within. There is something real within, where the words come from, but it is temporary—like a passing infection—real, painful, but not the true person.

Let us learn to discern whether the words spoken against us or against God or against the truth are merely for the wind—spoken not from the soul, but from the sore. If they are for the wind, let us wait in silence and not reprove. Restoring the soul, not reproving the sore, is the aim of our love. ❧

5

THE SLOW FIRES
OF MISERY

Enduring the Pain of a Flawed Marriage

braham Lincoln's marriage was a mess, and accepting the pain
brought deep strength in the long run.

I write this not because it is wrong to seek refuge from physical
abuse, but because, short of that, millions of marriages end over the agony
of heartbreaking disappointments and frustrations. They do not need to.
There is much to gain in embracing the pain for Christ and his kingdom.

Our culture has made divorce acceptable and therefore easier to justify
on the basis of emotional pain. Historically, the misery of painful emotions
was not a sanction for divorce in most cultures. Marriage durability—with
or without emotional pain—was valued above emotional tranquillity for the
sake of the children, the stability of society, and in the case of Christians, for
the glory of Christ. In Christianity such rugged, enduring marriages,
through pain and heartache, are rooted in the marriage of God to his rebellious people whom he has never finally cast off.

"'Your husband is your Maker.... For the LORD has called you, like a
wife forsaken and grieved in spirit, even like a wife of one's youth when she
is rejected,' says your God. 'For a brief moment I forsook you, but with great
compassion I will gather you'" (Isaiah 54:5–7).

Abraham Lincoln brought debilities to his marriage with Mary Todd.
He was emotionally withdrawn and prized reason over passion. She said
that he "was not a demonstrative man.... When he felt most deeply, he

expressed the least." He was absent, emotionally or physically, most of the time. For years before his presidency, he spent four months each year away from home on the judicial circuit. He was indulgent with the children and left their management almost entirely to his wife.

Mary often flew into rages.

She pushed Lincoln relentlessly to seek high public office; she complained endlessly about poverty; she overran her budget shamelessly, both in Springfield and in the White House; she abused servants as if they were slaves (and ragged on Lincoln when he tried to pay them extra on the side); she assaulted him on more than one occasion (with firewood, with potatoes); she probably once chased him with a knife through their backyard in Springfield; and she treated his casual contacts with attractive females as a direct threat, while herself flirting constantly and dressing to kill. A regular visitor to the White House wrote of Mrs. Lincoln that "she was vain, passionately fond of dress and wore her dresses shorter at the top and longer at the train than even fashions demanded. She had great pride in her elegant neck and bust, and grieved the president greatly by her constant display of her person and her fine clothes."[1]

It was a pain-filled marriage. The familiar lines in his face and the somber countenance reveal more than the stress of civil war. But the two stayed married. They kept at least that part of their vows. They embraced the pain, even if they could not (or would not) remove it.

What was the gain? God will give the final answer, but here are two historical assessments. (1) How was it that Lincoln, when president, could work so effectively with the rampant egos who filled his administration? "The long years of dealing with his tempestuous wife helped prepare Lincoln for handling the difficult people he encountered as president." In other words, a whole nation benefited from his embracing the pain. (2) "Over the slow fires of misery that he learned to keep banked and under heavy pressure deep within him, his innate qualities of patience, tolerance, forbearance, and forgiveness were tempered and refined." America can be glad that Lincoln did not run from the fires of misery in his marriage. There were resources for healing he did not know, and short of healing, embracing the fire is better than escape.

Increasingly, contemporary culture assumes the opposite. Pain-free relationships are assumed as a right. But God promises his people something better. "Blessed is the man who endures trial, for when he has stood the test he will receive the crown of life which God has promised to those who love him" (James 1:12 , RSV). ∾

6

FUTURE GRACE

Pondering the Power We Need for Obedience

G ratitude is a joyful emotion for worship but a dangerous motive for obedience. We are commanded in no uncertain terms to be thankful. "And let the peace of Christ rule in your hearts.... And be thankful" (Colossians 3:15, RSV). "In everything give thanks; for this is God's will for you in Christ Jesus" (1 Thessalonians 5:18). How can we not be thankful when we owe everything to God?

But when it comes to obedience, gratitude is a dangerous motive. It tends to get expressed in debtors' terms—or what I sometimes call the debtor's ethic. For example, "Look how much God has done for you. Shouldn't you, out of gratitude, do much for him?" Or, "You owe God everything that you are and have. What have you done for him in return?"

I have at least three problems with this kind of motivation. First, it is impossible to pay God back for all the grace he has given us. We can't even begin to pay him back, because Romans 11:35-36 says, "Who has given a gift to him [God] that he might be repaid? [Answer: nobody.] For from him and through him and to him are all things. To him be glory for ever." We can't pay him back because he already owns all we have to give him.

Second, even if we succeeded in paying him back for all his grace to us, we would only succeed in turning grace into a business transaction. If we can pay him back, it was not grace. "To the one who works, his wage is not reckoned as grace, but as what is due" (Romans 4:4, author's translation). If you try to do wage negotiations with God, you nullify grace. If friends try to show you a special favor of love by having you over for dinner, and you end the evening by saying that you will pay them back by having them over next week, you nullify their grace and turn it into a trade. God does not like to have his grace nullified. He likes to have it glorified (Ephesians 1:6, 12, 14).

Third, focusing on gratitude as an empowerment for obedience tends to overlook the crucial importance of future grace. Gratitude looks back to grace received in the past and feels thankful. Faith looks forward to grace promised in the future and feels hopeful. "Faith is the assurance of things hoped for" (Hebrews 11:1, RSV).

This faith in future grace is the power for obedience that preserves the gracious quality of human obedience. Obedience does not consist in paying God back and thus turning grace into a trade. Obedience comes from trusting in God for more grace—future grace—and thus magnifying the infinite resources of God's love and power. "I worked harder than any of them, though it was not I, but the grace of God which is with me" (1 Corinthians 15:10, RSV). The grace that enabled Paul to work hard in a life of obedience was the daily arrival of fresh supplies of grace. This is what faith trusts in—the continuing arrivals of grace. Faith looks to the promises like, I will be with you wherever you go (Joshua 1:9), and in that confidence faith ventures, in obedience, to take the land.

The biblical role of past grace—especially the cross—is to guarantee the certainty of future grace: "He who did not spare his own Son but gave him up for us all [past grace], will he not also freely give us all things with him [future grace]?" (Romans 8:32, RSV). Trusting in future grace is the enabling strength of our obedience. The more we trust in future grace, the more we give God the opportunity in our lives to show the glory of his inexhaustible grace. So take a promise of future grace and do some radical act of obedience on it. God will be mightily honored.[2] ❧

7

GIFT AND GRIT

(IN THAT ORDER)

Thoughts on Human Effort and Divine Enabling

Question: If God is the one who gives our varied measures of faith, should we pursue greater faith?

Answer: Yes! With all our might! Through prayer, word, fellowship, and obedience.

Faith is a gift of God. Romans 12:3 says, "Think with sober judgment, each according to the measure of faith which God has assigned to him" (RSV). God measures to each believer a measure of faith. Ephesians 2:8 says, "By grace you have been saved through faith; and this is not your own doing, it is the gift of God" (RSV). The word "this" refers to the whole act of God, including the accomplishment of salvation on the cross and the application of salvation through faith. Philippians 1:29 says, "To you it has been granted for Christ's sake, not only to believe on Him, but also to suffer for His sake." Believing and suffering are both gifts from God. Similarly repentance (the flip side of faith) is called a gift of God (2 Timothy 2:25; Acts 11:18). The revelation of Christ to the heart that makes faith possible is also a gift (Matthew 16:17; 2 Corinthians 4:4, 6).

This does not mean faith is static or that we should not pursue it more and more. In 2 Thessalonians 1:3, Paul says, "Your faith is growing abundantly, and the love of every one of you for one another." In 2 Corinthians 10:15, Paul says that he hopes their faith will "increase."

Therefore it is clear that faith should grow and not remain static. The fact that God gave you yesterday's level of faith does not mean that his will for you today is the same measure of faith. His purpose for you today may be far greater faith. His command is to "trust in him at all times" (Psalm 62:8, RSV) and to "grow in the grace and knowledge of our Lord and Savior Jesus Christ" (2 Peter 3:18, RSV).

God commands what he wills and grants in measure what he commands, but we should always pursue what he commands. He says, "Work out your salvation...for it is God who is at work in you, both to will and to work for His good pleasure" (Philippians 2:12–13). God does not say, "Since I work, you shouldn't." He says, "Because I do, you can." God's gift does not replace our effort; it enables and carries it.

We say with Paul, "[God's] grace toward me was not in vain. On the contrary I worked..." (1 Corinthians 15:10, RSV). The gift of grace produced the grit of hard work. It is not the other way around. He goes on, "I worked harder than any of them, though it was not I, but the grace of God which is with me." Even Paul's working is a gift of grace. Yes, it feels like our effort. It is an effort! But that is not all it is. That is not what it is at root. If it is virtuous, it is God's "working in us to will and to do his good pleasure." God "fulfill[s] every good resolve and work of faith by his power" (2 Thessalonians 1:11, RSV). He equips us "with everything good that [we] may do his will, working in [us] that which is pleasing in his sight" (Hebrews 13:21, RSV).

Therefore let us press on to the greatest faith possible with all the means of grace God has given. Let us be like Paul and strive "with all the energy which he mightily inspires within [us]" (Colossians 1:29, RSV). And when we have labored, let us not think more highly of ourselves than is necessary, but say with Paul, "I will not venture to speak of anything except what Christ has wrought through me...by the power of the Holy Spirit" (Romans 15:18–19, RSV). There is a place for grit in the Christian life ("I worked hard"), but it is preceded by and enabled by gift ("It was the grace of God"). Therefore all grit is living by faith in future grace. ❧

8

DOES IT PAY
TO VISIT VERMIN?

Meditation on James 1:27

*Pure and undefiled religion in the sight of
our God and Father is this:
to visit orphans and widows in their distress,
and to keep oneself unstained by the world.*

Local businessmen in Brazil call them "vermin." Garbage. "If we let them grow up, they will be criminals, a blight on our society." There are an estimated twelve million homeless children on the streets of Brazil. Their parents lost them in the crowds, put them out, died. However they got there, they are there. They beg, they steal, they sell their bodies. They eat garbage. They start scared and end scarred, hard, and dead.

Some policemen and others moonlight by contracting to kill street children so that they will not menace the city. In 1992 an average of four hundred of these children were killed monthly in Brazil.

It's the same in other big cities. The Philippine government estimates that there are fifteen thousand child prostitutes in Manila between the ages of nine and twelve. One estimate suggests that in Thailand there are eight hundred thousand girls between twelve and sixteen years old involved in prostitution.

Is your first thought merely human? Like, "If I can barely rear my own children to walk worthy of the gospel, what hope would there be to change the lives of these street kids?" Or, "If it takes ten thousand dollars' worth of Christian counseling to stabilize a mature American Christian who was sexually abused, what in the world would we do with thousands of adolescents who knew nothing but abuse and lawlessness and violence on the streets?"

Do you find yourself looking (in good American fashion) at the bottom line and saying, "The turnaround on this investment would not be good"? Or, "The growth potential in planting churches among street kids is not very great. There are too many obstacles."

Shift your thinking a minute (or a lifetime). What about the widow who put in her last two pennies? Jesus said she gave more than anyone (Luke 21:3). What about John the Baptist who lost his head on a dancer's whim and never did a miracle? Jesus said, "Among those born of women there has arisen no one greater than John" (Matthew 11:11, RSV). What about the poor in spirit? Theirs is the kingdom of heaven. What about the meek? They inherit the earth. What about those who receive one child in the name of Jesus? At that moment they receive God (Mark 9:37).

What effect does it have on your longings when you think that God says true religion is to visit orphans (James 1:27)?

The effect it has on me is to make me want to love like Jesus loved and not always be thinking of the earthly payoff. Face it. A few kids are cute, but most street kids will be thankless, rude, dirty, diseased, scar-faced, shifty-eyed, lice-infested, suspicious, smelly, and have rotten teeth. If we minister mainly for the earthly payoff, we will burn out in a year.

Jesus did not say, "True religion is converting orphans." He did not say, "True religion is making orphans mature and successful adults." He said, "True religion is visiting orphans." Results are God's business alone. Obedience is ours by his grace. More specifically, by faith in future grace. Perhaps when we grasp this, we will be freed from our earthbound way of thinking and released to minister to the ones who are least likely to thank us.[3]

9

Is Zeal for Good Praised or Persecuted?

—◈◈◈—

Meditation on 1 Peter 3:13–16

> *Now who is there to harm you if you are zealous*
> *for what is right? But even if you do suffer for righteousness' sake,*
> *you will be blessed. Have no fear of them, nor be troubled,*
> *but in your hearts reverence Christ as Lord. Always be*
> *prepared to make a defense to any one who calls you to account for the hope*
> *that is in you, yet do it with gentleness and reverence;*
> *and keep your conscience clear, so that, when you are abused, those who revile*
> *your good behavior in Christ may be put to shame. (RSV)*

Now who is there to harm you if you are zealous for what is right? (Verse 13)

Christians should be "zealots for the good." Can you do something good for someone? Can you help him? Can you change something bad and make it good? Then do it—and do it with zeal!

Will you be harmed? Not ultimately. "If God is for us, who can be against us?" (Romans 8:31). "The Lord is my helper, I will not fear. What can man do to me?" (Hebrews 13:6). "Do not fear those who kill the body, and after that have no more that they can do.... Are not five sparrows sold for two pennies? And not one of them is forgotten before God. Why, even the hairs of your head are all numbered. Fear not, you are of more value than many sparrows" (Luke 12:4, 6–7, RSV).

Verse 14a: *But even if you do suffer for righteousness' sake, you will be blessed.*

Yes, there will be opposition, even if you are zealous for what is good and righteous, but never forget the Beatitudes: "Blessed are those who are persecuted for righteousness' sake, for theirs is the kingdom of heaven" (Matthew 5:10, RSV).

Verses 14b–15a: *Have no fear of them, nor be troubled, but in your hearts reverence Christ as Lord.*

You pay homage to what you fear. So cowering in fear before men is the opposite of bowing in reverence before the Lord of glory.

Verse 15b: *Always be prepared to make a defense to any one who calls you to account for the hope that is in you, yet do it with gentleness and reverence.*

Why would they ask about hope? Because the craving for happiness in the human heart is so strong that the only explanation for our willingness to suffer for righteousness' sake must be some hope on the other side. That's exactly what Jesus said: "Rejoice and be glad, for your reward is great in heaven" (Matthew 5:12, RSV). Hope sustains zeal for the good under persecution. People know that intuitively. So they ask about hope.

Verse 16: *And keep your conscience clear, so that, when you are abused, those who revile your good behavior in Christ may be put to shame.*

There is a lag between the time when a good deed is done and the time when the deed is recognized as good by our opponents. First, they "revile" our deed. Then sometime later, they are "put to shame." How much later? Perhaps not until the final judgment will some people see things as they really are. For some, that recognition may come sooner. Peter describes this change from reviling to glorifying God: "Maintain good conduct among the

Gentiles, so that in case they speak against you as wrongdoers, they may see your good deeds and glorify God on the day of visitation" (1 Peter 2:12, RSV). So, for a while they slander us as wrongdoers, but then later they will glorify God for the very good deeds they once reviled. This may mean they are converted here, or it may mean they are constrained at the judgment.

Ours is not to make that final determination. Ours is to speak from a clear conscience and give a gentle and reverent answer.

Do you have zeal for a worthy cause? Is there some good for which you are being slandered? Or is your routine so harmless in this evil world that it fits nicely with the way things are going, and so nobody is asking you anything? ∿

VIOLENCE, UGLINESS, FAITH, AND GRATITUDE

Thoughts on Arrogance and Sacrilege

I n the omnipotent mercy of God, it might turn around. There have been despairing moments in history that looked like the end was near, but God intervened and rolled back the tidal wave of wickedness. Nevertheless, it seems today that week after week new forms of violence come to the surface.

Our newspaper documents how more and more teenage boys ridicule their girlfriends in public and hit them in private. Advocates of family values tell of the increasing violence of some special interest groups, like the one that overpowered the police in San Francisco, smashed windows where the police were retreating, and threw shards of broken glass like flying discs at the officers. Teenage murder rates increased 232 percent from 1950 to 1990, and murder has become the leading cause of death among fifteen- to nineteen-year-old minority youths.

Television's heroes are increasingly vicious in their sacrilege. One actress not only opens a show with a lesbian kiss, but says, concerning her role in a movie, "I'm an atheist, so it was actually a joy. Spitting on Christ was a great deal of fun—especially for me, being a woman.... I can't embrace a male god who has persecuted female sexuality throughout the ages."

The Bible warns that "in the last days there will come times of stress. For men will be lovers of self, lovers of money, proud, arrogant, abusive, disobedient to their parents, ungrateful..." (2 Timothy 3:1–2, RSV). Notice how ingratitude goes with pride, abuse, and insubordination. This is worth pondering.

In another place Paul says, "Let there be no obscenity, foolish talk or coarse joking...but rather thanksgiving" (Ephesians 5:4). So it seems that "thanksgiving" is somehow the opposite of ugliness and violence.

The reason this is so is that the feeling of gratitude, like faith in God's promises, is a humble feeling, not a proud one. It is other-exalting, not self-exalting. It calls attention to our need and the goodwill of another. It is glad-hearted, not angry or bitter.

The key to unlocking a heart of gratitude and overcoming bitterness, ugliness, disrespect, and violence is a strong sense of dependence on God the Creator, Sustainer, Provider, and Hope-Giver. If we do not believe that we are deeply dependent on God for all we have or hope to have, then the very spring of gratitude and faith runs dry. Remembering our dependence on past mercies kindles gratitude. Pondering the promises of tomorrow's mercies kindles faith. Gratitude is past-oriented dependence; faith is future-oriented dependence. Both forms of dependence are humble, self-forgetting, and God-exalting. That is one reason they are the opposite of meanspiritedness and violence.

The rise of violence, sacrilege, ugliness, insubordination is a God-issue. The basic issue is a failure to feel dependence on God with gratitude toward the past and faith toward the future. When the high springs of gratitude and faith toward God dry up at the top of the mountain, soon all the pools of happy thankfulness and courage begin to dry up farther down. When gratitude and faith go, the sovereignty of the self condones more and more corruption for its pleasure.

O that we might guard our hearts from the arrogance that unleashes a thousand evils in the world! Humble gratitude for all God has done for us in the past, and humble trust in all he promises to do for us in the future—this is the key. ❧

II

YOU SHALL TAKE UP YOUR TAMBOURINES

———◆◆◆———

On the Whole Counsel of God:
A Hedonistic Defense of Doctrine

I have loved you with an everlasting love;
Therefore I have drawn you with lovingkindness....
Again you will take up your tambourines,
And go forth to the dances of the merrymakers.
JEREMIAH 31:3–4

In my preaching I stress doctrine. One reason is that the apostle Paul stressed doctrine. It was his mission strategy. When he had finished his church-planting labor in Ephesus, he said, "I am innocent of the blood of all of you, for I did not shrink from declaring to you the whole counsel of God" (Acts 20:26, RSV). So on Sundays I preach doctrine.

Today is Monday. The sun is shining. The sky is deep-sea blue. The temperature is in the seventies. The wind is gentle. The air is crystal clear and clean. The tulips are halfway up. At times like this you want to leap for joy, not study doctrine.

Me too.

I am not interested in a religion that offers anything less than fullness of joy and pleasures for evermore (Psalm 16:11). I don't just mean deep, weighty delights that come in moments of heart-heaving discoveries of God's faithfulness in tragedy. I do mean that! There is too much cancer and killing in the world not to mean that—until the curse is finally lifted—but not just that.

I also mean what baby cows do: "You shall go forth leaping like calves from the stall" (Malachi 4:2, RSV). I love the April sunshine and the warmth on my skin and the breeze in my face. I love the yelping of my little ones as they come home from school, testing their high notes. I love the fast-fading, uninhibited affection of preadolescents. I love the exuberance of some of the young people in my church unleashed in drama for Jesus' sake.

Exuberance!

That's a rare word, isn't it? We grow out of it about eleven, I think. We try to find it again in a hundred artificial ways, but it's gone. We've grown up. We know too much now.

Or could it be that we know too little? Could it be that we have grown up halfway? Out of the naive exuberance of childhood into the cloud-covered realism of half-adulthood.

Reenter doctrine. The whole counsel of God. What is it?

It's the new foundation of exuberance when the naiveté of childhood won't work anymore, but it's different. The old foundation could not handle reality, but the new foundation sees everything—cancer, nuclear weapons, environmental crises, terrorism, abortion, burned-out cities, broken marriages, bummed-out kids, depression—it sees and feels everything. Nevertheless, it does not break or sink—not in the hospital and not in jail.

This is the whole counsel of God. If you intend to dance in the April sun, just remember, either you do it with your eyes closed or you do it on the great granite tableland of the whole counsel of God, also known as doctrine.

"Blessed are you when men hate you, and when they exclude you and revile you, and cast out your name as evil, on account of the Son of man! Rejoice in that day, and leap for joy, for behold_____" (Luke 6:22–23). Yes, the blank is filled with "your reward is great in heaven," but how you come to hope in this reward, how this reward was purchased for you by

Christ, what the nature of faith is that lays hold on this reward, what the content of the reward is, and how you maintain daily confidence in the surety of the reward—that is all doctrine. Without it, we will not leap for long. And surely not in jail. ❧

IT IS GREAT GAIN TO DIE

FIVE REASONS WHY

———

Meditation on Philippians 1:21

For to me to live is Christ, and to die is gain. (RSV)

For every morbid person who thinks pathologically about death, there are probably a million people who don't think about it enough. When Moses contemplated the brevity of life he prayed, "Teach us to number our days" (Psalm 90:12, RSV). It is good to ponder our death. We should live well that we might die well. Part of living well is learning why death is gain. Here are five reasons, but they represent only a few of the glories. For example, they do not contemplate the greater glory of resurrection, but even short of that great day, there is enough to take our breath away and cause Paul to say, "To live is Christ, and to die is gain."

1. *At the moment of death, spirits will be made perfect.*

There will be no more sin in us. We will be done with the inner war and the heartrending disappointments of offending the Lord who loved us and gave himself for us.

"But you have come to Mount Zion and to the city of the living God, the heavenly Jerusalem, and to myriads of angels, to the general assembly and church of the first-born who are enrolled in heaven, and to God, the Judge of all, and to the spirits of the just which have been made perfect" (Hebrews 12:22–23).

2. *At the moment of death, we will be relieved of the pain of this world.*

The joy of the resurrection will not yet be ours, but the joy of freedom from pain will be. Jesus tells the story of Lazarus and the rich man to show the great reversal that is coming: "[The rich man] cried out and said, 'Father Abraham, have mercy on me, and send Lazarus so that he may dip the tip of his finger in water and cool off my tongue, for I am in agony in this flame.' But Abraham said, 'Child, remember that during your life you received your good things, and likewise Lazarus bad things; but now he is being comforted here, and you are in agony'" (Luke 16:24–25).

3. *At the moment of death, we will be given profound rest in our souls.*

There will be a serenity beneath the eye and care of God that surpasses anything we have known here on the softest summer evening beside the most peaceful lake at our most happy moments.

"I saw underneath the altar the souls of those who had been slain because of the word of God, and because of the testimony which they had maintained; and they cried out with a loud voice, saying, 'How long, O Lord, holy and true, will You refrain from judging and avenging our blood on those who dwell on the earth?' And there was given to each of them a white robe; and they were told that they should *rest* for a little while longer" (Revelation 6:9–11).

4. *At the moment of death, we will experience a deep at-homeness.*

The whole human race is homesick for God without knowing it. When we go home to Christ there will be a contentment beyond any sense of security and peace we have ever known: "We are of good courage, I say, and prefer rather to be absent from the body and to be at home with the Lord" (2 Corinthians 5:8).

5. *At the moment of death, we will be with Christ.*

Christ is a more wonderful person than anyone on earth. He is wiser, stronger, and kinder than anyone you enjoy spending time with. He is endlessly interesting. He knows exactly what to do and what to say at every moment to make his guests as glad as they can possibly be. He overflows with love and with infinite insight into how to use that love to make his loved ones feel loved. Therefore Paul said, "For to me, to live is Christ, and to die is gain. But if I am to live on in the flesh, this will mean fruitful labor for me; and I do not know which to choose. But I am hard-pressed from both directions, having the desire to depart and be with Christ, for that is very much better" (Philippians 1:21–23).

With these five reasons for counting death gain, we only scratch the surface of wonder. There is more—so much more! ❧

ENJOYING GOD'S BEING GOD

Can God Be Impressed by Man?

uman strength can never impress an omnipotent God, and human bigness can never impress a God of infinite greatness. This is bad news for God's competitors, but it is very good news for those who want to live by faith.

Psalm 147 is a thrilling statement of hope for people who enjoy God's being God. It says, "He determines the number of the stars, he gives to all of them their names" (verse 4, RSV). Now this is more than we can absorb! "Such knowledge is too wonderful for me; it is high, I cannot attain it" (Psalm 139:6, RSV).

The earth, where we live, is a small planet revolving around a star called the sun which has a volume 1.3 million times that of the earth. There are stars a million times brighter than the sun. There are about a hundred billion stars in our galaxy, the Milky Way, which is one hundred thousand light years across. (A light year is six million million miles.) The sun travels about 155 miles per second, and so it would take two hundred million years to make a single revolution on its orbit in the Milky Way. There are millions of other galaxies besides ours.

Now hear it again: Psalm 147 says that God determined the number of all the stars. Not only that, it says that he named them all. Like naming hamsters or puppies or bunnies. You look them over, note their distinctives, and then think up something to call them that fits. When we sing Katherine Davis's hymn "Let All Things Now Living," I smile with great satisfaction at the words,

> *His law He enforces:*
> *The stars in their courses,*
> *The sun in His orbit*
> *Obediently shine.*

Yes, I thought, "obediently" is just the right word! The sun has a name in God's mind. He calls it by name and tells it what to do. It obeys. And so do the trillions of other stars. (As well as all the electrons in all the molecules of the elements of the stars and planets, including the ones in the gills of a dogfish beneath the rock off Providence, Rhode Island.)

Now what would impress a God like this? Psalm 147:10–11 (RSV) tells us very plainly.

> *His delight is not in the strength of the horse,*
> *   nor his pleasure in the legs of a man;*
> *But the LORD takes pleasure in those who fear him,*
> *   in those who hope in his steadfast love.*

Imagine some Olympic weightlifter feeling proud that he had picked up five hundred pounds. Or imagine some scientist feeling proud that he had figured out how some molecule is affected by another. It takes no genius to know that God is not impressed.

The good news for those who enjoy God's being God is that he enjoys them. He delights in those who hope in his immeasurable power. It is therefore no literary coincidence that the verses on either side of God's greatness in Psalm 147:4–5 show him caring for the weak (verses 3 and 6, RSV):

> ³ *He heals the brokenhearted,*
> *   and binds up their wounds.*
> ⁴ *He determines the number of the stars;*
> *   he gives to all of them their names.*
> ⁵ *Great is our Lord, and abundant in power;*
> *   his understanding is beyond measure.*

⁶ The Lord lifts up the downtrodden.

O may the truth grip us that God is God and that he works omnipotently for those who wait for him (Isaiah 64:4), hope in him (Psalm 147:11), and love him (Romans 8:28). He loves to be God for the weak and childlike, who look to him for all they need. ❧

14

One Way to Wield the Weapon of the Word

——◦◦◦——

What Happened at Luke 18

Discipline and spontaneity. We need both in reading the Bible: discipline to move steadily through books of the Bible, and spontaneity to go to a part of the Bible that we sense will meet a particular need. Both can be powerful with encouragement for faith. Sometimes in the midst of discipline, unexpected power will spring forth, and the line between spontaneity and discipline disappears.

Early one Sunday morning my discipline was taking me through Luke 18. It was one of those times when God came near with unusual force. Christ stood out from the pages as irresistibly compelling. Every paragraph made my soul yearn to be radically obedient to Jesus. I felt that no one ever spoke like this man. No one ever lived free like this man. No one ever demanded what he demanded and gave what he gave.

So I wanted to take this chapter with me all day and feed on it and fight unbelief with it. I didn't have time to memorize it. What could I do?

I decided to tag each paragraph and remember a key statement from each paragraph under that tag. I noticed that I could think of tags that began with the letter P. This is what I came up with when I finished:

Prayer (Luke 18:1–8)

God will vindicate his elect who cry to him day and night.

Pride (Luke 18:9–14)

"God, be merciful to me a sinner!" Jesus said, "This man went down to his house justified;...for every one who exalts himself will be humbled, but he who humbles himself will be exalted" (RSV).

Pusillanimity (Luke 18:15–17)

(It's just as well if you don't know the word. It used to mean childlikeness. That's the way I mean it. Not cowardliness, which it means now. Jonathan Edwards used to commend a "holy pusillanimity.") Jesus said, "Whoever does not receive the kingdom of God like a child shall not enter it" (RSV).

Prosperity (Luke 18:18–30)

Jesus said, "How hard it is for those who have riches to enter the kingdom of God.... There is no man who has left [anything] for the sake of the kingdom of God, who will not receive manifold more in this time, and in the age to come eternal life" (RSV).

Pain (Luke 18:31–34)

Jesus said, "The Son of Man...will be mocked and shamefully treated and spit upon; they will scourge him and kill him, and on the third day he will rise" (RSV).

Perspective (Luke 18:35–43)

Jesus asked a blind man, "'What do you want me to do for you?' He said, 'Lord, let me receive my sight.' And immediately he received his sight and followed him, glorifying God" (RSV).

With these six P's I was able to carry the power of these paragraphs with me all day. I have loved Christ in his pain. I have hated the destructive power of riches. I have feared pride. I have craved to be like a child. I have yearned for my eyes to be opened to the glory of God. I have prayed for the vindication of the church around the world.

O come with me to the Word of God! If this way of carrying it with you does not work for you, then find your own way. Whatever it costs, do not read it and leave it. It transforms us by its presence in our minds, not by staying on the bedside table. ❧

15

THE RIPPLE EFFECT
OF THE WORD

Thoughts on Reading and Writing

I've been thinking again about the importance of reading and writing. There are several reasons I write. One of the most personally compelling is that I read. I mean, my main spiritual sustenance comes by the Holy Spirit from reading. Therefore reading is more important to me than eating. If I went blind, I would pay to have someone read to me. I would try to learn Braille. I would buy books on tape. I would rather go without food than go without books. Therefore, writing feels very life-giving to me, since I get so much of my own life from reading.

Combine this with what Paul says in Ephesians 3:3–4 (RSV): "By revelation there was made known to me the mystery, as I wrote before in brief. And by referring to this, when you read you can understand my insight into the mystery of Christ." The early church was established by apostolic writing as well as apostolic preaching. God chose to send his living Word into the world for thirty years, and his written Word into the world for two thousand years. Think of the assumption behind this divine decision. People in each generation would be dependent on those who read. Some people, if not all, would have to learn to read—and read well in order to be faithful to God.

So it has been for thousands of years. Generation after generation has read the insights of its writers. This is why fresh statements of old truth are always needed. Without them people will read error. Daniel Webster once said,

If religious books are not widely circulated among the masses in this country, I do not know what is going to become of us as a nation. If truth be not diffused, error will be; if God and His Word are not known and received, the devil and his works will gain the ascendancy; if the evangelical volume does not reach every hamlet, the pages of a corrupt and licentious literature will.[4]

Millions of people are going to read. If they don't read contemporary Christian books, they are going to read contemporary secular books. They will read. It is amazing to watch people in an airport. In airports alone, at any given moment, there must be hundreds of thousands of people reading. One of the things we Christians need to be committed to, besides reading, is giving away thoughtful books to those who might read them but would never buy them.

The ripple effect is incalculable. Consider this illustration:

A book by Richard Sibbes, one of the choicest of the Puritan writers, was read by Richard Baxter, who was greatly blessed by it. Baxter then wrote A Call to the Unconverted *which deeply influenced Philip Doddridge, who in turn wrote* The Rise and Progress of Religion in the Soul. *This brought the young William Wilberforce, subsequent English statesman and foe of slavery, to serious thoughts of eternity. Wilberforce wrote his* Practical Book of Christianity *which fired the soul of Leigh Richmond. Richmond, in turn, wrote* The Dairyman's Daughter, *a book that brought thousands to the Lord, helping Thomas Chalmers the great preacher, among others.*[5]

It seems to me that in a literate culture like ours, where most of us know how to read and where books are available, the biblical mandate is to keep on reading what will open the Holy Scriptures to you more and more, and to keep praying for Bible-saturated writers. There are many great old books to read, but each new generation needs its own writers to make the message fresh. Read and pray. And then obey. ❧

16

WHAT IS A CHRISTIAN?

—⁓⁓—

Meditation on 2 Corinthians 5:14–15

The love of Christ constrains us, since we have made this judgment,
that one died for all; therefore all died.
And he died for all in order that the ones who live
might no longer live for themselves
but for the one who died for them and was raised. (author's translation)

What does it mean to be a Christian? Charles Hodge, one of the great nineteenth-century Reformed theologians, sees the answer in this text: "It is being so constrained by a sense of the love of our divine Lord to us, that we consecrate our lives to him."[6]

Being a Christian does not mean merely believing with our head that Christ died for us. It means "being constrained" by the love shown in that act. The truth presses in on us. It grips and holds; it impels and controls. It surrounds us and won't let us run from it. It cages us into joy.

How does it do that? Paul says that the love of Christ constrains him because of a judgment that he formed about that death: "…since we have made this judgment, that one died for all; therefore all died" (author's translation). Paul became a Christian not only through a decision that Christ died for sinners, but also through the sober judgment that the death of Christ was also the death of all for whom he died.

In other words, becoming a Christian is coming to believe not only that Christ died for all his people, but that all his people died when he died—including me. Becoming a Christian is, first, asking the question: Am I persuaded that Christ died for me and I died in him? Am I ready to die that I might live in the power of his love and for the display of his glory? Second, becoming a Christian means answering yes from the heart.

The love of Christ constrains us to answer yes. We feel so much love flowing to us from Christ's death that we discover our death in his death—our death to all other competing allegiances. We are so overwhelmed ("constrained") by the love of Christ that the world fades, as before dying eyes. The future opens as a great, wide field of love.

A Christian is a person living under the constraint of Christ's love. Christianity is not merely believing a set of ideas about Christ's love. It is an experience of being constrained by that love—past, present, and future.

But that constraint comes from a "judgment" that we make about Christ's death: "When he died, I died." It is a profound judgment. "As the sin of Adam was legally and effectively the sin of his race; so the death of Christ was legally and effectively the death of his people."[7] Since our death has already occurred, we do not bear that condemnation (Romans 8:1–3). That is the essence of the love of Christ for us. Through his own undeserved death, he died our well-deserved death and opened his future as our future.

Therefore that "judgment" that we make about his death results in our being "constrained" by his love. Here is the way Charles Hodge expressed it again: "A Christian is one who recognizes Jesus as the Christ, the Son of the living God, as God manifested in the flesh, loving us and dying for our redemption; and who is so affected by a sense of the love of this incarnate God as to be constrained to make the will of Christ the rule of his obedience, and the glory of Christ the great end for which he lives."[8]

How shall we not live for the one who died our death that we might live by his life! To be a Christian is to be constrained by the love of Christ. ❧

17

MAKING ROOM FOR ATHEISM

———⟿———

*Thoughts on the Supremacy of God
in a Pluralistic World*

Our church exists "to spread a passion for the supremacy of God in all things for the joy of all peoples." That is our mission. "All things" means business, industry, education, media, sports, arts, leisure, government, and all the details of our lives. Ideally this means God should be recognized and trusted as supreme by every person he has made. But the Bible plainly teaches that there will never be a time before Jesus comes back when all people will honor him as supreme (2 Thessalonians 1:6–10).

So how do we express a passion for God's supremacy in a pluralistic world where most people do not recognize God as an important part of their lives, let alone an important part of government, education, business, industry, art, recreation, or entertainment? Here are five ways:

1. *Maintain a conviction at all times that God is ever-present and gives all things their most important meaning. He is the creator, sustainer, and governor of all things. We must keep in our minds the truth that all things exist to reveal something of God's infinite perfections. The full meaning of everything, from shoestrings to space shuttles, is the way they relate to God.*

2. *Trust God in every circumstance to use his creative, sustaining, governing wisdom and power to work all things together for the good of all who love him. This is faith in the future grace of all that God promises to be for us in Jesus.*

3. *Make life choices that reveal the supreme worth of God above what the world values supremely. The steadfast love of the Lord is better than life (Psalm 63:3). So we will choose to die rather than lose sweet fellowship with God. This will show his supremacy over all that life offers.*

4. *Speak to people of God's supreme worth in creative and persuasive ways, and tell people how they can be reconciled to God through Christ so that they can enjoy God's supremacy as protection and help, rather than fear it as judgment.*

5. *Make clear that God himself is the foundation for our commitment to a pluralistic democratic order—not because pluralism is his ultimate ideal, but because in a fallen world, legal coercion will not produce the kingdom of God. Christians agree to make room for non-Christian faiths (including naturalistic and materialistic faiths), not because commitment to God's supremacy is unimportant, but because it must be voluntary or it is worthless. We have a God-centered ground for making room for atheism. "If my kingship were of this world, my servants would fight" (John 18:36, RSV). The fact that God establishes his kingdom through the supernatural miracle of faith, not firearms, means that Christians in this age will not endorse coercive governments—Christian or secular.*

This is why we resist the coercive secularization implied in some laws that repress Christian activity in public places. It is not because we want to establish Christianity as the law of the land. That is intrinsically impossible because of the spiritual nature of the kingdom. It is rather because repression of the free exercise of religion and persuasion is as wrong against Christians as it is against secularists. We believe this tolerance is rooted in the very nature of the gospel of Christ. In one sense, tolerance is pragmatic: freedom and democracy seem to be the best political order humans have conceived. But for Christians, tolerance is not purely pragmatic. The spiritual, relational nature of God's kingdom is the ground of our endorsement of pluralism—until Christ comes with rights and authority that we do not have.

Let us spread a passion for the supremacy of God in all things, not by coercion, but by compelling conviction. Let us preserve a form of government where faith can speak freely, neither forced nor silenced by the point of a gun. ❧

18

Strong Enough to Care about the Weak

—⁓⁓—

Jesus and the Children—and Us

When Isaiah says that God "exalts himself to show mercy to you" (Isaiah 30:18, RSV), he teaches us that one mark of great, self-sufficient poise is the willingness to get down low with the weak. This is probably why Jesus was so taken with children. It is also why Christians care about children in church and children on the streets.

According to some estimates, there are probably one hundred million children who live on the streets of our cities around the world. Some estimates say that by the year 2000, half the global population will be children under the age of fifteen, and perhaps two billion of them will live in extreme poverty or be at risk. The United Nations estimates that one million children enter the trade of child prostitution each year.[9]

The impulse to move toward this need rather than away from it is a sign that the Spirit of Jesus is at work in us. Consider a few of his relations with children.

1. Jesus was a child.

> *For unto us a child is born, unto us a son is given: and the government will be upon his shoulder.* (Isaiah 9:6, KJV)

2. Jesus took children in his arms and blessed them.

> *"Let the children come to me, do not hinder them."*... *And he took them in his arms and blessed them, laying his hands upon them.*
> (Mark 10:14, 16, RSV)

3. Jesus healed a child of a foreign woman.

> *"O woman, great is your faith! Be it done for you as you desire." And her daughter was healed instantly.* (Matthew 15:28, RSV)

4. Jesus cast a demon out of a child.

> *And Jesus rebuked him, and the demon came out of him, and the boy was cured instantly.* (Matthew 17:18, RSV)

5. Jesus raised a child from the dead.

> *Taking her by the hand he said to her, "Talitha cumi," which means, "Little girl, I say to you, arise." And immediately the girl got up.* (Mark 5:41–42, RSV)

6. Jesus used a child's loaves and fish to feed five thousand people.

> *"There is a lad here who has five barley loaves and two fish; but what are they among so many?" Jesus said, "Make the people sit down."* (John 6:9–10, RSV)

7. Jesus said you should become like a child.

> *"Truly, I say to you, unless you turn and become like children, you will never enter the kingdom of heaven. Whoever humbles himself like this child, he is the greatest in the kingdom of heaven."* (Matthew 18:3–4, RSV)

8. When Jesus came, children cried, "Hosanna to the Son of David."

> *The chief priests saw...the children crying out in the temple, "Hosanna to the Son of David!"* (Matthew 21:15, RSV)

9. Jesus predicted the terrible days when fathers would give their children up to death.

> *"And brother will deliver up brother to death, and the father his child."*
> (Mark 13:12, RSV)

10. Jesus said that if you receive a child in his name, you receive him and the one who sent him.

> *"Whoever receives one such child in my name receives me; and whoever receives me, receives not me but him who sent me."* (Mark 9:37, RSV)

The question is not whether caring for children is easy and safe, or whether they are responsive and thankful, or whether caring is depleting. The question is whether Jesus is the same yesterday, today, and forever, and whether we can say with the apostle Paul, "I can do all things through Him who strengthens me" (Philippians 4:13). ✺

19

O Spare Us This Rebuke in Worship!

—⁓—

Thoughts on the Handicapped Heart

> *This people honors me with their lips,*
> *but their heart is far from me;*
> *But in vain do they worship me.*
> MATTHEW 15:8

We need to start with a confession—honest, sober, non-judgmental, straightforward, humble, realistic—we are all emotionally crippled to some degree. This is no finger pointing. I mean ALL, and I include myself. I don't mean we are all emotional quadriplegics. Our emotional disabilities range from hyperactivity to paralysis. They include peculiar protuberances, clubfoot, odd gaits, dizzy spells, curious spasms, limps, blackouts, and so on.

I took a survey in a church service and asked, "How many of you grew up in homes where a regular, significant part of family life was glad-hearted singing to the Lord?" About 10 percent raised their hands. Then I asked, "How many of you grew up in homes where spontaneous praise and thanks to each other was more common than correction and criticism?" Fewer raised their hands.

From this I conclude that, in the homes we grew up in, probably 90 percent of us were hindered as much as helped to feel and express emotions of thanks and love and praise in a natural and authentic way. Add to this that we are all sinners with fallen natures that do not naturally delight in God and goodness and beauty and truth. None of us by nature is a person of praise and thanks and love. Put these two together (our fallen nature and our critical, unpraising, songless families), and you have most of the explanation for the emotional disabilities we bring to worship.

We sometimes think that some ethnic groups are exempt from this crippled condition. I doubt it. I attended a three-and-a-half-hour worship service at our neighboring African-American church, which I love to be a part of. I was the last of nine pastors who spoke in celebration of the pastor's thirty-fourth anniversary in that ministry. They clapped a lot. My hands got numb. They swayed a lot. They said, "Amen!" "Yes!" "All right!" "Well, well!" "Come on!" "Say that here!" "Bring it on home!" They sang very loud. They played the organ as background music to a couple of the messages. They shouted. I loved it. I wish our church would learn a few things from them.

But, you know what? I don't think they are any less crippled emotionally than we are. We are all partially disabled in our hearts—white and black, brown and yellow, Italians and Swedes, Hispanic and Teutonic, southern and northern, male and female.

So what's the point? The point is that we need not be satisfied with the way we are. There ought to be a holy dissatisfaction with whatever our own personal emotional disability is. We should seek to grow up into the fullness of the stature of Christ emotionally as well as spiritually and morally. We should refuse to settle for the emotional limp inherited from our parents, as though God were unable to heal and strengthen.

Christians are not fatalists. We do not believe that heredity and environment are the only components that shape us. We believe in God. We believe in the Holy Spirit. We believe in change from glory to glory (2 Corinthians 3:18). The most powerful worship will be among people whose minds linger in the light of truth and whose hearts—whose emotions—are as near the fire of God as they can be without being consumed. Let us rise and go forward from where we are to the next place of freedom, limping forward in the therapy of grace. ❧

20

GRACE FOR A
WELL-TIMED HELP

―――∾∾∾―――

Meditation on Hebrews 4:16

*Let us approach with boldness the throne of grace that we might receive mercy
and find grace for a well-timed help.* (author's translation)

Did you notice that my translation of this verse is a little different
from the traditional one? Usually it is translated, "and find grace
to help in time of need." But "grace for a well-timed help" is literal
and accurate. There is no contradiction between these translations. The
traditional one draws attention to our need; the literal one draws attention
to God's timing.

I think we need to be focused on the grace of God's timing. When we
have a need, we feel very strongly about when God should meet it. We want
him to act now! It is not natural for us to think that God's grace will be
shown as much in its timing as in its form. But Hebrews 4:16 reminds us
to seek God not only for the kind of grace we need, but also for the timing
of grace we need.

This can change our attitude in praying. God's timing is often odd,
which is not surprising since "with the Lord one day is like a thousand
years, and a thousand years like one day" (2 Peter 3:8). The Lord can pack
a thousand years of impact into one day, and he can take a thousand years
to do a day's work. In the one he is not taxed, and in the other he is not

hurried. As Peter says, "The Lord is not slow about His promise, as some count slowness" (2 Peter 3:9).

So it's not surprising that "a well-timed help" might be different from God's perspective than it is from ours, but his perspective is always best. It is always grace to us. It should always be trusted for what it is and when it is.

I need help. Always. In everything. I am simply kidding myself if I think I can move an inch without God's help. For God gives to all "life and breath and all things" (Acts 17:25). I need it for the sake of my own weak faith. I need it to inflame the smoldering wick of my zeal. I need it for empowering in evangelism. I need it for authentic worship. I need it for courage in righteous living. I need it to transform my teenagers into God-centered, humble, respectful young people. I need it so that I can minister hope and joy and boldness to our missionaries. I need it for guidance in future planning. I need it for a thousand other demands and stresses and joyful possibilities.

I love to think of the Lord's sovereign timing. For example, Daniel says that the Lord "changes the times and the epochs" (Daniel 2:21). That means that the seasons of modest or immense blessing in our lives, our homes, and our churches are in the hands of God. He generally times our blessing so that his wisdom, not ours, is highlighted. God is far more interested in the patience of faith than in our instant gratification. His timing will always pay dividends beyond what we can imagine. It is always "grace for a well-timed help." The timing and the content are gracious. Faith rests in the what and the when of God's grace.

So this invitation in Hebrews 4:16 is very precious to me. I need help, but I don't deserve it. Nevertheless, God provides help because his throne is a throne of grace, undeserved help. In every one of these needs the Lord has "grace for a well-timed help." Our duty is to approach him boldly, "find" it, and "receive" it from the throne of grace. We have every reason to believe he will hear us and help us at the proper time.

So let us come boldly to his throne of grace and receive what he has for us—a grace sovereignly designed and sovereignly timed for our greatest good. ❧

21

THE PLACE OF THE HOLY SPIRIT IN THE TRINITY

Foundation for Adoration

uring a series of messages on the Book of Hebrews, someone asked about my conception of the Holy Spirit. The reason is that he had not come in for as much attention as the Father and the Son. It is a heavy matter, but I tried, and here is what I wrote in response.

I have stressed (from texts like Hebrews 1:3; Colossians 1:15; 2:9; Philippians 2:6; 2 Corinthians 4:4; and John 1:1) that the Son of God is the mirroring-forth of God the Father himself in his own self-consciousness. God has a perfectly clear and full idea of all his own perfections. This image of God is so complete and perfect that it is, in fact, the standing forth of God the Son, a person in his own right.

Thus God the Son is not created or made. He is co-eternal with the Father because the Father has always had this perfect image of himself. The Son is thus dependent on the Father as an image is to the original, but he is not inferior in any divine attributes, because he is a complete and living duplicate of the Father's perfections. This of course is a great mystery—how an idea, or reflection, or image of the Father can actually be a person in his own right—and I do not presume to be able to make the infinite completely manageable.

Now what about the Holy Spirit? I find it helpful to observe that the mind of God, as reflected in our own, has two faculties: understanding and will (with emotions being the more lively acts of the will). In other words, before creation God could relate to himself in two ways: God could know himself and God could love himself. In knowing himself he begot the Son, the perfect, full, and complete personal image of himself. In loving himself the Holy Spirit proceeded from the Father and the Son.

So the Son is the eternal image that the Father has of his own perfections, and the Holy Spirit is the eternal love that flows between the Father and the Son as they delight in each other.

How can this love be a person in his own right? Words fail, but can we not say that the love between the Father and the Son is so perfect, so constant, and carries so completely all that the Father and Son are in themselves that this love stands forth itself as a person in his own right?

C. S. Lewis tries to get this into a conceivable analogy—but it is only an analogy:

> You know that among human beings, when they get together in a family, or a club or a trades union, people talk about the "spirit" of that family, club or trades union. They talk about its spirit because the individual members, when they're together, do really develop particular ways of talking and behaving which they wouldn't have if they were apart. It is as if a sort of communal personality came into existence. Of course it isn't a real person: it is only rather like a person. But that's just one of the differences between God and us. What grows out of the joint life of the Father and Son is a real Person, is in fact the Third of the three Persons who are God.[10]

These are great mysteries, but in order to know and love God, I find it helpful to have at least some conception in my mind when I affirm that there is only one God and that he exists in three Persons. It is our duty and delight to adore our great God, but he is not honored by ignorant adoration, for that can only be a charade. Adoration must be based on some knowledge, otherwise it is not God himself whom we adore. ❧

22

TRANSCENDENT SPRINGS
OF TENDERNESS

Meditation on Deuteronomy 10:17–19

The LORD your God is the God of gods and the Lord of lords, the great,
the mighty, and the awesome God who does not show partiality nor take a bribe.
He executes justice for the orphan and the widow,
and shows His love for the alien by giving him food and clothing.
So show your love for the alien, for you were aliens in the land of Egypt.

God's tenderness toward the lowly is rooted in his transcendent self-sufficiency. This means that those who love to make much of God's greatness (which we all should, according to Psalm 40:16) ought to delight in tenderness to the lowly. God exalts his transcendent self-sufficiency by loving the orphan, the widow, and the alien.

God is God over all other gods. He is Lord over all other lords. He is "great." He is "mighty." He is "awesome." Then Moses says, on the basis of this greatness, that God "does not show partiality nor take a bribe." All this stresses his transcendent self-sufficiency. God does not take a bribe because he has no motive to take a bribe: He already owns all the money in the universe, and he has control over the briber. He is above bribes the way the sun is above candles, or the way beauty is above mirrors.

Moses also says God shows no partiality. That is, he doesn't try to curry anyone's favor through special treatment. Showing partiality is another kind of bribery, only not with money but with favored treatment. God is above that, because he has no need to do it. If he wants to get something done, he is not cornered into coercive strategies. He can just do it. Showing partiality is what you do when you can't cope with the consequences of justice. But God is not only able to cope, he is the source of all coping. He depends on no one outside himself. He is transcendently self-sufficient.

Now here comes the most precious part. On the basis of God's transcendent self-sufficiency, Moses says, "He executes justice for the orphan and the widow, and shows His love for the alien by giving him food and clothing." Since God cannot be bribed by the rich and has no deficiency to remedy through favoritism, therefore he works for those who can't afford bribes and have nothing to attract his partiality—the orphan, the widow, and the refugee. This is why I said God's tenderness toward the lowly is rooted in his transcendent self-sufficiency.

Then comes the application in verse 19: "So show your love for the alien, for you were aliens in the land of Egypt." This is not because we are transcendently self-sufficient. It is because we are the beneficiaries of the overflow of God's transcendent fullness. Because our transcendent God works for us and satisfies us with himself, we can join him in lowliness. There is every reason to believe that we will continue to be his beneficiaries if we do not try to bribe him with our works or show off to win his partiality. If we will recognize our widow-like, orphan-like, refugee-like condition of helplessness and rely on the freedom of future grace from a self-sufficient Savior, then we will be loved forever. And being loved like this, we will have power and pleasure in loving as we are loved.

This is what lies behind James 1:27: "Pure and undefiled religion in the sight of our God and Father is this: to visit orphans and widows in their distress...." This is religion because it flows from God's transcendent self-sufficiency and is sustained by his grace and echoes to his glory. It is not social do-goodism. It is evidence of God's abundant provision. May God make us a tender people to the glory of his transcendent self-sufficiency. ❧

23

Very Calmly Say, "Your Outrageous Opinions Are Not Based on Truth"

Meditation on Ephesians 5:11

Take no part in the unfruitful works of darkness, but instead expose them. (RSV)

Our job as Christians is not to control government and education. Our job is to speak God's truth at every level. We may or may not change minds or laws. That is not our responsibility. Our responsibility is to speak with boldness and clarity what God would say.

Don't be muzzled by the comment that you can't force your religion or morality on others. You are not forcing it; you are commending it for serious consideration. Declaring and persuading are not forcing. Commending is not coercion. The fact is this: Everybody's idea about what should be done is guided by some kind of prior commitment. Secularists as well as Christians have a world-view that governs their opinions. Every policy suggestion is rooted in a view of how things should be.

Since Christianity is true, there is an echo of it (however faint) in every heart. You never know when the open statement of your conviction will strike a deep chord of rightness in some secular group. Don't feel burdened with having to control. Just stand up and say what God would say about the issue. You may be surprised that others were waiting for someone to say it.

For example, are your biblical convictions no less defensible than the incredibly unfounded moral pronouncements made below?

Recently a private mental-health counseling service in Minneapolis published a booklet to "give information about a variety of very personal problems that are hard to talk about." This booklet was distributed to the students of at least one high school as part of their sex education program. Here are some examples of the "information" imparted.

Choosing when, how and with whom to be sexual, is a big part of preparing to be an adult. Choose your partners carefully.

Mutual masturbation with your partner is enjoyable and safe.

Talking with and meeting other gays can help you understand how your sexual preference can be a healthy and important part of your life.

Terminate the pregnancy through abortion.... Medically it is best to have an abortion after the sixth week and before the twelfth week of pregnancy. ("Pregnancy Options"— #3)

HIV can be prevented. It may mean making some changes in the way you have sex, but it does not mean that you have to stop having sex.

When you meet this in the public square, you may simply stand up and calmly say: "This morality is not based on truth. It is the opinion of men, not God. Therefore it is false and harmful. God's will for human sexuality is abstinence until marriage; then heterosexual monogamy without adultery. This brings justice, health, and happiness to the world. I recommend that the counsel we give our teenagers correspond to truth. Thank you." Then be seated. ❧

THE LORD'S TOUCH

Meditation on 1 Samuel 10:26

Saul also went to his house at Gibeah;
and the valiant men whose hearts God had touched went with him.

Reading these words has moved me to pray for a new touch from God. What a wonderful thing to be touched in the heart by God! There is nothing unusual about the Hebrew word here: it is simply "touch" in the ordinary sense. God touched their hearts.

The touch of God on one's heart is an awesome thing. It is awesome because the heart is so precious to us—so deep and intimate and personal. When the heart is touched, we are deeply touched. Someone has gotten through protective layers to the center. We have been known. We have been uncovered and seen.

The touch of God is an awesome thing because God is God. Just think of what is being said here! God touched them. Not a wife. Not a child. Not a parent. Not a counselor. But God. The One with infinite power in the universe. The One with infinite authority, infinite wisdom, infinite love, infinite goodness, infinite purity, and infinite justice. That One touched their hearts. How does the circumference of Jupiter touch the edge of a molecule, let alone penetrate to its nucleus?

The touch of God is awesome because it is a touch. It is a real connection. That it involves the heart is awesome. That it involves God is awesome. That it involves an actual touch is awesome. The valiant men were not just spoken to. They were not just swayed by a divine influence. They were not just seen and known from outside. God, with infinite condescension, touched their hearts. God was that close. And they were not consumed.

I love that touch. I want it more and more. I want it for myself and for all of my people. I pray that God would touch me and all his church in a new, deep way for his glory. The text says that they were valiant men—"the valiant men whose hearts God had touched went with him." The Hebrew word carries strength and courage and substance. O that the saints of God would be valiant for the Lord—courageous and mighty and full of weighty truth and beauty!

Pray with me for that touch. If it comes with fire, so be it. If it comes with water, so be it. If it comes with wind, let it come, O God. If it comes with thunder and lightning, let us bow before it. O Lord, come. Come close enough to touch. Shield us with the asbestos of grace, but no more. Pass through all the way to the heart, and touch. Burn and soak and blow and crash. Or, in a still, small voice. Whatever the means, come. Come all the way and touch our hearts. ᴥ

A COMPELLING REASON
FOR RIGOROUS TRAINING OF
THE MIND

---ᕯᕤᕥ---

Thoughts on the Significance of Reading

I was reading and meditating on the Book of Hebrews recently, when it hit me forcefully that a basic and compelling reason for education—the rigorous training of the mind—is so that a person can read the Bible with understanding.

This sounds too obvious to be useful or compelling, but that is because we take the preciousness of reading for granted. We fail to appreciate the kind of thinking that a complex Bible passage requires.

The Book of Hebrews, for example, is an intellectually challenging argument based on Old Testament texts. The points that the author makes hang on biblical observations that come only from rigorous reading, not light skimming. Understanding these Old Testament interpretations in the text of Hebrews requires rigorous thought and mental effort. The same could be said for the extended arguments of Romans, Galatians, and the other books of the Bible.

This is an overwhelming argument for giving our children a disciplined and rigorous training in how to think an author's thoughts after him from a text—especially a biblical text. An alphabet must be learned as well as vocabulary, grammar, syntax, the rudiments of logic, and the way meaning is imparted through the sustained connections of sentences and paragraphs.

The reason Christians have always planted schools where they have planted churches is because we are a people of the book. It is true that the book will never have its proper effect without prayer and the Holy Spirit. It is not a textbook to be debated. It is a fountain for spiritual thirst and food for the soul. It is a revelation of God, a living power, and a two-edged sword. None of this, however, changes the fact that apart from the discipline of reading, the Bible is as powerless as paper. Someone might have to read it for you, but without reading, its meaning and power are locked up.

Is it not remarkable how often Jesus settled great issues with a reference to reading? For example, in the issue of the Sabbath he said, "Have you not read what David did?" (Matthew 12:3). In the issue of divorce and remarriage he said, "Have you not read that He who created them from the beginning made them male and female?" (Matthew 19:4). On the issue of true worship and praise, he said, "Have you never read, 'Out of the mouth of infants and nursing babes you have prepared praise for yourself'?" (Matthew 21:16). On the issue of the resurrection, he said, "Did you never read in the Scriptures, 'The stone which the builders rejected, this became the chief cornerstone'?" (Matthew 21:42). To the lawyer who queried him about eternal life, he said, "What is written in the Law? How does it read to you?" (Luke 10:26).

The apostle Paul also gave reading a great place in the life of the church. For example, he said to the Corinthians, "We write nothing else to you than what you read and understand, and I hope you will understand until the end" (2 Corinthians 1:13). To the Ephesians he said, "When you read you can understand my insight into the mystery of Christ" (Ephesians 3:4). To the Colossians he said, "When this letter is read among you, have it also read in the church of the Laodiceans; and you, for your part read my letter that is coming from Laodicea" (Colossians 4:16). Reading the letters of Paul was so important that he commanded it with an oath: "I adjure you by the Lord to have this letter read to all the brethren" (1 Thessalonians 5:27).

The ability to read does not come intuitively. It must be taught. And learning to read with understanding is a lifelong labor. The implications for

Christians are immense. Education of the mind in the rigorous discipline of thoughtful reading is a primary goal of education. The church of Jesus is debilitated when his people are lulled into thinking that it is humble or democratic or relevant to give a merely practical education that does not involve the rigorous training of the mind to think hard and to construe meaning from difficult texts. The issue of earning a living is not nearly so important as whether the next generation has direct access to the meaning of the Word of God.

We need an education that puts the highest premium under God on knowing the meaning of God's Book and growing in the abilities that will unlock its riches for a lifetime. It would be better to starve for lack of food than to fail to grasp the meaning of the Book of Romans. Lord, let us not fail the next generation! ❧

26

MONDAY MORNING
MEDITATION ON THIRST

—⟨∾⟩—

Hearing Jesus in John 4:14

Whoever drinks of the water that I shall give him shall never thirst;
but the water that I shall give him shall become in him
a well of water springing up to eternal life.

As I knelt that Monday morning in my study, I said, "O Lord, have mercy on me, a sinner. Help me. Please come and restore my soul." Then I asked quietly, "Lord Jesus, what did you mean that those who drink the water that you give will never thirst again (John 4:14)? I thirst this morning. I heard my associate, David Livingston, say last night that he thirsts. Almost every believer who comes into my office thirsts. What did you mean, that those who drink will never thirst? Have we not drunk? Is the promise vain?"

The Lord answered. He showed me the rest of the verse and shed on it a light I had never seen before. John 4:14 begins, "Whoever drinks of the water that I will give him shall never thirst." This is what caused me to cry out, "What do you mean? I am so thirsty! My church is thirsty! The pastors whom I pray with are thirsty! O Jesus, what did you mean?"

Jesus answered the only way I know him to answer. He opened my eyes to see the meaning of what he said in the Bible. I had rememorized the verse early Sunday morning for my own soul and for possible use in the pastoral prayer. So as I prayed, the materials of divine communication were in place. (O what insight we forfeit by not memorizing more Scripture!)

As I cried out, the second half of the verse spoke. Jesus spoke. "But the water that I shall give him shall become in him a well of water springing up to eternal life." With it came an answer. Not an audible voice, but the voice of Jesus in the Word illumined and applied by the Holy Spirit.

It went like this: When you drink my water, your thirst is not destroyed forever. If it did that, would you feel any need of my water afterward? That is not my goal. I do not want self-sufficient saints. When you drink my water, it makes a spring in you. A spring satisfies thirst, not by removing the need you have for water, but by being there to give you water whenever you get thirsty. Again and again and again. Like this morning. So drink, John. Drink.

Now as I sit here writing, I see this precious truth in Psalm 23: "The LORD is my shepherd, I shall not want." Nevertheless, we cry out, "O Lord, today I have wants! I know a hundred people who have wants who count you as their Shepherd. What do you mean, 'We shall not want'?"

But now I have learned a lesson. First, cry out, then read on. "He makes me lie down in green pastures; He leads me beside quiet waters. He restores my soul." Restores. That means the wants rise in my soul and then Jesus satisfies. They rise again, and he resatisfies. Life is a rhythm of need and nourishment—and sometimes even a rhythm of danger and deliverance. "Though I walk through the valley of the shadow of death..." The valley will (again) break forth onto green pastures, and the still waters will flow (again!). The spring is even now welling up within and will forever. For the spring within is not ourselves but God: "He who believes in Me, as the Scripture said, 'From his innermost being will flow rivers of living water.' But this He spoke of the Spirit, whom those who believed in Him were to receive" (John 7:38–39).

Thirst is quenched by the Spirit of Christ revealing himself and his promises to us for our soul's satisfaction. But the thirst is not obliterated, lest we lose our impulse to come to him again and again for all that God promises to be for us in Jesus.

Let the one who is thirsty come and keep coming, until our fellowship is so close that there is no distance between. ❧

27

PRECIOUS AND
POWERFUL REBUKES

The Supremacy of Christ over Everything

O ver the fever of a faithful servant:

> *And standing over her, [Jesus] rebuked the fever, and it left her; and she immediately got up and waited on them.* (Luke 4:39)

Over the wildness of wind and waves:

> *They came to Jesus and woke Him up, saying, "Master, Master, we are perishing!" And He got up and rebuked the wind and the surging waves, and they stopped, and it became calm.* (Luke 8:24)

Over the cruelty of an unclean spirit:

> *While [his father] was still approaching, the demon slammed [the boy] to the ground and threw him into a convulsion. But Jesus rebuked the unclean spirit, and healed the boy and gave him back to his father.* (Luke 9:42)

There is a rebuke from Jesus that cannot be resisted. It carries in it, not just the will to stop a thing, but the force to stop it. A fever is a chemical reaction in the cells of the body, producing excessive heat in response to infection. It has to do with molecules and electrons and the laws of physics and chemistry. In his divinity Jesus designed those laws ages ago (Colossians 1:16), and in his divinity he sustains them so that they work for us daily

(Colossians 1:17; Hebrews 1:3). In his humanity he entered into those laws and became subject to them so that he could die by their ineluctable constancy. But from inside he revealed that his word is also above these laws of physics and chemistry. He spoke, and the force of his word reversed the fever-flaming effect of infection.

Waves are caused by wind, which is created by the expanding and contracting effects of heat and cold. That cold should contract things and heat should expand things was Christ's idea. These laws are not unlike the ones that cause a fever. These, too, Jesus rules with a word. His rebuke carries not only the will but the force that reverses the effect of physical laws.

At the bottom of reality is not matter but mind. When Christ thinks a thing with sufficient intentionality, it materializes. Winds calm and fevers cool when Christ's mind triumphs by his will over matter and its Christ-designed laws. He created matter with the mere intention of his mind. He upholds matter with the mere intention of his mind. He also alters matter with the mere rebuke of his mind. Matter is utterly dependent for its origin, existence, and stability on the thought of Christ.

There are other minds in the universe besides Christ's. There are, for example, unclean spirits. They are not matter. They are only immaterial mind. They have intentionality too, but the story of Christ's dealing with them in the Gospels is meant to show one thing very clearly. The Mind of Christ rules other minds. Created minds—whether rebellious or submissive—are subject to the creating Mind of Christ.

All minds and all matter have their existence at the behest of Christ. He created. He sustains. He governs. He does not need magic or enchantment to govern sicknesses, wind, or wicked minds. All he needs is to intend. There is no power above his own power that he must conjure up. All that exists hangs on his mere will. One thought, and it is extinguished. One thought, and it is altered. One thought, and it is sustained and healed and cherished forever.

Nothing you will touch or feel or see or think today is apart from Christ. What can this mean but deep humility before such an all-encompassing, all-sustaining, all-governing person, and, since he loves us, indomitable confidence? ~

28

TALKING TO YOUR TEARS

---ᘐᘉᘐ---

Meditation on Psalm 126:5–6

> *May those who sow in tears*
> *reap with shouts of joy!*
> *He that goes forth weeping,*
> *bearing the seed for sowing,*
> *shall come home with shouts of joy,*
> *bringing his sheaves with him.* (RSV)

There is nothing sad about sowing seed. It takes no more work than reaping. The days can be beautiful. There can be great hope of harvest. Yet Psalm 126 speaks of "sowing in tears." It says that someone "goes forth weeping, bearing the seed for sowing." Why is he weeping?

I think the reason is not that sowing is sad or that sowing is hard. I think the reason has nothing to do with sowing. Sowing is simply the work that has to be done, even when there are things in life that make us cry. The crops won't wait while we finish our grief or solve all our problems. If we are going to eat next winter, we must get out in the field and sow the seed whether we are crying or not.

This psalm teaches the tough truth that there is work to be done whether I am emotionally up for it or not, and it is good for me to do it. Suppose you are in a season of heartache and discouragement, and it is time to sow seed. Do you say, "I can't sow the field this spring, because I am brokenhearted and discouraged"? If you do that, you will not eat in the winter.

Suppose you say instead, "I am heartsick and discouraged. I cry if the milk spills at breakfast. I cry if the phone and doorbell ring at the same time. I cry for no reason at all, but the field needs to be sowed. That is the way life is. I do not feel like it, but I will take my bag of seeds and go out in the fields and do my crying while I do my duty. I will sow in tears."

If you do that, the promise of this psalm is that you will "reap with shouts of joy." You will "come home with shouts of joy, bringing your sheaves with you," not because the tears of sowing produce the joy of reaping, but because the sheer sowing produces the reaping. We need to remember this even when our tears tempt us to give up sowing.

George MacDonald counseled the troubled soul, "Bethink thee of something that thou oughtest to do, and go to do it, if it be but the sweeping of a room, or the preparing of a meal, or a visit to a friend. Heed not thy feelings: Do thy work."[11]

So here's the lesson: When there are simple, straightforward jobs to be done, and you are full of sadness and the tears are flowing easily, go ahead and do the jobs with tears. Be realistic. Say to your tears: "Tears, I feel you. You make me want to quit life, but there is a field to be sown (dishes to be washed, a car to be fixed, a sermon to be written). I know you will wet my face several times today, but I have work to do and you will just have to go with me. I intend to take the bag of seeds and sow. If you come along, then you will just have to wet the rows."

Then say, by faith in future grace, on the basis of God's Word, "Tears, I know that you will not stay forever. The very fact that I just do my work (tears and all) will in the end bring a harvest of blessing. God has promised. I trust him. So go ahead and flow if you must. I believe (I do not yet see it or feel it fully)—I believe that the simple work of my sowing will bring sheaves of harvest, and your tears will be turned to joy." ❧

29

YUPPIES MAKE YUCKY MISSIONARIES

Thoughts on a Morning Meeting with Jesus

O ne morning I was meditating on the appearance of Jesus to the disciples after his resurrection. Incomprehensibly he called them "Brothers"! They had deserted him. They were hiding in fear. They were like…me. So I heard the Lord of the universe call me "Brother" that morning (John 20:17, author's translation).

Then I read on. Again, incomprehensibly, he said, "Peace to you!" They had deserted him. They were hiding in fear. They deserved to be rebuked. They were just like…me. So I heard the Lord of the universe speak peace to me that morning (John 20:19, 21).

Then I read on. Once more, incomprehensibly, he said, "As the Father sent me, I also am sending you." They had deserted him. They were hiding in fear. They were unfit to be sent. They were just like…me. So I heard the Lord of the universe say to me that morning: "Yuppies make yucky missionaries."

Actually, the reason I heard the word of God in these peculiar words was that just as I was meditating, my wife, Noël, showed me an anniversary card sent to us by a missionary couple from our church. It contained a little touch-and-feel booklet called "Pat the Yuppie."

On one page you could pat the soft sheepskin seat covers in Robert and Kathleen's brand-new luxury car. On another page you could feel the pasta strips coming out of their brand new pasta maker. Next you could touch the rough exposed bricks on the wall in their new four-hundred-thousand-dollar high-rise condo. "See how rough they are. Sooooo rough!" It concluded with a head-shaped mirror: "Now you can be a Yuppie, too!"

So there they were on my desk. The touch-and-feel invitation to join Robert and Kathleen for pasta in their condo and the invitation to join the mission force of Jesus Christ "as the Father sent him."

Crisis.

I turned the anniversary card over and read our friends' conclusion on the matter: "Yuppies make yucky missionaries."

The "yes" in my soul was strong and filled with longing to be more like Paul the missionary than like Robert the Yuppie.

> ...in much endurance, in afflictions, in hardships, in distresses, in beatings, in imprisonments, in tumults, in labors, in sleeplessness, in hunger...by glory and dishonor, by evil report and good report; regarded as deceivers and yet true; as unknown yet well-known, as dying yet behold, we live; as punished yet not put to death, as sorrowful yet always rejoicing, as poor yet making many rich, as having nothing yet possessing all things.
> (2 Corinthians 6:4–5, 8–10)

That last phrase settles the matter. Kathleen and Robert, the Yuppies, think they know the way to "have it all." But Paul teaches another way: "as having nothing yet possessing all things." How can this be?

Well, Jesus said, "Truly I say to you, there is no one who has left house or brothers or sisters or mother or father or children or farms, for My sake and for the gospel's sake, but that he will receive a hundred times as much now in the present age, houses and brothers and sisters and mothers and children and farms, along with persecutions; and in the age to come, eternal life" (Mark 10:29–30).

Paul explained further, to help us fight the force of consumer culture: "All things belong to you, whether Paul or Apollos or Cephas or the world or life or death or things present or things to come; all things belong to you, and you belong to Christ; and Christ belongs to God" (1 Corinthians 3:21–23).

This is what makes for mighty missionaries—and radically God-satisfied senders at home. ❧

30

SWEARING TO
YOUR OWN HURT

What to Do When You Make an Expensive Mistake

> *O LORD, who may abide in Your tent?*
> *Who may dwell on Your holy hill?...*
> *He [who] swears to his own hurt*
> *and does not change.*
>
> PSALM 15:1,4

There is a tremendous temptation to break your word when a pledge or a contract turns out to be a financial fiasco. But when Psalm 15 describes the kind of person who "may dwell on [God's] holy hill," one of the marks of that person is that "he swears to his own hurt and does not change."

In other words, he makes a promise, and even if it hurts to follow through on it, he does not go back on his commitment. His word is more valuable than his money. His integrity is more precious than his wealth. He stands by his word even if it hurts.

Where do we get the strength of character to do that?

There is a story in the Old Testament that gives an answer. It's found in 2 Chronicles 25:5–9. Amaziah was the king of Judah. He was being threatened by the Edomites. So he counted the men in his country above twenty years old and formed an army of three hundred thousand men.

He also went to the Northern Kingdom of Israel and hired one hundred thousand valiant warriors. He paid them one hundred talents of silver (about sixty-six hundred pounds of silver). But this displeased the Lord, and a man of God came to Amaziah and said, "O king, do not let the army of Israel go with you, for the Lord is not with Israel.... God will bring you down before the enemy" (25:7–8).

You can imagine Amaziah's first thought. "Amaziah said to the man of God, 'But what shall we do for the hundred talents which I have given to the troops of Israel?'" (25:9). It was a reasonable question. It is the question we all ask when we have made a rash commitment of money and things go wrong. Should Amaziah stand by his financial commitment to the warriors of Israel when he tells them to go home? What should he do?

The answer of the man of God was simple: "The LORD has much more to give to you than this" (25:9). In other words: Trust God and keep your word! Stand by your commitment because the Lord will take care of you and see that your integrity is rewarded in ways that you can never imagine.

The issue at a moment like this is our trust in God. Will we trust God to act for us? Will we take Psalm 37:5 to heart and bank on it: "Commit your way to the LORD. Trust also in Him and He will do it"? The issue is living by faith in the future grace of God's promise to work it out. Will we trust God to come through for us in his way and in his time?

Human promises are broken because people do not trust God. In fact they don't even think of God. He is not in the equation. Money is in the equation. Shrewdness is in the equation. Human probabilities are in the equation. But God is forgotten. He is just not as real as the money we might lose.

That is not the way we want to be. So, with the assurance of God's reality and the promise of his help, I call you to reckon with him. Take seriously the powerful, relevant, present, promising reality of God. Be holy. Be faithful. Keep your promises. Fulfill your commitments. Swear to your own hurt and do not change. God will be there for you. His smile is worth more than any gain from broken promises. Be people of unimpeachable integrity. For God's sake. "He is a shield to those who walk in integrity" (Proverbs 2:7). ❧

31

ON ADVERTISING
SEXY MOVIES

An Open Letter to an Advertiser

Dear Sirs:

Your numerous signs promoting the film _____
are harmful to our society and a symptom of irresponsible business ethics. The sign in my neighborhood pictures a headless woman lying almost naked in a pile of money. I know that your team of advertisers is capable of some very clever and even enjoyable creativity. This sign, however, reveals only an apparent aim to make money at the cost of spreading prurient interests. There are reasons why this kind of indecency is harmful.

1. For no good reason, it seems, you join the sex industry in stirring up erotic appetites that in our culture need no added assistance, but, if anything, need some means of free and healthy abatement.

2. Making matters worse, the sign closest to my home is across the street from Elliot Park and just above the local Dairy Queen. This means that it is seen especially by the children who play in the park. What do you think this communicates to little inner-city boys and girls where I live? Does it in any way help them to relate to each other in respectful and wholesome ways? Or does it help set the stage for seamy thoughts, crude language, belittling attitudes, and abusive behaviors? What possible good thing is being communicated to our sons and daughters by this sign?

3. Add to that the fact that there are children in our society who are already dysfunctionally obsessed with nudity, bathroom functions, and sexual anatomy. Parents are struggling to help them see that sexuality can be a healthy, God-given joy in marriage, while they try to overcome the jaded preoccupation with sex that degenerates into repulsive vulgarity that is void of beauty and tenderness and respect and commitment and love.

4. The fact that the almost-nude woman in your sign has no head is typical of the sexual depersonalizing of women and the abuse of them as mere bodies to be exploited for the gratification of men who do not want to deal with a true woman who has a head with thought and moral conviction.

5. The fact that she is lying in money communicates that she is to be bought. Again she is a thing, not a person. Her body is like a Blizzard at the Dairy Queen—you buy it to create some temporary pleasure.

6. If you are a young, insecure male who desperately wants to be strong and admired by his virile peers—and if you have no money to buy a desperate woman's body—what do you do? That is, what trajectory does your sign give to this young man's mind? This: "If there are women who don't mind having their pictures made like that, and if she has no head anyway, and if her body is a pleasure to be bought, and if society (and bill-board executives) think it's okay to show it at the Dairy Queen and to stir up my visceral appetites every day, then…" This sentence will be completed in a dozen destructive ways in our society.

7. Small and easy steps lead from saying it's okay to advertise with an alluring, headless woman's body in a bed of money, to saying it's okay to buy a woman's body, to saying it's okay to coerce a woman, to saying it's okay to force a woman.

If you do not care about our neighborhoods and the greater issues of social justice, personal respectability, family stability, and sexual wholesomeness, then at least think about your daughters. Do you want them to be thought of in this way? If not, why would you promote this sleazy mind-set in thousands of men and boys in Minneapolis?

You have an important hand in shaping as well as exploiting the tastes and standards of our community. You can do better. We hope you will.

John Piper

LIVING SUPERNATURALLY AS THE CHURCH OF CHRIST

———

The Necessity of Living on God

C hristian living is supernatural or it is nothing. The church is made of "living stones...built into a spiritual house" (1 Peter 2:5, RSV). "Spiritual" is the opposite of merely "natural." It means being inhabited and guided and empowered by the supernatural Spirit of Christ.

Paul distinguished between a "natural person" and a "spiritual person" (1 Corinthians 2:14–15). He called those who act like natural persons "mere humans" (1 Corinthians 3:4). Christians are not mere humans. They are "spiritual humans." God resides in them (1 Corinthians 6:19). They have new, supernatural life flowing through them. They live with power that is not merely their own.

There is no way we can be the church without this experience. The call to deny ourselves for the sake of love, to return good for evil, to forgive seventy times seven, to endure one another, and to keep on doing this with joy for fifty or sixty or eighty years is not possible to the natural human. It is only possible supernaturally.

To be the church we must live on God. "I am the vine, you are the branches. He who abides in me, and I in him, he it is that bears much fruit, for apart from me you can do nothing" (John 15:5, RSV). It takes supernatural power to endure patiently in the kind of love that defines us as the church of Christ. So Paul prays that we might be "strengthened with all power according to the might of [God's] glory for all endurance and patience with joy" (Colossians 1:11, author's translation). It takes power that accords with divine glory to endure joyfully and patiently in love until we die.

So we must seek to live on God. We must seek to experience supernatural power daily in order to be the church. One of the crucial steps in this direction is to be fully persuaded of this. This means we need to meditate on passages of Scripture that stress the supernatural reality of the Christian life. Consider the following.

Every life devoted to godliness will suffer persecution and affliction. "All who desire to live a godly life in Christ Jesus will be persecuted" (2 Timothy 3:12, RSV). "Through many tribulations we must enter the kingdom of God" (Acts 14:22). How is this suffering to be endured? Paul answers: "Do not be ashamed then of testifying to our Lord,...but take your share of suffering for the gospel in the power of God" (2 Timothy 1:8, RSV). In God's power, not ours. Christian living is supernatural.

The Christian life is not only punctuated with persecutions and afflictions, it is a life of joyful and meaningful labor in the cause of Christ. "Be steadfast, immovable, always abounding in the work of the Lord" (1 Corinthians 15:58). Where shall we get the energy to persevere and not grow weary in this labor? Again Paul answers: "For this I toil, striving with all the energy which he mightily inspires within me" (Colossians 1:29, RSV). We exert ourselves and toil, but the energy comes from God when we trust in him and seek his glory. It is a supernatural toil.

Time would fail to unpack all the texts where this is Paul's concern. "I can do all things in him who strengthens me" (Philippians 4:13, RSV). "Work out your own salvation with fear and trembling; for God is at work in you, both to will and to work for his good pleasure" (Philippians 2:12–13, RSV). "Be strong in the Lord and in the strength of his might" (Ephesians 6:10, RSV). "I will all the more gladly boast of my weaknesses, that the power of Christ may rest upon me" (2 Corinthians 12:9, RSV). "But by the grace of God I am what I am, and his grace toward me was not in vain. On the contrary, I worked harder than any of them, though it was not

I, but the grace of God which is with me" (1 Corinthians 15:10, RSV). "For I will not venture to speak of anything except what Christ has wrought through me to win obedience from the Gentiles, by word and deed" (Romans 15:18, RSV).

Once we are persuaded that normal Christian living is supernatural, if we desire to be Christians, we will be on our knees in obedience to Jesus' command to pray "that you may have strength!" (Luke 21:36). ❧

33

PUTTING THE GODS
IN THEIR PLACE

Meditation on Psalm 82

History is being played out on two levels. One is seen; the other is unseen. One has humans as the main actors; the other has "gods." The two scripts are interwoven but not identical. What happens among the gods affects what happens among us, and what happens among us affects what happens among them. The pattern of evil in the visible human fabric is a pattern woven by the invisible gods. Nevertheless, the pattern comes from the "inventions" of human hearts, and we are responsible moral agents, not mere pawns of the "principalities and powers."

Psalm 82 is an amazing exposé of the gods—what the New Testament calls "principalities," and "powers," and "world rulers of this present darkness" (Ephesians 6:12). In this psalm, the one true God comes to the assembly of the gods and rebukes them for the pattern of evil in the world.

> *God takes his stand in the assembly of God; He judges in the midst of the gods.* (verse 1, author's translation)

Then here is what he says to the "gods," not to mere humans:

> *How long will you judge unjustly, and show partiality to the wicked? Selah. Vindicate the weak and fatherless; do justice to the afflicted and destitute. Rescue the weak and needy; deliver them out of the hand of*

> *the wicked. They do not know nor do they understand; they walk about*
> *in darkness; all the foundations of the earth are shaken.* (verses 2–5)

Verse 5 refers to the victims of the darkness caused by the "world rulers of this present darkness." They are the people whom Hosea says are "destroyed for lack of knowledge" (Hosea 4:6). Paul says that the "god of this world" darkens the minds of unbelievers (2 Corinthians 4:4). Now in Psalm 82, God is calling to account the powers of darkness for this destructive darkening, which even shakes the foundations of the earth. The foundations are light and truth. If darkness prevails, the foundations are shaken.

Then God warns the gods that, although they are "sons of the Most High" (that is, they are angels; see Job 1:6; 38:7), nevertheless, they will "die like men."

> *I said, "You are gods, and all of you are sons of the Most High. Nevertheless,*
> *you will die like men, and fall like any one of the princes."* (verses 6–7)

This is what Jesus was referring to when he said that "the eternal fire [was] prepared for the devil and his angels" (Matthew 25:41, RSV)—that is, for the gods. In other words, their end will be as ignominious and horrible as the ordinary sinners on earth whom they have used to weave their fabric of evil.

Finally, God asserts the truth we must hold to through all the cosmic conflict of this age: All the nations belong to God! Satan is a deceiver (speaking a half-truth) when he says to Jesus in Luke 4:6 that the earth is his and he gives it to whomever he wills. The ultimate truth is:

> *Arise, O God, judge the earth!*
> *For it is Thou who dost possess all the nations.* (verse 8)

Our God owns the nations. The gods are permitted for a season to wreak havoc. We are called to see beyond their suicidal schemes of sin. We are called to stand with God and bear witness to his truth against the darkness. In due time he will defeat all his enemies and "the earth will be filled with the knowledge of the glory of the LORD, as the waters cover the sea" (Habakkuk 2:14, RSV). ❧

34

SETTING OUR MINDS ON THINGS ABOVE IN SUMMER

Thoughts on Colossians 3:1–2

If then you have been raised up with Christ, seek the things that are above, where Christ is, seated at the right hand of God. Set your minds on things that are above, not on things that are on earth. (RSV)

Every season is God's season, but summer has a special power.

Jesus Christ is refreshing, but flight from him into Christless leisure makes the soul parched. At first it may feel like freedom and fun to skimp on prayer and neglect the Word, but then we pay: shallowness, powerlessness, vulnerability to sin, preoccupation with trifles, superficial relationships, and a frightening loss of interest in worship and the things of the Spirit.

Don't let summer make your soul shrivel. God made summer as a foretaste of heaven, not a substitute. If the mailman brings you a love letter from your fiancé, don't fall in love with the mailman. That's what summer is: God's messenger with a sun-soaked, tree-green, flower-blooming, lake-glistening letter of love to show us what he is planning for us in the age to come—"things which eye has not seen and ear has not heard, and which have not entered the heart of man, all that God has prepared for those who love him" (1 Corinthians 2:9). Don't fall in love with the video preview and find yourself unable to love the coming reality.

Jesus Christ is the refreshing center of summer. He is preeminent in all things (Colossians 1:18), including vacations, picnics, softball, long walks, and cookouts. He invites us in the summer: "Come to Me, all who are weary and heavy-laden, and I will give you rest" (Matthew 11:28). This is serious summer refreshment.

Do we want it? That is the question. Christ gives himself to us in proportion to how much we want his refreshment. "You will seek me and find me; when you seek me with all your heart" (Jeremiah 29:13, RSV). One of the reasons to give the Lord special attention in the summer is to say to him, "We want all your refreshment. We really want it."

Peter's word to us about this is: "Therefore repent and return, so that your sins may be wiped away, in order that times of refreshing may come from the presence of the Lord" (Acts 3:19). Repentance is not just turning away from sin; it is also turning toward the Lord with hearts open, expectant, and submissive.

What sort of summer mind-set is this? It is the mind-set of Colossians 3:1–2, "Therefore if you have been raised up with Christ, keep seeking the things above, where Christ is, seated at the right hand of God. Set your mind on the things above, not on the things that are on earth."

In the summer the earth is very much with us. It is God's earth, but it is all prelude to the real drama of heaven. It is a foretaste of the real banquet. It is a video preview of the reality of what the eternal summer will be like when "the city has no need of sun or moon to shine upon it, for the glory of God is its light, and its lamp is the Lamb" (Revelation 21:23, RSV). So, you see, the summer sun is a mere pointer to the sun that will be: the glory of God. Summer is for seeing and showing that.

Will we have eyes to see? Do you want to have eyes to see? Lord, let us see the Light beyond the campfire. ❧

35

WHY BEING TRUTH-DRIVEN IS SO CRUCIAL

Loving God by Loving Truth

Our concern with truth is an inevitable expression of our concern with God. If God exists, then he is the measure of all things, and what he thinks about all things is the measure of what we should think. Not to care about truth is not to care about God. To love God passionately is to love truth passionately. Being God-centered in life means being truth-driven in ministry. What is not true is not of God. What is false is anti-God. Indifference to the truth is indifference to the mind of God. Pretense is rebellion against reality, and what makes reality is God. Our concern with truth is simply an echo of our concern with God.

Biblically, the urgency of being truth-driven is seen at least three ways. First, God is truth. The entire Trinity is the truth. God the Father is true, and nothing can nullify this utter faithfulness and reliability behind all his statements and promises. "What then? If some did not believe, their unbelief will not nullify the faithfulness of God, will it? May it never be! Rather, let God be found true, though every man be found a liar" (Romans 3:3–4a).

God the Son, who is the very image of the Father, is true. Jesus said, "I am the way, and the truth, and the life; no one comes to the Father but through Me" (John 14:6). In Revelation 19:11, John saw Jesus glorified as faithful and true: "And I saw heaven opened, and behold, a white horse, and He who sat on it is called Faithful and True, and in righteousness He judges and wages war" (Revelation 19:11).

God the Spirit, who personally lives out the life of the Father and the Son in ministry to us, is the Spirit of truth. Jesus said, "When the Counselor comes, whom I shall send to you from the Father, even the Spirit of truth, who proceeds from the Father, he will bear witness of me.... When the Spirit of truth comes, he will guide you into all the truth" (John 15:26; 16:13a).

To love God the Father, the Son, and the Spirit is to love the truth. To pursue them is to pursue truth. Passion for their vindication in the world involves a passion for the truth. There is no separating God and truth, as if one can put relationship against truth. "God is" precedes "God is love," and "God is" has content and meaning. God is one thing and not another thing. He has character. His nature has contours that define him. Concern with the true God, who is not created in our own image, is at the bottom of a truth-driven life.

The second way the biblical urgency of being truth-driven is seen is in the terrible warning that not to love truth is eternally suicidal. Paul speaks of a lawless one at the end of the age who will come with "all power and signs and false wonders, and with all the deception of wickedness for those who perish, because they did not receive the love of the truth so as to be saved" (2 Thessalonians 2:9–10). Loving the truth is a matter of perishing or being saved. Indifference to the truth is a mark of spiritual death.

Paul goes on and contrasts believing the truth with taking pleasure in wickedness. "They all [will] be judged who did not believe the truth, but took pleasure in wickedness" (2 Thessalonians 2:12). This shows that believing truth involves the affections, since its alternative is "taking pleasure" in something else. It also shows that truth is moral and not just cognitive, since its alternative is wickedness and not just falsehood. The overwhelming impact of this text, however, is that loving the truth—believing the truth with your whole heart—is a matter of eternal life and death.

The third reason I say that being truth-driven is so urgent is that the New Testament portrays Christian living as the fruit of knowing truth. For example, when Paul says, "Do you not know?" as a rebuke or an incentive in relation to some behavior, he is showing that true knowledge would change the behavior. "Do you not know that your bodies are members of Christ? Shall I then take away the members of Christ and make them members of a prostitute? May it never be!" (1 Corinthians 6:15). This means that knowing the truth about the redeemed body of a Christian is a powerful source of chastity.

"Or do you not know that the one who joins himself to a prostitute is one body with her? For He says, 'The two will become one flesh.'...Or do you not know that your body is a temple of the Holy Spirit who is in you, whom you have from God, and that you are not your own?" (1 Corinthians 6:16, 19). Not knowing the truth is a great cause of irreverence and immorality. Truth is a fountain of holy Christian living. You will know the truth, and the truth will make you free—from sin for God.

Loving truth is a mark of the God-entranced world-view. It is obedience to the first and great commandment. ᴥ

36

THE PAINFUL LESSON OF
LEARNING JOY

There Is No Serving Like This Serving

Serving God is utterly different from serving anyone else. God is extremely jealous that we understand this—and enjoy it. For example, he commands us, "Serve the LORD with gladness!" (Psalm 100:2, RSV). There is a reason for this gladness. It is given in Acts 17:25 (RSV), "[God is not] served by human hands, as though he needed anything, since he himself gives to all men life and breath and everything." We serve him with gladness because we do not bear the burden of meeting his needs. Rather, we rejoice in a service where he meets our needs.

The psalmist compares it to a servant's dependence on a gracious master: "Behold, as the eyes of servants look to the hand of their master, as the eyes of a maid to the hand of her mistress; so our eyes look to the LORD our God, till he have mercy upon us" (Psalm 123:2, RSV). Serving God always means receiving grace from God.

To show how jealous God is for us to get this and glory in it, there is a story in 2 Chronicles 12. Rehoboam, the son of Solomon, who ruled the Southern Kingdom after the revolt of the ten tribes, "forsook the law of the LORD" (verse 1). He chose against serving the Lord and gave his service to other gods and other kingdoms. As judgment, God sent Shishak, king of Egypt, against Rehoboam with twelve hundred chariots and sixty thousand horsemen (verse 3).

In mercy, God sent the prophet Shemaiah to Rehoboam with this message: "Thus says the LORD, 'You abandoned me, so I have abandoned you to the hand of Shishak'" (verse 5, RSV). The happy upshot of that message was that Rehoboam and his princes humbled themselves in repentance and said, "The LORD is righteous" (verse 6, RSV).

When the Lord saw that they humbled themselves, he said, "They have humbled themselves, so I will not destroy them, but I will grant them some measure of deliverance, and My wrath shall not be poured out on Jerusalem by means of Shishak" (verse 7). Yet as a discipline to them, he said, "They will become his slaves so that they may learn the difference between My service and the service of the kingdoms of the countries" (verse 8).

There it is. God's zeal that we know the difference between serving him and serving anyone else. The lesson they had to learn was that serving God is a glad service, or as Jesus said, a light burden and an easy yoke (Matthew 11:30). From this we may learn, as Jeremy Taylor said, that God threatens terrible things if we will not be happy. This is what Moses said in Deuteronomy 28:47–48: "Because you did not serve the LORD your God with joy and a glad heart...therefore you shall serve your enemies."

The point is plain: Serving God is a receiving, a blessing, a joy, and a benefit. This is why I am so jealous to say that at our church the worship of Sunday morning and the worship of daily obedience are not, at bottom, a giving to God but a joyful getting from God.

Beware of serving God in a way that makes him look like the gods of the nations. Let all your serving be in the strength that he supplies (1 Peter 4:11). ❧

37

THE AMERICAN REVIVAL
OF 1905

Observing the Spirit Blowing Where He Wills

Revival is the sovereign work of God to awaken his people with fresh intensity to the truth and glory of God, the ugliness of sin, the horror of hell, the preciousness of Christ's atoning work, the wonder of salvation by grace through faith, the urgency of holiness and witness, and the sweetness of worship with God's people. Revival is what happens when the sovereign Spirit wills to blow on large numbers at one time (John 3:8). No one has documented these movements of God in more detail than J. Edwin Orr.[12] One of the great stories he tells is of the American Revival of 1905.

Many have heard of the Great Welsh Revival of 1904–5. It touched all classes and ages. Newspapers kept tally as the churches swelled with new converts—more than 100,000 in one six-month period. In Cardiff, police reported a 60 percent decrease in drunkenness and 40 percent fewer people in jail on New Year's Day of 1905. In Glamorgan the convictions for drunkenness decreased from 11,282 in 1904 to 5,615 in 1907. Stocks of Welsh Bibles were sold out. Profanity had disappeared in the coal mines to the extent that the pit ponies dragging the coal carts in the tunnels did not understand their commands anymore and stood still, confused. Even children held their own meetings in homes and barns.

What is not as well known is that the power of revival spread to America and to many other countries. Welsh immigrants in Pennsylvania received news of the revival from the homeland. Suddenly in December

1904 an awakening began in Wilkes-Barre, and the Reverend J. D. Roberts in one month instructed 123 converts.

By early spring, the Methodists of Philadelphia were claiming ten thousand converts, the greatest ingathering since 1880. In Schenectady, New York, the local ministerial association heard reports of the great revival in Wales and united all evangelical denominations in meetings for prayer and evangelistic rallies. By January 22, 1905, all the evangelical congregations in the city were packed with awakened and seeking people. In Troy, New York, the awakening began during the January week of prayer held in the Second Presbyterian Church. The revival spread to twenty-nine other churches in the city.

Throughout New England the revival spread during the spring of 1905. J. Edwin Orr wrote that "the movement was characterized by an intense sensation of the presence of God in the congregations, as in the Welsh Revival."

The southern states were not overlooked by the Lord. Late in 1904 the Atlanta newspapers reported that nearly a thousand businessmen had united in intercession for an outpouring of the Holy Spirit. On November 2, with unprecedented unanimity, stores, factories, and offices closed at midday for prayer. Georgia's Supreme Court adjourned.

In Louisville, Kentucky, the press reported, "The most remarkable revival ever known in the city is now interesting Louisville.... Fifty-eight of the leading business firms of the city are closed at the noon hour" for prayer meetings. In March 1905 Henry Clay Morrison said, "The whole city is breathing a spiritual atmosphere.... Everywhere in shop and store, in the mill and on the street, salvation is the one topic of conversation."

The story goes on and on, but, of course, 1905 was only one of many movings of the sovereign Spirit. "The wind blows where it wills, and you hear the sound of it, but you do not know whence it comes or whither it goes; so it is with every one who is born of the Spirit" (John 3:8, RSV). God is free in the worst of times to do this beyond all our calculations and expectations. O to be among the number of those who pray and proclaim in this hope. ❧

38

IRVING HETHERINGTON, SELF-PITY, AND SERVICE

Learning to Follow the Man of Sorrows

Self-pity in suffering is the taste left after your sacrifice goes un-admired. There are two ways to get rid of it. One is to make sure you get admiration. The other is to make no sacrifices. Or could there be a third way? Like seeing the sacrifice in a new way?

Take being a pastor, for example. Are there sacrifices? Is there any suffering? Well, that depends. Let me tell you a story that has punched (for a season, at least) the air out of my self-pity.

Irving Hetherington was born on July 23, 1809, in Scotland. He became a preacher in 1835 and felt called to leave Scotland for missions in Australia. He wondered if his fiancée would go with him. Her name was Jessie Carr, and she said, "Where you wish to take me, there I wish to go." They sailed for Sydney on March 24, 1837, aboard the *John Barry*, immediately after their wedding.

In the first week of May, Jessie developed a sore throat and then the dreaded fever. "Have you no fear of death, Jessie?" Irving asked.

"No, dear," she replied.

"And how is it that you are not afraid to die?" he asked.

"I have long taken Christ for my portion and set my hopes on Him," she said.

Irving wept. Jessie died that night, and in the morning they buried her at sea.

In Sydney, alone, Hetherington was assigned to a district fifty miles long and thirty miles wide. He rode a horse to his little groups of believers in rain and heat.

When a drought weakened the horse, he walked. He tried to study on the way and get his sermons ready. His biographer tells the following story: "One Saturday night he had to walk thirty miles; and, after climbing a hill, and while resting on a log at the summit, the idea of ministers in Scotland complaining of being Mondayish after two services, and without other fatigue, struck him as so ludicrous that he could not help bursting out into a loud 'guffaw' of laughter, which sounded strange in the darkness and loneliness of the bush."[13]

What this powerful story did for me was to put the pressures of my ministry into missionary—and biblical—perspective. How easy it is to begin to assume that I should be comfortable. How quickly I can start to expect an easy and hassle-free ministry.

But I tell missionaries just the opposite. Life is war. Life is stress: the language-learning is stress; the culture is stress; the food is stress; the kids' education is stress; relationships are stress. Get ready for incarnation and crucifixion.

Yet here in America, where everybody speaks English and eats pizza, I bellyache over an extra meeting, an ill-timed hospital call, and too many choices. Then I read of Irving Hetherington, and I think of "normal" missionary life. I see my "sacrifices" in a new way. I recall Jesus' rebuke of Peter's pitiful, "Behold, we have left everything and followed You," (Mark 10:28). Jesus was not impressed by the sacrifice. He said, "Truly I say to you, there is no one who has left house or brothers or sisters or mother or father or children or farms, for My sake and for the gospel's sake, but that he will receive a hundred times as much now in the present age, houses and brothers and sisters and mothers and children and farms, along with persecutions; and in the age to come, eternal life" (Mark 10:29–30).

Before the words of Jesus and the example of Irving Hetherington, my self-pity goes up the chimney. And in its place? A passion to have the mind of Christ. "The Son of man came not to be served, but to serve, and to give his life as a ransom for many.... It is more blessed to give than to receive" (Matthew 20:28; Acts 20:35, RSV). ❧

39

PRAYING FOR WHAT
CANNOT FAIL

Pondering the Promises beneath the Prayers

Unbiblical cynics say, "If it is sure, why pray for it?" Biblical saints say, "Pray for it with joy, because God has promised and cannot fail." For example, it is absolutely certain that God's kingdom is going to come. The apostle John sees it as virtually done: "The kingdom of the world has become the kingdom of our Lord and of his Christ, and he shall reign for ever and ever" (Revelation 11:15, RSV). Yet we are told to pray, "Thy kingdom come" (Matthew 6:10, RSV).

Or consider another example: Jesus promised with absolute certainty, that "this gospel of the kingdom will be preached throughout the whole world as a testimony to all nations; and then the end will come" (Matthew 24:14, RSV). In other words, the great commission will be completed. There is no doubt. Yet Jesus commanded us to make disciples of all nations (Matthew 28:19) and to "pray therefore the Lord of the harvest to send out laborers" (Matthew 9:38, RSV).

What this means is that God appoints prayer as the means of finishing a mission that he has promised will certainly be finished. Therefore we pray, not because the outcome is uncertain, but because God has promised and cannot fail. Our prayers are the means God has appointed to do what he most certainly will do—finish the great commission and establish his kingdom.

Those who pray for the kingdom to come will receive the kingdom, but those who don't love the kingdom and the appearing of the Lord probably will not bother themselves with this prayer. Paul's words in 2 Timothy 4:8 are ominous: "In the future there is laid up for me the crown of righteousness, which the Lord, the righteous Judge, will award to me on that day; and not only to me, but also to all who have loved His appearing." Not to love the appearing of the Lord (that is, not to pray passionately, "Thy kingdom come") means that some will not receive the crown of righteousness.

One of the few Aramaic words that the Greek-speaking early church preserved from the very words of Jesus (who probably spoke Aramaic during most of his ministry) was *Maranatha*. It probably means "Our Lord, come!" There was no doubt that he would come. He promised that he would ("I will come again" [John 14:3]). The timing of his coming was fixed by the Father in heaven: "But of that day or hour no one knows, not even the angels in heaven, nor the Son, but the Father alone" (Mark 13:32). Nevertheless the early church prayed, "Maranatha!" This is the way one who loves Jesus prays: "If anyone does not love the Lord, let him be accursed. Maranatha" (1 Corinthians 16:22).

Let us then pray the way the apostle taught us to pray for what cannot fail. Let us not stand by and watch as skeptics or fatalists. Let us pray with all our hearts, as Paul says, "that the word of the Lord may run and be glorified" (2 Thessalonians 3:1, author's translation). The promise is there that the word does not come back void but accomplishes what God appoints for it (Isaiah 55:11). Therefore (not "nevertheless"), let us pray that this mighty word will run and triumph.

Anyone who says, "It is meaningless to pray, because the promise is certain," will be left out. Such soldiers will not share in the spoils of victory, for they have not shared in the battle. Let us pray and triumph with him in the battle that cannot fail! ❧

40

WHEN UNCLOTHED
IS UNFITTING

Thoughts on Selling with Sex

Jonathan Edwards once said that godly people can smell the depravity of an act before they can explain why it is evil. There is a spiritual sense that something is amiss. It does not fit in a world permeated with God. Ephesians 5:3 says that some things are not "fitting among saints." Fittingness is not always easy to justify with arguments. You discern it before you can defend it, which is good because we have to make hundreds of choices every day with little time for extended reflection.

From time to time, however, we need to pause and give rational, biblical expression to why something is not fitting. Some years ago I came to that point when, week after week, a local newspaper put scantily clad women on the second page of the first section in order to sell underclothes. I wrote a letter to the editors with nine reasons why they should stop using this kind of advertising. Perhaps my reflections will help you deal with the hundreds of abuses of God's good gift of sexuality in our culture. Here is what I wrote.

> *As a fourteen-year subscriber and reader of your newspaper, I am writing to express the persuasion that your sexually explicit ads that often turn up in Section A are increasingly offensive and socially irresponsible. The effectiveness of catching people's attention by picturing a woman in her underclothes does not justify the ads. The detrimental effects of such mercenary misuse of the*

*female body are not insignificant. The harm I have in mind is described in
the following nine persuasions.*

*1. This woman could not go out in public dressed like that without
being shamed or being mentally aberrant. Yet you thrust her out, even in
front of those of us who feel shame for her.*

*2. This portrayal of a woman sitting in her underclothes at a table
with a cup of tea disposes men to think of women not as persons but mainly
in terms of their bodies. It stimulates young boys to dwell on unclothed
women's bodies and thus lames their ability to deal with women as dignified
persons. I have four sons.*

*3. The ad stimulates sexual desire which in thousands of men has no
legitimate or wholesome outlet through marriage. In other words, it feeds a
corporate, community lust that bears no good fruit outside marriage, but in
fact many ills.*

*4. The ad makes sensibilities callous so that fewer and fewer offenses
against good taste feel unacceptable, which spells the collapse of precious
and delicate aspects of personhood and relationships.*

*5. The ad makes thousands of women subconsciously measure their
attractiveness and worth by the standard of rarefied, unrealistic models,
leading to an unhealthy and discouraging preoccupation with outward looks.*

*6. The ad feeds the prurient fantasies of ordinary men, lodging a
sexual image in their minds for the day which can rob them of the ability to
think about things greater and nobler than skin.*

*7. The ad condones the proclivity of males to mentally unclothe
women by reminding them what they would see if they did, and it suggests
that there are women who want to be unclothed publicly in this way. This
reminder and this suggestion support habits and stereotypes that weaken
personal virtue and jeopardize decorous relationships.*

*8. The ad encourages young girls to put excessive focus on their
bodies and how they will be seen, adding to the epidemic of depression and
eating disorders.*

9. *The ad contributes to dissatisfaction in men whose wives can't produce that body and thus adds to the instability of marriages and homes.*

I realize that the bottom line is big bucks for page 2 and lots of attention for the department store, but please know that at least one assessment of your standards of fitness for print is that it is part of a tragic loss of modesty and decency that may, for now, feel like mature liberation, but in generations to come will reap a whirlwind of misery for all of us.

If you love God's good gift of sexuality, take a stand for treating it like precious gems rather than common gravel. Guard it in the velvet-lined safe of steel commitment. Don't strew it on the street or in the press.

John Piper

41

HOW I WAS MOVED TO TEARS

The Commitment of a Lifetime

Not long ago a phone call moved me to tears. I had never received one like it in my life. Never. I can hardly believe it even now. It was more gracious than I could have legitimately hoped for.

A friend of mine called from out of state. He is a pastor and a school administrator. He is busy in multiple ministries and has a family. He told me that he was at a conference recently and the speaker challenged those present to consider the impact they might have if they devoted themselves to praying for someone every day.

He said that as he was praying, the Lord brought my name to mind. He had given it thought and prayer, and he wanted to tell me that from now until he dies or I die—or Jesus comes back—he is going to pray for me every day.

I could hardly believe it. No one but Noël, my parents, and Jesus has ever made such a commitment to me. Imagine it. That means, if he and I live out our three score and ten years, he will pray for me more than eight thousand times. It means rain or shine, he is praying. For better or for worse, he is praying. If I succeed or fall, he is praying. If I lose my mind and become a vegetable, he is praying. If I make shipwreck of my faith and commit apostasy, he is praying.

This kind of commitment takes my breath away. It brought tears of joy and gratitude. It made me tremble. It was, in fact, an inexpressible demonstration of God's covenant love to me. I feel that I have been loved with bands that cannot be broken. I am overwhelmed.

How is such a thing possible? It is possible because it really is a part of God's covenant and not just a human imitation of it. This kind of love is an overflow of God's commitment to be everything my friend needs in this life and the next. God has said to him and me: "I will make an everlasting covenant with them that I will not turn away from them, to do them good; and I will put the fear of Me in their hearts so that they will not turn away from Me" (Jeremiah 32:40). This means that God is the guarantor of our constancy. If we do not turn away from what we promise to do, it is God's work; "I will not turn away from doing them good."

I hung up the phone and prayed: "Thank you, Lord. I need this power and this guidance so much. O that I might be docile in the Lord's hands. Lord, bless my friend in his intercession for me. Strengthen him. Use me for his good in the way you touch me through him. May we be mutually empowered by this commitment."

What an amazingly foreign thing this is in our unstable culture! Someone who says, "Not just if it feels good, not just if I think of it, not just if you respond well, and not just if I am fulfilled by it—John, you can count on it, every day until the Lord returns or until I die, I will pray for you, whether it's one minute or one hour."

What prayer promise might God be leading you to make? This is not the only good kind of commitment you can make. There are all kinds. For example, I am committed to pray for our church staff by name every day as long as I am the pastor of this church.

Pause and ponder the possibilities. ❧

42

THINK DEEPLY AND CLEARLY

A Dialogue on 2 Timothy 2:7

*Think over what I say, for the Lord will grant you
understanding in everything.* (RSV)

Timothy: Wait a minute, Paul. You tell me to think, but isn't the organ of our thinking fallen and unreliable?

Paul: Yes, your mind is fallen and fallible. Yes, it is prone to self-justifying errors. But Christ is in the business of renewing the mind (Romans 12:2; Ephesians 4:23). Do you think there is some *unfallen* part of you that you could substitute for your mind? We are fallen and depraved in every part. You cannot retreat from thinking into some other safe, untainted faculty of knowing. Take note, Timothy; even in raising the objection against thinking, you are thinking! You cannot escape the necessity of thinking. God's call is to do it well.

Timothy: But, Paul, I don't want to become a cold, impersonal intellectual.

Paul: There is danger on both sides, Timothy. There is cold knowledge, and there is a red-hot zeal that is not according to knowledge (Romans 10:2), but thinking does not have to cool your zeal. In fact, in my life, the vigorous exercise of my mind in spiritual things causes me to boil inside, not to freeze. You are right not to want to become impersonal. That happens when thinking is emphasized to the exclusion of feeling about people and when reason is exalted above love, but note this, Timothy: The abandonment of thinking is the destruction of persons. Yes, there is more to personal relationships than thinking, but they are less human without it. God honored his image in us when he said, "Come now, let us reason together" (Isaiah 1:18). Should we do less?

Timothy: But, Paul, shouldn't I just take you at your word and not ask so many questions? You're an apostle and speak for God.

Paul: Take what, Timothy?

Timothy: Your words, what you say in your letters.

Paul: Do you mean the black marks on the parchment?

Timothy: No. What they stand for. You know, what they mean.

Paul: How do you know what I mean, Timothy?

Timothy: I read what you write.

Paul: You mean you pass your eyes over the black marks on the parchment?

Timothy: No, I...I think about it. I ask how the words and sentences fit together. I look for what it means.

Paul: That's right, Timothy. Thinking and asking questions are the only ways you will ever understand what I want to communicate in my letters. Either you will do it poorly, or you will do it well. So do not be a child in your thinking. Be a babe in evil, but in thinking be mature (1 Corinthians 14:20, RSV). As the Master said, "wise as serpents and innocent as doves" (Matthew 10:16, RSV).

Timothy: But, Paul, won't I become arrogant and boastful if by using my mind I discover things on my own?

Paul: Timothy, you never have and never will discover anything "on your own." You would know this if you had thought more deeply about what I said. What I said was: "Think over what I say, for the Lord will grant you understanding in everything." The Lord, Timothy, the Lord! "From him and through him and to him are all things. To him be the glory!" (Romans 11:36, RSV). He is the ground and goal of all thought. So think, Timothy. Gird up your mind and think! ❧

43

A PASSION FOR HOLINESS

---~~~---

*The Key to Lasting Effectiveness in
the Life of John Owen*

Over the years I have heard thoughtful evangelical leaders like J. I. Packer, Roger Nicole, and Sinclair Ferguson say that the most influential writer in their lives (after the biblical authors) is John Owen. This is enough to send one hungry to the library to find out who this man was and what made him tick.

John Owen was born in 1616. He was probably the greatest pastor-theologian among the Puritans in England. As J. I. Packer would say, he was the tallest among the Puritan redwoods.[14] Owen's twenty-four thick volumes (including his biblical theology) are still in print, shaping and feeding today's shepherds (like me).

He was a man of incredible activity—politically (as Oliver Cromwell's chaplain and frequent speaker to Parliament), denominationally (as the point man for all the controversies between Congregational and Presbyterian Puritans), theologically (as the foremost Puritan defender of Calvinistic truth), academically (as dean and vice chancellor in the University of Oxford), pastorally (serving churches in and around London almost all his adult life, even when it was illegal to gather), and personally (with a family of eleven children, ten of whom died while young, followed by the eleventh when she was a young adult).

What amazed me about this man is that, in the midst of all this activity and tragedy, his passion was not public performance, but personal holiness.

He said, "My heart's desire unto God, and the chief design of my life…are that…universal holiness may be promoted in my own and in the hearts and ways of others."[15]

I need heroes like this. Not many leaders today state the goals of their lives in terms of holiness. More and more leaders openly confess that their personal holiness is of no significance to their public performance. For example, a president of the United States has communicated very clearly that he did not think his personal purity was a significant factor in his leadership of this nation. Similarly we read about a British leader who has had a longstanding adulterous affair. So, on both sides of the Atlantic, our statesmen say with their lives: personal holiness is relatively unimportant— public performance and personal purity are not related.

That was not the case with John Owen. The wonder, the power, and the beauty of his public life was the constancy of his personal communion with God in purity and joy. One of his biographers described it like this: "Amid the din of theological controversy, the engrossing and perplexing activities of a high public station, and the chilling damps of a university, he was yet living near God, and like Jacob amid the stones of the wilderness, [he was] maintaining secret intercourse with the eternal and invisible."[16]

In his own words he gave the secret to his personal holiness amid all the pressures and pains of life: "What better preparation can there be for [our future enjoyment of the glory of Christ] than in a constant previous contemplation of that glory in the revelation that is made in the Gospel."[17]

That is the key to purity and holiness, the key to lasting effectiveness in all of life: constant contemplation of the glory of Christ. ❧

44

THE LOVE OF GOD
PAST AND PRESENT

Meditation on Romans 5:8

God demonstrates His own love toward us,
in that while we were yet sinners, Christ died for us.

Notice in the text above that "demonstrates" is present tense and "died" is past tense. "God demonstrates His own love toward us, in that while we were yet sinners, Christ died for us." The present tense implies that this *demonstrating* is an ongoing act that keeps happening in today's present and tomorrow's present, which we call the future.

The past tense, "died," implies that the death of Christ happened once for all and will not be repeated. "Christ...died for sins once for all, the just for the unjust, so that He might bring us to God" (1 Peter 3:18).

Why did Paul use the present tense ("God demonstrates")? I would have expected Paul to say, "God demonstrated [past tense] His own love toward us, in that while we were yet sinners, Christ died for us." Was not the death of Christ the demonstration of God's love? Did not that demonstration happen in the past? So why does Paul say, "God demonstrates," instead of "God demonstrated"?

I think the clue is given a few verses earlier. Paul has just said that "tribulation brings about perseverance; and perseverance, proven character; and proven character, hope; and hope does not disappoint" (verses 3–5). In other words, the goal of everything God takes us through is hope. He wants us to feel unwaveringly hopeful through all tribulations.

But how can we? Tribulations by definition are anti-hope. If they felt hopeful in themselves, they wouldn't be tribulations. What's the underlying secret of actually growing in hope through tribulation?

Paul answers in the next line: "Because the love of God has been poured out within our hearts through the Holy Spirit who was given to us" (verse 5). God's love has been poured out in our hearts. The tense of this verb means that God's love was poured out in our hearts in the past (at our conversion), and it is still present and active.

So Paul's point is that the Spirit-given assurance and enjoyment of the love of God are the secret to growing in hope through tribulation. Tribulation works perseverance and proven character and unashamed hope because, at every point along the way, the Spirit of God is assuring us of the love of God in and through all the trouble.

Now we can see why Paul uses the present tense in verse 8: "God demonstrates his own love toward us." This is the very work of the Holy Spirit referred to in verse 5: God the Holy Spirit is pouring out and shedding abroad in our hearts the love of God.

God did demonstrate his love for us in giving his own Son to die once for all in the past for our sins (verse 8). But he also knows that this past love must be experienced as a present reality (today and tomorrow) if we are to have patience and character and hope. Therefore he not only demonstrated it on Calvary, he goes on demonstrating it now by the Spirit. He does this by opening the eyes of our hearts to see the glory of the cross and the guarantee it gives that nothing can separate us from the love of God in Christ Jesus (Romans 8:39). ∼

45

SEEKING PEOPLE ON THE STRETCH FOR GOD

Thoughts on Being Fellow Workers with God

In his little book *The Master Plan of Discipleship,* Robert Coleman shows something amazing. In the Book of Acts, evangelistic strategy seems to focus mainly on people who have been prepared in some way by God to be receptive. God is the great evangelist. He is the one who prepares and persuades. He awakens sinners (Ephesians 2:5), opens their hearts (Acts 16:14), draws them (John 6:44), empowers the gospel (2 Thessalonians 3:1), and calls the lost (1 Corinthians 1:24). It is not surprising then that our part in evangelism would be to join with God as fellow workers in what he is doing. The Book of Acts points in this direction. For example:

- The outpouring of the Spirit at Pentecost unleashed the gospel on a host of spiritually sensitive Jews who had come from at least fifteen different nations to worship the God of the Old Testament.

- The next big harvest came in Samaria (Acts 8:4–25), where Jesus earlier had laid a foundation by his witness (John 4:4–42).

- The Holy Spirit sent Philip to an Ethiopian eunuch who was reading the scroll of Isaiah and was puzzling over who chapter 53 was talking about (Acts 8:26–39).

- The evangelistic breakthrough with Gentiles outside Jerusalem came

with Cornelius, who feared God and gave alms and prayed and had a
vision of God's messenger (Acts 10).

- When Paul launched his missionary career, he followed the pattern of
  going first to the synagogue in search of some receptive Jews or God-fearing
  Gentiles (Acts 13:5, 14, 42f; 14:1; 17:1f, 10, 17; 18:4, 7, 19, 26; 19:8).

- On his second missionary journey, Paul's planning was checked twice
  by the Lord. The Holy Spirit forbade him (for the moment) to speak
  the word in Asia (Acts 16:6), and the Spirit of Jesus did not allow them
  to go to Bithynia (Acts 16:7). Instead, Paul saw a vision with a man
  saying, "Come over to Macedonia and help us" (Acts 16:9). The focus
  again was on the spiritually receptive.

- In Philippi there was no synagogue. So Paul found a place where
  women prayed outside the city and joined them, where one was
  converted (Acts 16:12–14).

Of course, there were times when Paul simply "argued...in the market
place every day with those who chanced to be there" (Acts 17:17, RSV). Yet
there does seem to be enough of a pattern to encourage us in our own evangelism, as Coleman says, "to look for those who want to move for Christ. Life
is too short to expend excessive time and energy upon apathetic people."[18]

This seems right to me, not that we ignore the spiritually callous, but that
we focus mainly on the ones who seem to be groping for God. It's true that
God's purpose in world missions demands that we go to all peoples, including
the most resistant, since they are to be part of the glorious mosaic of all nations
who will be represented in heaven (Revelation 5:9; 7:9). Nevertheless, as
Coleman says, "Even in penetrating unreached peoples the principle applies.
Ministry to the larger community will disclose those sensitive to the message of
Christ. These persons then can receive more cultivation and teaching."[19]

To put it another way, we are partners with the Holy Spirit, and we should be alert to those who are beginning to be awakened by his grace. Seek out those who are on the stretch for God and concentrate energy on their development. Coleman is no doubt right when he says, "I am convinced that a few such persons are within the influence of every Christian."[20] ❧

46

WHY SOME SPIRITUAL GIFTS ATTRACT UNSTABLE PEOPLE

Thoughts on the Baby or the Bathwater

The Bible is aware of unstable people. For example, 2 Peter 3:16 says (RSV), "There are some things in [Paul's letters] hard to understand, which the ignorant and unstable twist to their own destruction, as they do the other scriptures." The apostle also speaks of evil men who "entice unstable souls" (2 Peter 2:14). James 1:8 speaks of a "double-minded man, unstable in all his ways."

None of us is perfectly stable. King David and the apostle Paul knew what it was like to be in the pit of discouragement and in the clouds of ecstasy. It is not always easy to separate the sick from the sound, nor should we always try, since the same therapy is prescribed for both: namely, love. Let me describe what I mean by "unstable people," and don't fret too much if one or two of these features fit you.

1. Unstable people tend to have excessive emotional mood swings without good reasons. They can be excessively cast down or highly excited when there is no sufficient reason to be so.

2. The emotions of unstable people are not adequately connected to their reasoning and perceiving faculties. In some measure this is true of all of us, but in a sound mind, emotions are guided by true observations about reality and right thinking about these observations. In the unstable person, perceptions are skewed, and the rudder of reason is spinning free under the boat. The ship of life is blown on the sea of emotion without the normal

control provided by the rudder. Even with a good rudder, you can be blown pretty badly, but when the rudder connection is broken, things are much worse. The unstable boat of life is blown here and there on the sea of emotions.

3. Therefore unstable people are excessively insecure. Without a deep root of knowledge, trust, and emotional satisfaction in God's sovereign grace, they draw an excessive amount of security from relational circumstances. Again, we are all like this in some measure: "I believe; help my unbelief!" (Mark 9:24). But in the unstable, the problem is greater, and they are therefore vulnerable to anything that looks even remotely like criticism, disapproval, or rejection.

4. One manifestation of these problems is that unstable people are often out of touch with relational dynamics. They do not realize how they are being perceived. The ordinary restraints and requirements of simple social interaction are not part of their framework.

Why does this kind of person feel attracted in a disproportionate degree to the extraordinary spiritual gifts like prophecy, knowledge, and tongues, as well as other unusual signs and miracles? This is not an attempt to belittle the gifts, nor to deny their validity today. It is based on a simple observation from one who has tried for years to be open to all the fullness of God (Ephesians 3:19).

One possible answer is that these gifts are, by and large, above the ordinary processes of objective observation and reasoning. Therefore they provide an atmosphere that seems free from the ordinary constraints in which these people find it so hard to live. They feel that here, at last, they can say what comes to their minds without the constraints of reason, careful biblical interpretation, and sober observation that ordinarily govern the give and take of life. These spiritual gifts seem to fit their way of life: unpredictable, less connected to reasoned processes, and free from the demands of objective observation.

But I do not get the impression from reading 1 Corinthians 14 that Paul saw the atmosphere of supernatural spiritual gifts as an unstable one—nor an unloving one. So the challenge before us is how to own up to the truth of the gifts without cultivating a forum for instability. It will not do to write off the gifts because of whom they attract any more than we write off serious lectures because they attract some cold intellectuals. ❧

47

RESOLUTIONS ON GROWING OLD WITH GOD

Savoring the Faith of an Old Psalmist
Reflections on Psalm 71

I do not want to be a grumpy old man. God threatens terrible things to those who grumble (Psalm 106:25–26). Murmuring dishonors the God who promises to work all things together for our good (Romans 8:28). Complaining puts out the light of our Christian witness (Philippians 2:14–15). A critical, anxious spirit dries up joy and peace (Philippians 4:6–7). That is not the way I want to grow old.

I want to be like the aging man in Psalm 71. We know he is getting old because he prays, "Even to old age and gray hairs, O God, do not forsake me" (verse 18, RSV) and "Do not cast me off in the time of old age; forsake me not when my strength is spent" (verse 9, RSV).

Looking at this man's approach to old age I have formed some resolutions:

1. I will remember with wonder and thanks the thousands of times I have leaned on God since my youth.

For you are my hope; O Lord GOD, you are my confidence from my youth. (verse 5)

O God, you have taught me from my youth, and I still declare your wondrous deeds. (verse 17)

2. I will take refuge in God rather than taking offense at my troubles.

In You, O LORD, I have taken refuge. (verse 1)

3. I will speak to God more and more (not less and less) of all his greatness until there is no room in my mouth for murmuring.

My praise is continually of You. (verse 6)

I will...praise You yet more and more. (verse 14)

4. I will hope (doggedly) and not give in to despair, even in the nursing home, and even if I outlive all my friends.

I will hope continually. (verse 14)

5. I will find people to tell about God's wonderful acts of salvation and never run out, because they are innumerable.

My mouth shall tell of Your righteousness, and of Your salvation all day long, for I do not know the sum of them. (verse 15)

6. I will stay on the lookout for younger people and tell them about the power of God. I will tell them that God is strong and can be trusted in youth and age.

Do not forsake me, until I declare Your strength to this generation. (verse 18)

7. I will remember that there are great things about God above my imagination, and soon enough I will know these too.

Your righteousness, O God, reaches to the heavens. (verse 19)

8. I will count all my pain and trouble as a gift from God and a path to glory.

You who have shown me many troubles and distresses will revive me again. (verse 20)

9. I will resist stereotypes of old people, and play and sing and shout with joy (whether it looks dignified or not).

I will praise You with the harp, even Your truth, O my God; to you I will sing praises with the lyre, O Holy One of Israel. (verse 22)

My lips will shout for joy, when I sing praises to You. (verse 23)

I invite you to join me in these resolutions and to bank your hope on the precious promise of God to his aged ones: "Even to your old age I am He, and to gray hairs I will carry you. I have made, and I will bear; I will carry and will save" (Isaiah 46:4, RSV). ❧

48

CONTRACTS, COVENANTS, AND SELF-DEIFICATION

Thoughts on the Cost of Integrity

Minneapolis almost had to pay thirty-one million dollars to a French firm that intended to build two hundred stores under a dome at the south end of downtown along the Nicollet Mall. The city allegedly backed out on a signed deal. The jury originally said that this was a breach of contract and the city must pay up. Why did this happen? One local newspaper commentator said it happened because of "the city's casual ideas about contracts."

A contract is a form of commercial covenant. This failure to take covenants more seriously almost cost the city of Minneapolis $85 per citizen. The $510 that it might have cost my family at the time is not my concern here. It is only symbolic of a far deeper truth: Namely, the loss of covenant faithfulness destroys life.

The catch is that the destruction can feel good in the process. No one breaks a covenant (or contract) because it hurts to do so. No one sins out of duty. Covenants are broken because it feels good to be free from the commitment. Covenant breaking is a way of short-term pain reduction, but in the process of reducing our pain, we destroy life.

One might say that the whole Old Testament is written to persuade the world that the short-term happiness of covenant breaking leads to destruction and misery. The Lord God said,

If you...break my covenant...I will appoint over you sudden terror, consumption, and fever that...cause life to pine away. And you shall sow your seed in vain, for your enemies shall eat it. (Leviticus 26:15–16, RSV)

Can a man...break the covenant and yet escape?... Therefore thus says the Lord GOD: As I live, surely my oath which he despised, and my covenant which he broke, I will requite upon his head. (Ezekiel 17:15, 19, RSV)

But in America a whole religion of self-psychology has risen which makes covenant faithfulness almost unintelligible. The concept of God has been so reduced and internalized that whatever is left of the sacred has its center in the self, which means that today covenant commitment is primarily a commitment to "god," namely, self. And the primary duty of this "covenant" is to feel personally happy and fulfilled, even if vows are forsaken, promises are not kept, and contracts are broken.

An avalanche of books and articles on how to look out for number one and pull your own strings and be your own best friend have spread the root fallacy, as Daniel Yankelovich says, that "the human self can be wholly autonomous, solitary, contained and 'self-created.'"[21]

The truth is that true selfhood flourishes in covenant faithfulness. By "true" I mean the self that has been created in Christ Jesus and is being transformed into his likeness. For example, Paul says in Colossians 3:9–10, "Do not lie to one another, since you laid aside the old self with its evil practices, and have put on the new self." The true self does not emerge and flourish in the autonomy of self-gratification without regard to keeping promises. The true self is created by the Truth and flourishes in relationships of truth telling and covenant keeping.

Of course, this only makes sense if God is the central reality of our lives. Standing by our word in the face of great loss or pain would be self-destructive if God did not promise to set all things right and work for those who hope in him instead of hoping in expedient shrewdness (Psalm 37:5; Isaiah 64:4; Proverbs 3:5–6). Covenant breaking as a means of pain reduction always backfires, because it spurns the promises of the only One who can remove all mourning, crying, and pain (Revelation 21:4).

God is exalted in our honesty when we look to him and not to our schemes. And when God is exalted in our lives, we discover what we were created to be. No pursuit of self-enhancement without this exaltation of God will succeed. But if we humble ourselves with confidence in God's future grace, and by this faith submit to his command for promise-keeping integrity, then he will exalt us in due time (Luke 18:14). Because to exalt the one who keeps promises by trusting God is to exalt the One trusted. ∾

49

BREAKFAST, BENJAMIN, AND BABY-WORK

How to Receive Jesus

A
t the breakfast table God opened my eyes again. As a family we were reading through the Gospel of Luke. That morning we came to the part where the disciples were arguing (again!) about which of them was the greatest (9:46). Jesus did something surprising this time.

He took a child and put him by his side, and said to them, "Whoever receives this child in my name receives me, and whoever receives me receives him who sent me; for he who is least among you all is the one who is great." (Luke 9:47–48)

I read this to Karsten, Benjamin, Abraham, and Barnabas. Then I said, "This is strange. What does 'receiving a child' have to do with 'being least'? It looks like Jesus is saying that receiving a child is the same as being least. What does he mean?"

Karsten and I agreed: It must mean that spending time with children was a sort of low-priority, insignificant, demeaning work—at least that's the way Jesus' disciples were looking at it. So if you spent time receiving and caring for children, you were one of the "least" people.

Eleven-year-old Benjamin was listening to all this. You have to understand that Benjamin was a regular worker in Nursery I. His name and phone number stood on a list with 108 other "least" people who worked in Nursery I.

He would get an official postcard from Beth, the coordinator of all these "least" people, to remind him of his upcoming duty. He had a white sheet of nursery guidelines, a cream sheet of information for the nursery, and a gold sheet with the monthly schedule.

Benjamin heard us explain that "receiving a child in Jesus' name" is like "being least" because it was work nobody wanted to do. So he said, "But that's not the way it is at church! It's not low work."

At that moment, as I opened my mouth to respond, I found myself saying a most wonderful truth: "Benjamin, I think that's because God is creating a Christlike atmosphere at Bethlehem." At least that's the way it ought to be.

Jesus took the child-belittling culture of his day that defined greatness to exclude "receiving children," and he turned it upside down. He said: "Receiving children in my name may be the world's least, but the world's least is my great. So wherever the Spirit of Christ pervades, the people who receive children will no longer be the 'least.' They will be 'great.'"

Really? Why? Because Jesus says that when you receive a child in his name (that is, with love in Jesus' strength and for his glory), you receive Jesus himself. In that act of love for the glory of Christ, Jesus himself draws near and makes his fellowship more real and more sweet. Jesus continued by saying that when you receive him in this way, you also receive God the Father. Which means that Nursery I may be more full of God on Sunday morning than any other room in the church.

Yes, Benjamin, it is a great work. May you love it all your days! ❧

50

THE IRIS BY MY WALK

---❦---

Thoughts on God's
Direct Involvement in Creation

I have been picking up little things in reading the Scriptures that show God's intimate involvement in creation. For example, in 1 Corinthians 15:38, Paul is comparing how a seed is planted in one form and comes up in another form with a body different from all other bodies. He says, "God gives it a body just as He wished, and to each of the seeds a body of its own." This is a remarkable statement of God's involvement in the way he designed each seed to bring forth its own unique plant (not just species, but each individual seed!). Paul is not teaching about botany here; he is teaching about the resurrection. At the same time Paul shows how he takes God's intimate involvement with creation for granted. He cannot imagine that any natural process should be conceived without God's doing it.

In Psalm 94:9 it says, "He who planted the ear, does he not hear? He who formed the eye, does he not see?" (RSV). The psalmist assumes that God was the designer of the eye and that he designed the way the ear is planted in the head to do its hearing work. So when we marvel at the wonders of the eye and the remarkable structure of the ear, we are not to marvel at the processes of chance but at the wisdom and creativity of God.

Similarly in Psalm 95:5, "The sea is his, for he made it; for his hands formed the dry land" (RSV). The involvement of God in land and sea is such that the present sea is his. It is not as though he in some impersonal way set it all in motion a billion years ago. Rather he is the one who owns it because he made it. It is today his handiwork and bears the marks of his creator's claim on it—like a piece of art belongs to the one who painted it until he sells it or gives it away.

This is a call for us to be God-centered in our admiration of the wonders of the world. Charles Spurgeon was a great lover of nature as well as a great preacher in London over a hundred years ago. As with preaching, so with observing nature, he was radically God-centered and God-exalting:

> I believe that every particle of dust that dances in the sunbeam does not move an atom more or less than God wishes—that every particle of spray that dashes against the steamboat has its orbit, as well as the sun in the heavens—that the chaff from the hand of the winnower is steered as the stars in their courses. The creeping of an aphid over the rosebud is as much fixed as the march of the devastating pestilence—the fall of...leaves from a poplar is as fully ordained as the tumbling of an avalanche.[22]

Every wonder in the world is wrought by God. He decided exactly how the iris beside our fence should look this morning when it came to flower. God means for the beauty of that plant—not just that kind of plant, but that very plant—to be an occasion for our worshiping his specific creativity. "God gives it a body just as He wished, and to each of the seeds a body of its own." ∿

51

PRAYER AND PREDESTINATION

A Conversation between Prayerful and Prayerless

Prayerless: I understand that you believe in the providence of God. Is that right?

Prayerful: Yes.

Prayerless: Does that mean you believe, like the Heidelberg Catechism says, that nothing comes about by chance, but only by God's design and plan?

Prayerful: Yes, I believe that's what the Bible teaches. Job prays, "No purpose of Yours can be thwarted" (42:2). There are lots of texts like that.

Prayerless: Then why do you pray?

Prayerful: I don't see the problem. Why shouldn't we pray?

Prayerless: Well, if God ordains and controls everything, then what he plans from of old will come to pass, right?

Prayerful: Yes.

Prayerless: So it's going to come to pass whether you pray or not, right?

Prayerful: That depends on whether God ordained for it to come to pass in answer to prayer. If God predestined that something happen in answer to prayer, it won't happen without prayer.

Prayerless: Wait a minute, this is confusing. Are you saying that every answer to prayer is predestined?

Prayerful: Yes it is. It's predestined as an answer to prayer.

Prayerless: So if the prayer doesn't happen, the answer doesn't happen?

Prayerful: That's right.

Prayerless: So the event is contingent on our praying for it to happen?

Prayerful: Yes. I take it that by contingent you mean prayer is a real reason that the event happens, and without the prayer the event would not happen.

Prayerless: Yes, that's what I mean. But how can an event be contingent on my prayer and still be eternally fixed and predestined by God?

Prayerful: Because your prayer is as fixed as the predestined answer.

Prayerless: Explain.

Prayerful: It's not complicated. God providentially ordains all events. God never ordains an event without a cause. The cause is also an event. Therefore the cause is also foreordained. So you cannot say that the event will happen if the cause doesn't because God has ordained otherwise. The event will happen if the cause happens.

Prayerless: So what you are saying is that answers to prayer are always ordained as effects of prayer, which is one of the causes, and that God predestined the answer only as an effect of the cause.

Prayerful: That's right. Since both the cause and the effect are ordained together, you can't say that the effect will happen even if the cause doesn't, because God doesn't ordain effects without causes.

Prayerless: Can you give some examples?

Prayerful: Sure. If God predestines that I die of a bullet wound, then I will not die if no bullet is fired. If God predestines that I be healed by surgery, then if there is no surgery, I will not be healed. If God predestines heat to fill my home by a fire in the furnace, then if there is no fire, there will be no heat. Would you say, "Since God predestines that the sun be bright, it will be bright whether there is fire in the sun or not"?

Prayerless: No.

Prayerful: I agree. Why not?

Prayerless: Because the brightness of the sun comes from the fire.

Prayerful: Right. That's the way I think about answers to prayer. They are the brightness and prayer is the fire. God has established the universe so that in large measure it runs by prayer, the same way he has established brightness so that in larger measure it happens by fire. Doesn't that make sense?

Prayerless: I think it does.

Prayerful: Then let's stop thinking up problems and go with what the Scriptures say: "Ask, and you will receive" (John 16:24), and "You do not have, because you do not ask" (James 4:2). ❧

52

IT DOESN'T MATTER WHAT HAPPENS TO ME

Meditation on John 12:24–25

*Unless a grain of wheat falls into the earth and dies,
it remains alone; but if it dies, it bears much fruit. He who loves his life loses it,
and he who hates his life in this world will keep it to life eternal.*

I t doesn't matter what happens to me." Those are the words that keep coming back to me as I try to express what Jesus meant when he spoke the words of John 12:24–25.

First, there is the call to die. If we are to bear fruit for God, we must die. Now when I am dead, I will not care what they do with my body. It will make no difference to me. I will be home with Jesus. That's the way it is now, too, if I have died already with Christ, which all Christians have. "Those who belong to Christ Jesus have crucified the flesh with its passions and desires" (Galatians 5:24). Crucified means dead. So in a profound sense I am dead on the earth. "[My life] is hidden with Christ in God" (Colossians 3:3). So it just doesn't matter what happens to me here on earth.

Then there is this strange thing called "hating your life in this world." "He who hates his life in this world will keep it to life eternal" (John 12:25). What does that mean? It means, at least, that you don't take much thought for your life in this world. In other words, it just doesn't matter much what happens to your life in this world.

If men speak well of you, it doesn't matter much. If they hate you, it doesn't matter much. If you have a lot of things, it doesn't matter much. If you have little, it doesn't matter much. If you are persecuted or lied about, it doesn't matter much. If you are famous or unknown, it doesn't matter much. If you are dead, these things just don't matter much.

Yet this is even more radical. There are some choices to be made here, not just passive experiences. Jesus goes on to say, "If anyone serves Me, he must follow Me" (John 12:26). Where to? He is moving into Gethsemane and toward the cross. Jesus is not just saying: If things go bad, don't fret, since you are dead anyway. He is saying, "Choose to die with me. Choose to hate your life in this world the way I have chosen the cross."

This is what Jesus meant when he said, "If anyone wishes to come after Me, he must deny himself, and take up his cross, and follow Me" (Matthew 16:24). He calls us to choose the cross. People did only one thing on a cross. They died on it. "Take up your cross," means, "Like a grain of wheat, fall into the ground and die." Choose it. "Hate your life in this world."

What's the point of all this? Is it aimless masochism? No. It is the path of true love, true life, and true worship. Our aim in dying is fruit: "But if it dies, it bears much fruit" (John 12:24). Our aim in dying is life: "He who hates his life in this world shall keep it to life eternal" (John 12:25). Our aim in dying is to exalt the worth of Christ: "I count all things to be loss in view of the surpassing value of knowing Christ Jesus my Lord, for whom I have suffered the loss of all things" (Philippians 3:8).

Paul is the great example of what it means to die. He said, "[We carry] about in the body the dying of Jesus, so that the life of Jesus also may be manifested in our body" (2 Corinthians 4:10), and "[Through] the cross of our Lord Jesus Christ...the world has been crucified to me, and I to the world" (Galatians 6:14).

But why? For the sake of radical commitment to ministry: "I do not consider my life of any account as dear to myself, so that I may finish my course and the ministry which I received from the Lord Jesus, to testify solemnly of the gospel of the grace of God" (Acts 20:24). I think I hear Paul saying, "It doesn't matter what happens to me if I can just live to the glory of his grace."

Can you speak Paul's words as your own? Can you desire to? Ask God earnestly that it would be so more and more. ❧

53

BACK TO SCHOOL:
A BIBLICAL PERSPECTIVE

————

Thinking about Thinking and God

R eadin', writin', and 'rithmetic have to do with thinking.

Reading well does not mean moving your eyes quickly over the letters on a page. It means grasping facts and ideas accurately, assessing their truth and beauty correctly, and making use of them to lead a good life.

Arithmetic, at the simplest levels, means stocking the mind with tools for thought (the tables of addition, subtraction, multiplication, and division). At more advanced levels, math is the exercise of logic for building things and living wisely: How many windows will we have to enlarge to bring the room up to code if one window is required for every 144 square feet of floor space? Which is the better buy, three eight-ounce boxes at $1.00 each or two twelve-ounce boxes at $1.40 each?

Writing is what you learn so you can preserve for yourself and communicate to others what you are thinking.

This business of education is God's business. He gave us minds that think. He created the world we think about. He wrote the book of nature. He made the rules of logic. He is the standard of true and false, good and bad, beautiful and ugly. To ignore him is to be profoundly undereducated. Meditate (and help your children meditate) on the following biblical truths.

• We are commanded to love the Lord with our minds.

[Jesus] said to him, "You shall love the Lord your God with all your heart, and with all your soul, and with all your mind." (Matthew 22:37, RSV)

• Without God as the highest value of education, all thinking becomes futile, dark, and sordid.

Although they knew God they did not honor him as God or give thanks to him, but they became futile in their thinking and their senseless minds were darkened.... Since they did not see fit to acknowledge God, God gave them up to a base mind and to improper conduct. (Romans 1:21, 28, RSV)

• We are commanded to be mature in our thinking.

Brethren, do not be children in your thinking; be babes in evil, but in thinking be mature. (1 Corinthians 14:20, RSV)

• The failure to love truth will lead to destruction.

They refused to love the truth and so be saved. (2 Thessalonians 2:10, RSV)

• Wise people seek to grow in knowledge.

The mind of him who has understanding seeks knowledge, but the mouths of fools feed on folly. (Proverbs 15:14, RSV)

An intelligent mind acquires knowledge, and the ear of the wise seeks knowledge. (Proverbs 18:15, RSV)

Incline your ear, and hear the words of the wise, and apply your mind to my knowledge. (Proverbs 22:17; see Proverbs 2:1–6; 23:12, RSV)

• Thinking does not replace God, and God does not replace thinking.

Think over what I say, for the Lord will grant you understanding in everything. (2 Timothy 2:7, RSV)

Everything, absolutely everything, has to do with God. All things are from him and through him and to him (Romans 11:36). Therefore going to school is from his design of human thinking, through his gift of life and breath and motivation, and for his glory. This is the most important lesson our children should learn about school. ∾

54

O CROSS OF CHRIST, MY LIBERTY AND POWER!

Meditation on My Remaining Corruption

I could not go on without the cross. Why? Because periodically I discover surprising sinfulness in me that I did not know anything about. Without the cross to cover all that, I would despair because I am sure that in the folds of my heart there remains unknown corruption.

For example, on a Monday afternoon, I considered making a crucial visit to one of our members. It would be a hard visit, but I knew that I should probably do it. I had to write a lecture the next day (Tuesday), and so I put off until another day making the appointment.

Before I left the church that Monday, our business administrator gave me a copy of the newest version of our word processing program. I was really excited to see what this new version could do.

The next morning I got up, ate, spent some time in the Scriptures, and could hardly wait to experiment with the new program. As I was about to set it up, something hit me: If I "have to" write a lecture today, why am I about to take two hours to install and play with this new program? There is absolutely no pressure to install it today. None.

Why was the pressure of lecture preparation an infallible reason for not making that tough visit today, but no reason at all for not playing with the new computer program?

The answer was too plain—painfully plain. I put the visit off because I didn't feel like making it. But the computer program was like a new toy and

I really wanted to play with it. My mind was able to support my desire not to visit by supplying the necessary "reason." No time on Tuesday. Lecture preparation.

Yet as soon as there was a special chance to play with my computer on Tuesday, my mind was quite ready to withdraw the reason. By the sheer grace of God, I saw what was happening.

What a wretch, I thought to myself. What a fickle wretch! Is that how my mind works—simply passing out rational permission slips for what I already want to do? How many times has this happened?

This time the Lord opened my eyes to my irrational self-justifying effort to sanction what I already felt like doing. I repented, set aside the new program, and called the church member to ask if I could come over.

I thank God for that moment of victory over the exceedingly deceptive power of sin. But I do not kid myself. The remaining corruption that twists the mind to justify our desires on the basis of ostensible principle is deep and elusive. I hate it.

And when, by the grace of God, I see its effects, I kiss the cross and kill my flesh. What would I do without the grand assurance: "Christ died for the ungodly.... We are now justified by his blood" (Romans 5:6, 9, RSV). O Cross of Christ, my liberty and power! In you, I face this day anew, a sinner justified and free! ∾

55

COMBUSTIBLE SOUND BITES FROM THE BATTLEFIELD

———◆◆◆———

Recollections from Lausanne II

O ne of the great moments of my life was the Second Lausanne Congress on World Evangelization in Manila in 1989. It mightily renewed my zeal to spread a passion for the supremacy of God in all things for the joy of all peoples. I jotted down explosive sentences that landed on me with power day after day. Many of them still burn in my heart. A few others were brought up from my memory and made to live again. Here they are. Read at your own risk.

There is not an inch of any sphere of life over which Jesus Christ does not say, "Mine." (Os Guiness quoting Abraham Kuyper)

No local church can afford to go without the encouragement and nourishment that will come to it by sending away its best people. (David Penman)

In America the most important thing is that people have freedom. In restricted countries the most important thing is what people do with freedom. (George Otis)

Jesus will judge us not only for what we did, but also for what we could have done and didn't. (George Otis)

Expect great things from God, attempt great things for God. (William Carey)

We cannot preach good news and be bad news. (Tekmito Adegemo)

Far away is far away only if you don't go there. (George Otis)

Is our failure to thrive in Muslim countries the absence of martyrs? Can a covert church grow in strength? Does a young church need martyr models? (George Otis)

God almost never calls his people to a fair fight. (George Otis)

The cross is not the terrible end to an otherwise God-fearing and happy life, but it meets us at the beginning of our communion with Christ. When Christ calls a man, he bids him come and die. (Dietrich Bonhoeffer)

I tell you, my friends, do not fear those who kill the body, and after that have no more that they can do. (Jesus; see Luke 12:4)

He is no fool who gives what he cannot keep to gain what he cannot lose. (Jim Elliot)

For to me, to live is Christ, and to die is gain. (Apostle Paul; Philippians 1:21)

I am immortal until God's work for me to do is done. The Lord reigns. (Henry Martyn)

Some of you they will put to death; you will be hated by all for my name's sake. But not a hair of your head will perish. (Jesus; Luke 21:16–18, RSV)

Lord, make me free from fear and greed, to be like Jesus. (John Piper— my prayer today) ✑

56

BORN TO DIE
FOR OUR FREEDOM

―∽∾∿―

Meditation on Hebrews 2:14–15

Therefore, since the children share in flesh and blood,
He Himself likewise also partook of the same,
that through death He might render powerless him who had the power of death,
that is, the devil, and might free those who through fear of death
were subject to slavery all their lives.

Some passages of Scripture are so thick with crucial truth that they deserve more than others to be memorized and pondered and proclaimed. These two verses in Hebrews set before us a sequence of the greatest realities in the world. To know these two verses by heart and to know what they mean is a benefit greater than the biggest windfall on earth. Linger for a few moments over each phrase.

Therefore, since the children share in flesh and blood...

The term *children* is taken from the previous verse and refers to the spiritual offspring of Christ, the Messiah (see Isaiah 8:18; 53:10). These are also the children of God. In sending Christ, God has the salvation of his children specially in view. It is true that "God so loved the world, that he gave [Jesus]" (John 3:16), but it is also true that God was especially gathering "the children of God who are scattered abroad" (John 11:52), and that he lays down his life for his sheep (John 10:15). God's design was to offer Christ to the world and to effect the salvation of his "children" (see 1 Timothy 4:10). You may experience adoption as children of God by receiving Christ (John 1:12).

...He Himself likewise also partook of the same [flesh and blood]...

Christ existed before the incarnation. He was spirit. He was the eternal Word. He was with God and was God (John 1:1; Colossians 2:9), but he took on flesh and blood and clothed his deity with humanity. He became fully man and remained fully God. It is a great mystery in many ways. But it is at the heart of our faith and is what the Bible teaches.

...that through death...

The reason he became man was to die. As God, he could not die for sinners, but as man he could. His aim was to die. Therefore he had to be born a man. He was born to die. Good Friday is the reason for Christmas. Christ embraced death willingly. It was his intention. It did not take him off guard. His suffering and death were planned by the Father from of old. Isaiah 53 describes it in some detail hundreds of years before it happened. Jesus chose to become man that he might die.

...He might render powerless him who had the power of death, that is, the devil...

In dying, Christ defanged the devil. How? By covering all our sin. This means that Satan has no legitimate grounds to accuse us before God: "Who will bring a charge against God's elect? God is the one who justifies" (Romans 8:33). On what grounds does he justify? Through the blood of Jesus (Romans 5:9). Satan's ultimate weapon against us is our own sin. But what happened on the cross nullifies the condemning power of our sin: "[God] canceled out the certificate of debt consisting of decrees [the Law] against us, which was hostile to us; and He has taken it out of the way, having nailed it to the cross" (Colossians 2:14). If the death of Jesus takes away the condemning power of our sin, then the chief weapon of the devil is taken out of his hand. He cannot make a case for our death penalty, because the Judge has acquitted us by the death of his Son! The sting of death is gone: Our sin is forgiven and the Law is fulfilled (1 Corinthians 15:56–57).

...and might free those who through fear of death were subject to slavery all their lives.

So we are free from the fear of death. God has justified us. Satan cannot overturn that decree. And God means for our ultimate safety to have an immediate effect on our lives. He means for the happy ending to take away the slavery and fear of the now. If we do not need to fear our last and greatest enemy, death, then we do not need to fear anything. We can be free. Free for joy. Free for others.

Christ died—ponder this price—that you might not fear. Measuring by the sacrifice, the intensity of God's commitment to your fearlessness—your freedom—is immeasurable. Take it. Enjoy it. His liberating power will shine as you savor the liberty of life. ❧

57

MAGNIFICENT MANUMISSION

Meditation on Romans 6:17–18

> *But thanks be to God that though you were slaves of sin,*
> *you became obedient from the heart to that form of teaching to which you were*
> *committed, and having been freed from sin,*
> *you became slaves of righteousness.*

Manumission: \man-ye-'mish-en\ n [fr. Latin *manumissio*]: the act or process of formal emancipation from slavery.

We are either slaves of sin or slaves of God; there is no third alternative. You can call it different things, but it boils down to this: We serve sin or we serve God. Sin reigns or God reigns.

Therefore Romans 6 describes conversion as a change of slave masters. "Thanks be to God that though you were slaves of sin...you became slaves of righteousness...having been freed from sin and enslaved to God" (verses 17–18, 22).

But watch out! Don't carry over all the implications of sin-slavery to God-slavery. There are radical dissimilarities. Consider these crucial verses from Romans 6:20–23: "When you were slaves of sin, you were free in regard to righteousness. 21But then what fruit did you get from the things of which you are now ashamed? The end of those things is death. 22But now that you have been set free from sin and have become slaves of God, the fruit you get is sanctification and its end, eternal life. 23For the wages of sin is death, but the free gift of God is eternal life in Christ Jesus our Lord" (author's translation).

OLD SLAVERY	NEW "SLAVERY"
slave master is sin (20)	slave master is God (22)
free from righteousness (20)	free from sin (22)
benefit? none (21)	fruit? sanctification (22)
the final end? death (21)	the final end? eternal life (22)
the master pays wages (23)	the master gives gifts (23)
the wage is death (23)	the gift is eternal life (23)

There is a radical breakdown in the parallels here. The whole concept of slavery as we know it is transformed when God becomes the "Slave Master."

The old slave master pays wages, but God gives gifts. "The wages of sin…but the free gift of God…." This is all important! We do not relate to God as wage earners. We relate to him as gift receivers. Our "slave role" is not working for wages, but walking submissively where the gifts are, which means walking by faith.

Why didn't Paul answer his own question in verse 21, "What fruit did you get from the things of which you are now ashamed?" The answer is that sin does not bear fruit; it demands works and pays wages. But when you are a "slave" of God, the fruit you get is sanctification, and the "payoff" for this from God is not a wage but a free gift—eternal life.

So our new "Slave master" does not demand "work"; he produces fruit. He does not pay wages for work; he gives gifts in reward for his own fruit. And the gift is eternal life, while the only wage a sinner can earn is death. Beware of a wage relation to God. There is no such thing. The master in spiritual wage relations is always sin, and the wage is always death.

In view of this magnificent manumission, I urge you to the obvious: "Do not go on presenting the members of your body to sin as instruments of unrighteousness, but present yourselves to God as those alive from the dead, and your members as instruments of righteousness to God" (Romans 6:13). ❧

58

WHAT CONDOM ADS
PRODUCED

An Exchange of Letters

A few years ago the *Minneapolis Star Tribune* printed an editorial I wrote titled, "Condom Ads Promote Promiscuity, Not Good Health." There had been a brouhaha in our town about whether such ads were a good idea. Somehow the media got to me for an opinion, and then with some other pastors I wrote to say that the advertising was a bad idea. Two days later I received the following letter. It shows a slice of "real world" sexual amorality.

The letter: "After reading your commentary on condom ads I for one am glad I am not a member of an organization that thinks on the same lines as you folks do. You all have your heads deep in the sand. I am single and thirty-eight years old, so according to you I am not to have sex until the day I get married. What if I never marry? Am I never to have sex? I for one like to have sex, and so does my girlfriend. And physical stimulation of the sexual nature is one of the greatest feelings one can have. Without it you lose something from your general well-being."

My response: "I appreciate your honesty and your willingness to sign your letter to me. Not everyone has the courage to stand behind his opinion.

"Yes, you are right in concluding that I think people should not engage in sexual intercourse outside marriage. I certainly agree that our sexual nature is good and that the experience of consummation in sexual relations is a 'great feeling.'

"What I don't agree with is that these good physical feelings can be pursued without regard to larger issues in life, like commitment and loyalty. Or, to put it another way, I'm profoundly convinced that since sexuality is a gift of God, we should look to God for guidance in how to handle this remarkably precious gift.

"When I look to God's written Word, the Bible, I find the teaching that premarital and extramarital sex are forbidden. Since God is a God of love and wisdom, I take that to mean that it would be good for me to abstain from sexual intercourse outside of marriage.

"Yes, in a sense, those who don't marry experience 'loss'—the loss of a physical sensation—but they also experience great gain. The moral and emotional thrill of being master over your own impulses is like reaching a snow-swept mountain peak against all the odds of ice and wind. The greatest pleasures in life do not come from giving in to bodily impulses that we share with animals. The greatest pleasures in life come by rising to that moral, personal, spiritual conformity with our Creator, in whose image we were made.

"I wonder if you would want to say that because Jesus was never married and never experienced sexual intercourse, he was somehow less admirable, less worthy of our trust, obedience, and praise?

"Please know that I do not resent your writing to me, nor do I despise you because of your opinions. My deep desire is that you would simply take more seriously the possibility that our sexuality may be an expression of extraordinary love rather than Victorian prudery."

He wrote back a conciliatory letter saying he respected my views. I still pray he will stop settling for mud pies in the slum when a holiday in the Alps is offered in allegiance to Jesus. ❦

59

NO PRAYER, NO POWER

---~~~---

Thoughts on the Offense and Defense
of Spiritual Life

I rearranged my study at home, but I did not remove the prayer corner
or the prayer bench. I made it more private. All I have ever read and
experienced teaches me that deep spiritual influence for the good of
sinners and the glory of God comes from men and women who give themselves to prayer and meditation. My longings often exceed my actions, I
admit, but I will not give up without a fight, and making a place is part of
the war effort.

I just read, for example, about the secret of Charles Simeon, who
endured great hardships in his powerful fifty-four-year pastorate in
Cambridge, England (1782–1836). His friend, R. Housman, stayed with
him for a few months and tells us something of this man's devotion: "Never
did I see such consistency, and reality of devotion, such warmth of piety,
such zeal and love…. Invariably he arose every morning, though it was the
winter season, at four o'clock; and after lighting his fire, he devoted the first
four hours of the day to private prayer and the devotional study of the
Scriptures…. Here was the secret of his great grace and spiritual strength.
Deriving instruction from such a source, and seeking it with such diligence,
he was comforted in all his trials, and prepared for every duty."[23]

It is true for individuals and churches. No prayer, no power. Consider
the story in Mark 9. The disciples had been unable to cast out an unclean
spirit from an afflicted boy. Jesus came on the scene and cast it out. The disciples ask, "Why could we not cast it out?" Jesus answers, "This kind cannot

be driven out by anything but prayer"[24] (Mark 9:29, RSV). There are spiritual forces that Jesus says are very hard to overcome. His disciples asked why they could not overcome the evil. Jesus answered, "Insufficient prayer!"

What did he mean? Probably not that they hadn't prayed over the demonized boy; it seems that would have been the first and basic approach. Probably he means that they had not lived in prayer. They had been caught in a prayerless period of life or a prayerless frame of mind. Notice that Jesus cast out the demon without praying: "You dumb and deaf spirit, I command you, come out of him, and never enter him again" (Mark 9:25, RSV). Yet Jesus had prayed. He lived in prayer. He spent whole nights in prayer. He was ready when evil came. But apparently the disciples had become weak and negligent in their praying, so they were powerless in the face of strong evil forces: "This kind cannot be driven out by anything but prayer."

In other words, without persistent prayer we have no offense in the battle with evil. Individually and as churches we are meant to invade and plunder the strongholds of Satan. But no prayer, no power.

The same is true of defense. Consider the words of the Lord to Peter, James, and John when they fell asleep in the garden instead of keeping up their guard on the defense against evil. "Watch and pray," Jesus said, "that you may not enter into temptation" (Mark 14:38, RSV). If we are not vigilant, we will be ensnared by temptation. Our defense and our offense is an active, persistent, earnest, believing prayer force.

Let the example of Charles Simeon, the words of our Lord, and the chastisement of the disciples spur us on not just to periodic prayers, but to a life of prayer. As Housman said, to "a consistency and reality of devotion." ❧

60

WHY DO YOU BELIEVE JESUS
ROSE FROM THE DEAD?

On Having an Answer for the Hope in Us

T he odd thing about this question, "Why do you believe Jesus rose from the dead?" is that I usually have to sit and ponder awhile to remember some answers that begin to sound compelling to non-Christian seekers. At first this seems phony: If I believe it, why do I have to study up to support it?

But when you think about it a little longer, it's not phony at all. If I can't remember how I met my wife, it doesn't mean I'm not married. If I can't find words to account for the affection in my heart, it doesn't mean there is no such thing as love. Memory lags. Words fail. But neither means that I have no basis for love.

Still, shouldn't we be able to give a simple answer to the question of why we believe that Jesus rose from the dead? If we deal with a Jesus living every day, shouldn't we be able to say why we believe that? Yes, I suppose we should.

What kind of answer might that be? Well, we might say, "I believe Jesus rose from the dead because the Bible says so." Someone will object: "That's just an appeal to authority." So it is, but that's the way most people answer questions about why they believe things they can't see.

Ask the typical secular American why he believes in viruses, radiation, pulsars, or evolution. Virtually everyone will say something like, "Because science has shown…"

What they mean is that they don't know how to demonstrate why certain unseen realities exist. So they are willing to base their belief on the testimony of an authority—in this case a group of scientists. This is especially true if the belief helps make sense out of the world.

The reason that saying, "Because the Bible tells me so," sounds unacceptable while, "Because the scientists tell me so," sounds acceptable is that more people appeal to scientific authority than to biblical authority. And large majorities always make opinions sound normative and obvious, but in principle, we are both doing the same thing.

So we must ask, Are the men who wrote the New Testament a good authority on the resurrection of Jesus? Are the scientists who write about unseen viruses a good authority? That question must be answered. Now we see that we are playing fair. Most of us are more comfortable telling others why we trust a witness than we are at demonstrating resurrections—or the reality of nuclear radiation.

I find Matthew, Mark, Luke, John, Paul, Peter, James, Jude, and the writer of Hebrews to be the sort of men I would trust with my life more quickly than a host of secular authorities. And when it comes to making sense out of the world (of guilt and fear and pain), the incarnation, the cross, and the resurrection of Christ go a lot farther than viruses or evolution.

There are good, solid historical arguments in favor of Jesus' resurrection from the dead. I gathered a few of these in a little essay, "Is the Bible a Reliable Guide to Lasting Joy?"[25] But the real-life problem is this: No matter how hard you study these historical arguments to become reasonably persuaded, it is simply unrealistic to think that these reasons or arguments will be in your mind and easily accessible when your faith is tested by death or challenged by unbelievers. It is the same with any secular philosophy of life. Christians are not unique in this.

In those moments of questioning, the sustaining strength of our faith will come reasonably from a history of finding God real and his Word trustworthy in our lives. We will say, "The witnesses to Christ in the Bible have won my trust. Christ shines through their word with such compelling authenticity that I have yielded to him. No other way of seeing the world answers as many of my pressing questions as the Christian way. There is a spiritual life God has given to me so that I love him and trust him and hope to be with him more than anything else." In this way we give expression to the reality of 1 John 5:11: "The testimony [of God] is this, that God has given us eternal life, and this life is in His Son." ❧

61

PICTURE JESUS PLAYING THE LOTTERY

~~~

12/6/04

Dallying with the Soul's Suicide

Can you picture Jesus playing the lottery? What would happen inside the soul of Jesus when he reads, "Win up to ten thousand dollars now—one million dollars later...Play anywhere, win anytime...For people who just can't wait to get rich"?

What does Jesus really long for? What should we really want in life? Lotteries are the litmus paper of many hidden motives.

The lottery is another opportunity to pierce your soul with many pangs. It is another chance to lead your children into ruin. It is being pushed beyond our worst expectations. Its effect is and will be terribly destructive on the moral life of our society. Here are some reasons why I urge you to resist the temptation to play. Make it a rule in your family not to play. Tell the children no and teach them why.

1. *The Bible teaches us not to want to be rich.*

Those who want to get rich fall into temptation and a snare and many foolish and harmful desires which plunge men into ruin and destruction. For the love of money is a root of all sorts of evil, and some by longing for it have wandered away from the faith and pierced themselves with many griefs. (1 Timothy 6:9–10)

The desire to be rich is suicidal. The heart that is hot after money is not pursuing God. This heart is the root of all evils. The passage goes on to say that we are to pursue "righteousness, godliness, faith, love" (verse 11). Jesus said, "Seek first [the kingdom of God] and all these things will be added to you" (Matthew 6:33). Our pursuit in life is not to get rich—neither quickly nor slowly. Our passion in life is to be pure, holy, loving, and sold out to the cause of Christ. Playing the lottery is not motivated by a "hunger and thirst for righteousness" (Matthew 5:6). It is driven by a love for the world, and that is deadly because the world and everything in it are passing away (1 John 2:17). Take heed: "Where your treasure is, there your heart will be also" (Matthew 6:21).

2. It is wrong to wager with a trust fund.

Good stewards do not handle their master's money in such a way. Faithful trustees may not gamble with a trust fund. They have no right. And everything we have is a trust from God, to be used for his glory (1 Corinthians 4:7; 6:19–20). How does it glorify God to wager with his money?

Faithful stewards do not gamble. They work and trade: value for value, just and fair. This is the pattern again and again in Scripture. Wage and benefits correspond to work done. And when you are handling the funds of another, how much more irresponsible it is to wager!

3. It is wrong to endorse and support an institution that is bound to confirm people in their weaknesses and to cultivate in others the greed that would lie latent without this outlet. The lottery will hook most easily those people who need just the opposite, namely, encouragement and guidance in fiscal diligence and responsibility.

Therefore, I urge you, for the honor of our treasure in heaven, for the good of our society, and for the safety and health of your own soul, don't play the lottery. ❧

62

DID GOD COMMAND A MAN TO EARN HIS LIFE?

Thoughts on the So-Called Covenant of Works

H as God ever commanded anyone to obey with a view to earning or meriting life? Would God command a person to do a thing that he uniformly condemns as arrogant?

In Romans 11:35–36, Paul describes why earning from God is arrogant and impossible. He says, "Who has first given to [God] that it might be paid back to him? For from Him and through Him and to Him are all things. To Him be the glory forever. Amen." The thought that anyone could give anything to God with a view to being paid back with merit or wages is presumptuous and impossible, because all things (including obedience) are from God in the first place. You can't earn from God by giving him what is already his. You can't merit anything from God by offering work which God freely enables (1 Corinthians 15:10; Philippians 2:12–13). All things are from God, and therefore there is no bartering, negotiating, or earning with God. There is only trust in his free provision, or treason.

It is true that God commanded Adam to obey him, and it is also true that failure to obey would result in death (Genesis 2:16–17): "In the day that you eat from it you will surely die" (verse 17). But the question is this: What kind of obedience is required for the inheritance of life—the obedience of earning or the obedience of trusting? The Bible presents two very different kinds of effort to keep God's commandments. One way is legalistic; it depends on our own strength and aims to earn life. The other way we might call evangelical; it depends on God's enabling power and aims to obtain life by faith in his promises, which is shown in the freedom of obedience.

These two ways of trying to keep God's commandments are described in Romans 9:31–32: "Israel, pursuing a law of righteousness, did not arrive at that law. Why? Because they did not pursue it by faith, but as though it were by works." Pursuing obedience by faith and pursuing obedience by works are opposite ways of life, even though both are trying to obey God. God does not command us to pursue obedience by works. That is legalism. It is arrogant in man, a dishonor to God, and in the end, impossible and suicidal. Adam had to walk in obedience to his Creator in order to inherit life, but the obedience required of him was the obedience that comes from faith. God did not command legalism, arrogance, and suicide.

What made Adam's sin so evil was that God had shown him unmerited favor and offered himself to Adam as an everlasting Father to be trusted in all his counsel for Adam's good. The command was that Adam trust God's goodness. Adam's test was whether he would prove the trustworthiness of God in reckoning God more to be desired than the prospect of Satan's offer. There was no hint that Adam was to earn or deserve. The atmosphere was one of testing faith in unmerited favor, not testing willingness to earn or merit. The command of God was for the obedience that comes from faith.

What then of the "second Adam," Jesus Christ, who fulfilled the obedience that Adam forsook (1 Corinthians 15:45; Romans 5:14–20)? What was Jesus' test? Should we think of the Son of God relating to his Father as a workman earning wages? Are we to think of the role of the "second Adam" as earning what the "first Adam" failed to earn? Is his role not rather to glorify the trustworthiness of his Father, which Adam so terribly dishonored? Was not Christ put forward to demonstrate the righteousness of God by an obedience and sacrifice that vindicated God's righteous allegiance to his own glory, which had been injured by Adam's unbelieving scorn of the merciful wisdom of God (Romans 3:25–26)? Christ rendered to God the obedience of faith that Adam forsook. He fulfilled the Law perfectly in the way that the

Law was meant to be fulfilled from the beginning, not by works, but by faith (Romans 9:32). Thus he obtained life for his people, not by wages, but by fulfilling the covenant conditions of a faithful Son.

We are called to walk the way Jesus walked and the way Adam was commanded to walk. Adam failed because he did not trust the grace of God to pursue him with goodness and mercy all his days (Psalm 23:6). He fell for the lie that God was holding back some really good thing and that he could decide on his own what was "good and evil." Faith does not do that. Faith is the assurance of things hoped for (Hebrews 11:1). It is the confidence that God withholds no good thing from us (Psalm 84:11). It is the firm hope that God works for those who wait for him (Isaiah 64:4) and will meet all our needs according to his riches in glory (Philippians 4:19). Believing this, we are freed from the lie of Satan that disobedience to God will bring more happiness or more significance. With Jesus we can then take up our cross and, for the joy set before us, lay down our lives in the cause of love (Mark 8:34; Hebrews 12:2). ⌘

63

THE UNMERITED, CONDITIONAL GRACE OF GOD

~~~

Reflections on Psalm 25

⁸*Good and upright is the LORD;*
Therefore <u>He instructs sinners in the way.</u>
⁹*He leads the* **humble** *in justice,*
And He teaches the **humble** *His way.*
¹⁰*All the paths of the LORD are <u>lovingkindness</u> and truth*
To **those who keep His covenant and His testimonies.**
¹¹*For Your name's sake, O LORD,*
<u>Pardon my iniquity, for it is great.</u>
¹²*Who is the man* **who fears the Lord?**
He will instruct him in the way he should choose....
¹⁶*Turn to me and <u>be gracious to me,</u>*
For I am lonely and afflicted....
¹⁸*Look upon my affliction and my trouble,*
And <u>forgive all my sins</u>....
²⁰*Guard my soul and deliver me;*
Do not let me be ashamed, for **I take refuge in You.**
²¹*Let* **integrity and uprightness** *preserve me,*
For **I wait for You.**

A ll the forgiveness and help of God are gracious and unmerited. But they are not all unconditional. Our election (Romans 9:11) and our regeneration (John 3:8) are unconditional, but subsequent blessings—like ongoing forgiveness and guidance and help in trouble—are conditional on our covenant keeping.

This does not mean we lose security or assurance, for God has pledged himself to complete the work he began in the elect (Philippians 1:6). He is at work within us to will and to do his good pleasure (Philippians 2:12–13). He works in us what is pleasing in his sight (Hebrews 13:21). He fulfills the conditions of the covenant through us (Ezekiel 36:27). Our security is as secure as God is faithful (1 Corinthians 1:8; 1 Thessalonians 5:24).

What this means is that most of the blessings of the Christian life are conditional on our (God-enabled!) covenant keeping. Consider the verses from Psalm 25. The words in bold type are all conditions that the psalmist says he fulfills in order to receive blessings. The underlined words are all references to the fact that these blessings are graciously given, not earned.

Read it carefully. Do you see that there are conditions we meet in order to receive God's guidance (verse 9), God's lovingkindness (verse 10), God's instruction (verse 12), and God's protection (verse 20)? But all this condition keeping is done by "sinners" (verses 8 and 11). And notice that these covenant-keeping sinners who receive God's guidance and protection are being preserved by their "integrity and uprightness" (verse 21). In other words, even though we sin every day in various ways, there is a profound difference between sinners who keep God's covenant (verse 10) and those who don't.

I urge you to search your heart in the light of this psalm to know if you "wait for the Lord" (verse 21), "take refuge in him" (verse 20), "fear" him (verse 12), are "humble" before him (verse 9), and "keep his covenant" (verse 10). These are the sinners whom God will guide and protect. Are you one of them? ❧

64

LORD-FOCUSED LIVING
AT WORK

—◆—

Who Is Your Supervisor?
Meditation on Ephesians 6:7–8

With good will render service,
as to the Lord, and not to men,
knowing that whatever good thing each one does,
this he will receive back from the Lord,
whether slave or free.

A Call to Radically Lord-Centered Living

What Ephesians 6:7–8 calls for is astonishing compared to the way we usually live. Paul says that all our work should be done as work for Christ, not for any human supervisor: "With good will render service, as to the Lord, and not to men." This means that we will think of the Lord in what we are doing at work. We will ask, Why would the Lord like this done? How would the Lord like this done? When would the Lord like this done? Will the Lord help me do this? What effect will this have for the Lord's honor? Being a Christian at work means radically Lord-centered living. What you are asked to do by a supervisor should generally be viewed as an appeal from the Lord.

A Call to Be a Good Person

Lord-centered living means being a good person and doing good things. Paul says, "With good will render service…whatever good thing each one does." Jesus said that when we let our light shine, men will see our good deeds and give glory to our Father in heaven. Lord-centered living does good deeds for the glory of the Lord.

Power to Do a Good Job for Inconsiderate Employers

Paul's aim is to empower Christians with Lord-centered motives to go on doing good for supervisors who are not considerate. How do you keep on doing good in a job when your boss ignores you or even criticizes you? Paul's answer: Stop thinking of your boss as your main supervisor and start working for the Lord (see 1 Peter 2:18–19). Do this in the very duties given to you by your earthly supervisor. Look through the supervisor to the sovereign Lord and don't worry about the supervisor's thoughtlessness. Think about the Lord's reward.

Encouragement That Nothing Good Is Done in Vain

Perhaps the most astonishing sentence of all is this: "Whatever good thing each one does, this he will receive back from the Lord." This is amazing. Everything. Every little thing you do that is good is seen and valued by the Lord. And he will "pay you back" for it. Not in the sense that you have earned anything by putting him in your debt; he owns you and everything in the universe. He owes us nothing, but he freely, graciously chooses to reward good things done in faith. Nothing we do—nothing, not one thing—is done in vain. "Whatever good thing each one does, this he will receive back from the Lord." Astounding!

Encouragement That Insignificant Status on Earth Is No Hindrance to Great Reward in Heaven

The Lord will reward every good thing you do—"whether slave or free." Your supervisor may think you are a nobody, or he may not even know you exist. That doesn't matter. The Lord knows you exist, and he is going to reward you on the same terms as the most famous Christian. There is no partiality with God (1 Peter 1:17). "Whether slave or free," your good is recorded and rewarded.

An employee at the Billy Graham headquarters told me once that Dr. Graham gave a devotional for the office staff and said that he believed some of them would be ahead of him in line for the Lord's rewards. They chuckled with skepticism. He became serious and said that he really meant it because the Lord rewards faithfulness above fruitfulness, which puts us all on the same footing, whether famous for our effectiveness or unknown in our faithfulness.

O how I long to live and do my ministry more and more with a view to the Lord's reward alone and not to man's. ❧

65

FROM MISPLACED SHAME TO MISSION FLAME

------◆◆◆------

Pondering Some Shame-Shattering Promises

Misplaced shame is a mountain standing in the way of world missions. Jesus means for us to cast it into the sea. "If you have faith...it will be done!" (Matthew 21:21, RSV). The jagged mountain of shame becomes a highway for missionary joy when we blast it away with the bombshells of Bible promises. How many megatons of power are in these shame-blasting promises!

> *Fear not, for you will not be ashamed; be not confounded, for you will not be put to shame; for you will forget the shame of your youth, and the reproach of your widowhood you will remember no more. For your Maker is your husband, the LORD of hosts is his name.* (Isaiah 54:4–5, RSV)

> *The Lord GOD helps me; therefore I have not been confounded; therefore I have set my face like a flint, and I know that I shall not be put to shame; he who vindicates me is near. Who will contend with me? Let us stand up together.* (Isaiah 50:7–8, RSV)

> *I am not ashamed of the gospel: it is the power of God for salvation.* (Romans 1:16, RSV)

> *I suffer [as a missionary!]. But I am not ashamed, for I know whom I have believed, and I am sure that he is able to guard until that Day what has been entrusted to me.* (2 Timothy 1:12, RSV)

> *If you are reproached for the name of Christ, you are blessed, because the spirit of glory and of God rests upon you.... If one suffers as a Christian, let him not be ashamed, but under that name let him glorify God.* (1 Peter 4:14, 16, RSV)

By faith in these promises God means to blast the mountain of shame out of the way and make it a highway for missionary zeal. "Every mountain and hill shall be brought low,...and all flesh shall see the salvation of God" (Luke 3:5–6, RSV).

Shame tries to cancel our missions commitment in two ways. We can feel that we are not good enough for missions, or we can feel that missions is not good enough for us. Being ashamed of sin can keep us away, and being ashamed of God can scare us away. We can feel crushed beneath the shame of sin, or we can feel comfortable above the shame of the cross. In either case, shame wins and we lose.

This is not the will of Christ for you. "Your sins are forgiven.... Your faith has saved you; go [forth to mission!] in peace [not in shame!]" (Luke 7:48, 50). Do not fear the world's shame. God's honor makes all the difference. "If any one serves me,...the Father will honor him" (John 12:26).

So let us go on from strength to strength in the courage of God's promises: "He who believes in him will not be put to shame" (1 Peter 2:6); "No one who believes in him will be put to shame" (Romans 10:11); therefore, "Do not be ashamed then of testifying to our Lord" (2 Timothy 1:8). ❧

66

THE LIMITS OF LOVE

Conflicting Claims and Incorrigible Sinners

One of my seminary professors, Lewis Smedes, wrote a book titled *Love within Limits*.[26] The point was that real life puts real limits on the good you *can* do for people and the good that you *should* do for people. Don't hold him accountable for what follows, but he did help me learn to think more biblically about these things. Consider two kinds of limits on love.

The first is the limit set by clashing claims. There are limits to the goodness love can do when doing good to one person will mean not doing good to another person. This limit happens virtually every time you do an act of love for someone, because in that moment you are not doing that act of love for someone else. To choose one course of love is always to leave a thousand other courses unchosen. When Jesus healed one leper, he left hundreds unhealed. His life was a continual series of choices to love one way and not another. To do is also to leave undone.

But clashing claims express themselves in other ways. Suppose you had captured the man who blew up the government building in Oklahoma City in 1995 and killed 168 adults and children. How should he be loved? Forgiveness and release would be one possible way, but two clashing claims are against this. One is the immediate claim of the safety of others who might be injured by his violence. Another is the less immediate, but more important, claim of a stable society based on the biblical principle that government exists for the restraint and punishment of evil (Romans

13:1–6). Maintaining a stable society that does not slip into anarchy is a great work of love to millions of citizens. The claim of this love limits the claim of our love for terrorists. The civil act of punishing criminals is an act of tender love to many people through severe justice to a few people.

A second kind of limit on love is the limit Jesus points to when he speaks of the unforgivable sin: "Whoever speaks against the Holy Spirit, it shall not be forgiven him, either in this age or in the age to come" (Matthew 12:32). This means that God's patience with unrepentant sinners will not last forever. They eventually cross a line beyond which God will not pursue them. He will let them go, and they will never be forgiven. At this point, whatever love he was pursuing them with (Romans 2:4) is gone, and they become the objects of his eternal wrath (Revelation 14:10–11).

How does this affect our love toward incorrigible sinners? Jesus calls us to imitate God's common grace toward his enemies, not his acts of judgment (Matthew 5:45). "'Vengeance is mine, I will repay, says the Lord.'... 'If your enemy is hungry, feed him'" (Romans 12:19–20, RSV). We are not to do all that God does. God may be planning vengeance according to his wisdom and justice for the sake of some greater work of love. That is not our business. Ours is to love our enemies.

There may be a rare instance when we discern that the line has been crossed into unforgivability: "If someone sees his brother sinning a sin not unto death, he shall ask and [God] will give him life—to those sinning not unto death. There is sin unto death; not concerning that do I say for you to ask" (1 John 5:16, author's translation). In other words, there may come a point when the prayers for your enemy will cease. I confess I have never had the confidence to recognize this point in anyone I have ever known. To me it is safer to keep praying. We are to do good while we can and hope that they will see our good deeds and give glory to our Father (Matthew 5:16; Luke 6:27). John does not command us not to pray. He only says, "I don't command you to pray in such cases."

This "sin unto death" may lie behind the psalms that are prayers for

God's judgment rather than for his mercy. It may be that, seeing with God's eye, the psalmists discerned the irrevocable rebellion of their enemy and spoke judgment with the very Spirit of God. ❧

67

ABORTION AS ANARCHY

*The Rights of the Weak
and the Will of the Strong*

I n the spring of 1987 in northern Minnesota, a teenager helped his pregnant girlfriend commit suicide. As the *Minneapolis Star Tribune* told the story, the girl put a .44–caliber magnum rifle in her mouth and the boyfriend counted. At first she didn't pull the trigger, but when he turned to walk away, he heard the shot. He covered her with some loose brush and walked away. She was six-and-a-half-months pregnant with a baby boy.

In 1994 a jury acquitted the boyfriend, then age twenty, of murdering his girlfriend, but found him guilty of aiding a suicide and of "inadvertently murdering the fetus during the commission of a felony." The four-year-old fetal homicide law carries a much stiffer penalty than aiding a suicide and could have required twelve years of prison for the fetal homicide. What was astonishing in this case is the following sentence from the newspaper: "The law makes it murder to kill an embryo or fetus intentionally, except in cases of abortion."

Try to translate that sentence. It could go like this: "It is illegal to kill a fetus except when it is legal." But that is not a satisfying translation because, while it is strictly true, it does not help us understand the difference between the two cases. Why is it illegal in some cases to kill an unborn child and not in other cases?

One might use war or capital punishment as an analogy here and show that there are some killings that most of society condones, namely, the killing of soldiers in an army of unjust aggression, or the execution of a cold-blooded murderer. The analogy would suggest that some killings are not murder because the person killed has forfeited the right to life by the kind of behavior he pursues.

But the analogy won't work because the embryo is doing nothing different in both cases—the case in which it is *legal* to kill it and the case in which it is *illegal* to kill it. So the difference must lie elsewhere.

Where? Evidently it lies in the will of the mother. If the mother wants her embryo to live, it is illegal to kill it. If she does not want it to live, it is not illegal to kill it. In our laws we now have made room for some killing to be justified, not on the basis of the rights or crimes of the one killed, but solely on the basis of another person's will. The distinguishing criterion of what is right and wrong is the will of the strong. This is the ultimate statement of anarchy. It is the essence of rebellion against objective truth and against God.

This is one of the most vivid illustrations of where subjectivism and relativism lead. "In those days there was no king in Israel; everyone did what was right in his own eyes" (Judges 17:6, NKJV). When the will of man becomes the criterion of right and wrong, your life is only as precious as your enemy thinks it is.

But we all know this is not true. All of us demand that we not be treated according to what others want to do with us, but rather according to some intrinsic sense of justice. We will not let people justify assaulting us on the basis that they don't like us, don't want us around, or consider us a nuisance. Our enemy's desire for our destruction is no justification for it.

But in the case of the unborn, it is precisely the desire of the mother that legally justifies killing the embryo. The will of the mother alone makes this killing legal or illegal. So in the case of abortion, we endorse a principle that we absolutely will not endorse in the way we are treated ourselves, and the reason for this is not that the unborn are not humans. The law does make killing the embryo an act of murder (see the newspaper quote above). The reason we will endorse a principle of anarchy in the case of a mother's will seems to be that the embryo cannot object and because there are so many abortion defenders who make the principle of anarchy sound like a noble right. ❧

68

PRACTICAL STEPS
TO KILL SIN

Thoughts on Mortification

I t is both relief and heartache to know that all true believers have sin remaining in them in this life. The great apostle said, "Not that I have already obtained it or have already become perfect, but I press on so that I may lay hold of that for which also I was laid hold of by Christ Jesus" (Philippians 3:12). In another place he said, "I see in my members another law at war with the law of my mind and making me captive to the law of sin which dwells in my members" (Romans 7:23, RSV). And Jesus taught us to pray daily, "Forgive us our debts" (Matthew 6:12, RSV).

This does not mean we should become complacent about sin. It means we must fight it daily. We are commanded to constantly kill the sin that remains in our lives: "If you live according to the flesh you will die, but if by the Spirit you put to death the deeds of the body you will live.... Put to death therefore what is earthly in you" (Romans 8:13; Colossians 3:5, RSV). This is not optional. This is mortal combat: Sin dies or we die. Not that we ever become perfect in this age, but we go on killing sins as they attack us from day to day. We do not settle in with sin. We fight and we kill.

How do we kill sin? Here are thirteen tactical steps in the battle.

1. Take heart from the truth that the old sinful you is decisively already dead (Romans 6:6; Colossians 3:3; Galatians 5:24). By faith we are united to Christ so that his death was our death (Romans 6:5; 2 Corinthians 5:14). This means three things: (a) The mortal blow to our "old man" has been

struck; (b) the old self will not succeed in domination now; and (c) his final obliteration is certain.

2. Consciously reckon the old man dead; that is, believe the truth of Scripture about the old man's death in Christ and seek to live in that freedom (Romans 6:11). Living out the reality that you are is the proof that you are. One clear illustration of becoming what you are is found in 1 Corinthians 5:7 (RSV): "Clean out the old leaven that you may be a new lump, as you really are unleavened." It sounds strange, but salvation is a strange and wonderful thing: Clean out the old leaven of sin, because it is really already cleaned out. If you try to play logic games with this reality and say, "I don't need to fight sin because it is already cleaned out," you will prove only that you are not among the number who are cleansed.

3. Cultivate enmity with sin! You don't kill friends (Romans 8:13). You kill enemies. Ponder how sin killed your best Friend (Jesus), dishonors your Father, and aims to destroy you forever. Develop more hatred for sin.

4. Rebel against sin's coup. Refuse to be bullied by its deceits and manipulations. "Do not let sin reign in your mortal body that you obey its lusts" (Romans 6:12). Temptations to sin are all half-truths and half-lies at best. Paul calls their fruit "lusts of deceit" (Ephesians 4:22).

5. Declare radical allegiance to the other side—God—and consciously put all your mind, heart, and body at his disposal for righteousness and purity. "Present yourselves to God as those alive from the dead, and your members as instruments of righteousness to God" (Romans 6:13).

6. Don't make any plans that open the door for sin's entry. "Make no provision for the flesh in regard to its lusts" (Romans 13:14). Don't prove your purity in a pornography shop or your commitment to simplicity at an upscale mall.

7. Know the spirit of the age and consciously resist conformity to it (Romans 12:2). As D. L. Moody said, "The ship belongs in the water of the world, but if the water gets in the ship, it sinks."

8. Develop mental habits that continually renew the mind in God-

centeredness (Romans 12:2; 2 Corinthians 4:16). Fix attention daily on "the things of the Spirit" (Romans 8:5, RSV), "things that are above" (Colossians 3:2, RSV). Let your mind dwell on "whatever is true,...honorable,...just,...pure,...lovely,...gracious,...excellen[t],...worthy of praise" (Philippians 4:8).

9. Admit failure and confess all known sin every day (1 John 1:9). Ask God for forgiveness (Matthew 6:12).

10. Ask for the Spirit's help and power in all these things. "By the Spirit put to death the deeds of the body" (Romans 8:13). All that is good in us is a "fruit of the Spirit" (Galatians 5:22). He causes us to walk as we should (Ezekiel 36:27; Isaiah 26:12).

11. Be part of a larger and a smaller fellowship where you are exhorted often to beware of the deceitfulness of sin (Hebrews 3:13). Perseverance in faith is a community project. We have no warrant to think we will make it to heaven if we neglect the appointed means of mutual encouragement and warning.

12. Fight your sinful impulses with all your might as a boxer fights an opponent and as a marathon runner fights fatigue (1 Corinthians 9:27; 2 Timothy 4:8).

13. Beware of "works of law," but let all your warfare be "the work of faith" (2 Thessalonians 1:11). That is, let your fight against sin spring from your confidence in the superior pleasures of all God promises to be for you in Christ. ❧

69

THE REPENTANCE OF GOD

Meditation on the Mind of God

T wice the Bible says that God repented for something he had done in the past (Genesis 6:6–7 and 1 Samuel 15:11), and at least fifteen times it says he repented or might repent of something he was about to do in the future (Exodus 32:12–14; 2 Samuel 24:16; 1 Chronicles 21:15; Psalm 106:45; Jeremiah 4:28; 18:8; 26:3, 13, 19; 42:10; Joel 2:13–14; Amos 7:3, 6; Jonah 3:9–10; 4:2).

Nevertheless, the Bible also says that God will not repent. For example, Psalm 110:4 says, "The Lord has sworn; he will not repent" (author's translation). In Ezekiel 24:14 God says, "I the LORD have spoken; it shall come to pass, I will do it; I will not go back, I will not spare, I will not repent" (RSV). In Jeremiah 4:28 God says, "The earth shall mourn, and the heavens above be dark, because I have spoken, I have purposed, and I will not change My mind, nor will I turn from it."

Even more important than these are the texts that say God would be like a man if he repented. In other words, God's freedom from a need to repent is based on his deity. Being God means that he cannot repent:

God is not a man, that he should lie, or a son of man, that he should repent. (Numbers 23:19, RSV)

The Glory of Israel will not lie or repent; for he is not a man that he should repent. (1 Samuel 15:29, RSV)

This last text comes in the very same story where it says God repented that he had made Saul king (1 Samuel 15:11, 35). So we must not think that these two views come from different authors of the Old Testament as if they disagreed with each other.

Rather, we should say that there is a sense in which God does repent, and there is a sense in which he does not. The strong declaration that God cannot repent (1 Samuel 15:29 and Numbers 23:19) is intended to keep us from seeing the repentance of God in a way that would put him in the limited category of a man.

God's repentance is not like ours. I take that to mean that God is not taken off guard by unexpected turns of events as we are. He knows all the future: "Behold, the former things have come to pass, and new things I now declare; before they spring forth I tell you of them" (Isaiah 42:9). Nor does God ever sin. So his repentance does not spring from a lack of foresight nor from folly.

Rather, the repentance of God is his expression of a different attitude and action about something past or future, not because events have taken him off guard, but because the turn of events (which he himself has ordered—Ephesians 1:11) makes a different attitude more fitting now than would have been the case earlier. God's mind "changes," not because it responds to unforeseen circumstances, but because he has ordained that his mind accord with the way he himself orders the changing events of the world.

Our confidence in the stability and constancy of God rests not on his inability to respond to emerging situations, but on his infallibly planning and knowing all that he responds to. Mingle this confidence with the preciousness of his promises, and we have a Rock on which to weather every wind. ❧

INSTITUTIONS:
HAZARDOUS AND HELPFUL

―――∿∿∿―――

The Danger of Trusting in Your Horse

A comment about Karl Marx set me to thinking about how ideas shape life. "Marx has had more impact on actual events, as well as on the minds of men and women, than any other intellectual in modern times. The reason for this is not primarily the attraction of his concepts and methodology but the fact that his philosophy has been institutionalized in two of the world's largest countries, Russia and China."[27] In other words, one of the factors that preserves and lengthens the influence of ideas is whether they are institutionalized.

A religious example of this is the Princeton Theology (the Reformed, Calvinistic, God-centered, Bible-based vision taught by men like B. B. Warfield and Charles Hodge). Mark Noll points out that "the Princeton Theology sprang from the minds of its exponents, but it flowed outward from Princeton through institutions which vastly transcended those individuals."[28] The institutions he has in mind are Princeton Seminary itself (for more than a century), Princeton College (for much of the nineteenth century), several scholarly Princeton journals, and the Presbyterian church. For almost a hundred years (before the influences of the modern mistrust of the Scriptures), these institutions embodied and spread the God-centered, Bible-saturated vision of the founders.

The question arises: Is it God's will, revealed in Scripture, to advance the influence of biblical truth through human institutions? Institutions like seminaries, colleges, parochial schools, mission agencies, publishing houses, journals, newsletters, hospitals, relief agencies, musical groups, drama troupes, conferences, camps, counseling centers, evangelistic associations, coffee houses, and radio and television networks, stations, and programs.

The reason the question is urgent is that institutions by nature develop self-sustaining power as opposed to God-sustained power. There are human expectations, human employees, procedures, traditions, money, brainpower, real estate, facilities, reputation, and a constituency. These all can keep an institution going even if the Holy Spirit has withdrawn. In this way, Christian institutions can become contradictions and artifacts of divine power that once was.

Thus the Bible repeatedly warns against relying on powers resident within human culture (institutional power). For example, Psalm 33:17: "A horse is a false hope for victory; nor does it deliver anyone by its great strength." Military institutional power is not to be trusted for deliverance.

On the other hand, the Bible does not say that institutions are therefore evil or useless. On the contrary, Proverbs 21:31 says, "The horse is prepared for the day of battle, but victory belongs to the LORD." Recognizing that institutions are not the decisive force for the triumph of truth does not mean that they are no force.

God never commanded Israel to abolish its army, but again and again he warned the people against relying on it when they went to battle. "Woe to those who go down to Egypt for help, and rely on horses, and trust in chariots because they are many, and in horsemen because they are very strong, but they do not look to the Holy One of Israel, nor seek the LORD!" (Isaiah 31:1).

It seems to me that institutions are virtually inevitable not just where people settle comfortably into this fallen world with self-reliant structures, but even more, wherever passionate believers dream of new ways to declare the Glory of Christ among the nations. Therefore I expect that until Jesus comes back there will always be tension among believers over where the line is crossed between God-ordained, Spirit-sustained institutional life and human-designed, human-sustained institutionalism.

Therefore let us be alert to the possibilities and the pitfalls of institutions. If you are part of one, ponder these things. Let us labor to permeate all our human structures with prayer and with a heartfelt reliance on God, "[who] gives to all men life and breath and everything" (Acts 17:25, RSV). ❧

71

TREMBLING WITH JOY
OVER MY ESCAPE

Thoughts about Hell at Christmastime

D o you remember a time you were lost as a child, or slipping over a precipice, or about to drown? Then suddenly you were rescued. You held on for dear life. You trembled for what you had almost lost. You were happy. O so happy and thankful. You trembled with joy.

That's the way I feel at the end of the year about my rescue from God's wrath. On cold Minnesota Christmas days we have a fire in the fireplace. Sometimes the coals are so hot that when I stoke them my hand hurts. I pull back and shudder at the horrendous thought of the wrath of God against sin in hell. How unspeakably horrible that will be!

Some years back on a Christmas afternoon I visited a woman who had been burned over 87 percent of her body. She had been in the hospital since August. My heart broke for her. How wonderful it was to hold out hope to her from God's Word! "The steadfast love [of the Lord] is better than life" (Psalm 63:3, RSV). And God never leaves and always helps those who trust in him (Isaiah 41:10; Hebrews 13:5). But I came away thinking not only about her pain in this life, but also about the everlasting pain I have been saved from through Jesus.

Test my experience with me. Is this trembling joy a fitting way to end the year? Paul was glad that the Lord from heaven is "Jesus who delivers us from the wrath to come" (1 Thessalonians 1:10, RSV). He warned that "for those who…do not obey the truth,…there will be wrath and fury" (Romans 2:8, RSV). "Because of [fornication, impurity and covetousness] the wrath of God comes upon the sons of disobedience" (Ephesians 5:6, RSV).

There at the end of the year I was finishing my trek through the Bible and reading the last book, Revelation. It is a glorious prophecy of the triumph of God and the everlasting joy of all who "take the water of life without price" (22:17, RSV). No more tears, no more pain, no more depression, no more sorrow, no more death (21:4).

But O the horror of not repenting and not holding fast to the testimony of Jesus! The description of the wrath of God by the "apostle of love" is terrifying. Those who spurn God's love will "drink the wine of God's wrath, poured unmixed into the cup of his anger, and [they] shall be tormented with fire and sulphur in the presence of the holy angels and in the presence of the Lamb. And the smoke of their torment goes up for ever and ever; and they have no rest, day or night" (14:10–11, RSV). "And if any one's name was not found written in the book of life, he was thrown into the lake of fire" (20:15, RSV). Jesus will "tread the wine press of the fury of the wrath of God the Almighty" (19:15, RSV). "Blood flowed from the wine press, as high as a horse's bridle, for [two hundred miles]" (14:20, RSV).

I tremble with joy that I am saved! The holy wrath of God is a horrible destiny. Flee this, brothers and sisters. Flee this with all your might. And let us save as many as we can! No wonder there is more joy in heaven over one sinner who repents than over ninety-nine righteous! (Luke 15:7). ❧

72

AN OUTPOURING OF
EXTRAORDINARY POWER

———◆◆◆———

What Is a Revival?

Martyn Lloyd-Jones said in 1959, "The greatest problem confronting us in the Church today is that the vast majority of professing Christians are not convinced of the reality and the desirableness of revivals."[29]

One reason for that is that we do not know what they are. We constantly confuse a revival with an evangelistic campaign. What's the difference? Lloyd-Jones puts it like this: "An evangelistic campaign is the Church deciding to do something with respect to those who are outside. A revival is not the church deciding to do something and doing it. It is something that is DONE to the Church...the whole essence of a revival is that it is something that happens to the Church, to the people inside. And they are affected and moved and tremendous things happen."[30]

What happens? Again Lloyd-Jones says, "The best way of answering that question is to say that it is in a sense a repetition of the day of Pentecost.... The essence of a revival is that the Holy Spirit comes down.... It is, if you like, a visitation of the Holy Spirit, or...an outpouring of the Holy Spirit.... What the people are conscious of is that it is as if something has suddenly come down upon them. The Spirit of God has descended into their midst, God has come down and is amongst them. A baptism, an outpouring, a visitation."[31]

What effect does this have on the people? "They immediately become aware of his presence and of his power in a manner that they have never known before.... The people present begin to have an awareness of spiritual things and clear views of them such as they have never had before.... Spiritual things become realities.... What they testify is this: 'You know, the whole thing suddenly became clear to me. I was suddenly illuminated, things that I was so familiar with stood out in letters of gold, as it were. I understood. I saw it all in a way that I had never done in the whole of my life.'"[32]

What are these things they become so aware of? "First and foremost, the glory and the holiness of God...and that leads inevitably to a deep and a terrible sense of sin, and an 'aweful' feeling of guilt.... Then they are given a clear view of the love of God and the Lord Jesus Christ, especially of his death upon the cross.... They begin to get a concern for the members of their own family.... There is a constraint that is driving them. They talk about it to people...and they begin to pray for them.... Others who are outside begin to join the meetings and to say, 'What is this?' So they come in, and they go through the same experience."[33]

Who would not rejoice if such a thing happened? This is not an evangelistic crusade. It is not something that can be organized or scheduled. This is a free and sovereign work of God. But what we can do, at least, is ask God to do it. This seems to be what Paul did in Ephesians 3:19 (RSV) when he prayed that we would be "filled with all the fullness of God." It can happen one at a time, which is wonderful, or it can happen in large-scale awakening. If we would love to see it happen to our children or our spouses and ourselves, how can we not yearn and pray for it to happen to many—how can we not pray for revival! ❧

73

WHY GOD IS NOT AN ABOMINATION TO HIMSELF

Meditation on Proverbs 17:15

*He who justifies the wicked and he who condemns the righteous
are both alike an abomination to the LORD.* (RSV)

Why is God not an abomination to God? Proverbs 17:15 tells us that whoever justifies the wicked is an abomination to God, yet according to Romans 4:5 (RSV), God "justifies the ungodly." Not only that, God condemns the righteous, namely, his Son Jesus. "He was wounded for our transgressions" (Isaiah 53:5, RSV). So the Bible says that he who justifies the wicked is an abomination, and he who condemns the righteous is an abomination, but the Bible also says that God justifies the ungodly and God put Jesus to death for sins that were not his. Why is this not an abomination?

Perhaps it would help to step back and ask, When a court acquits the wicked, what makes that an abomination?

Two things.

One is that it fails to require due compensation for the way that wickedness dishonors the law and society. Whenever a crime occurs, the law is demeaned and society is degraded. Usually an individual is also hurt. Justice says that recompense is necessary, which requires from the offender a loss of honor equal to the honor he took from the law or society or the individual. For example, he may be fined, imprisoned, or executed. The problem with justifying (that is, acquitting) the guilty is that it does not require any just recompense. It treats the law and the person who was assaulted as though they were unworthy of vindication—the same way the criminal treated them. So it is an abomination.

The other reason acquitting the wicked is an abomination is that it unleashes on society a person who is very likely to commit the same crime again. Letting him go free is no guarantee that he will reform. So it is an abomination to let him go.

Condemning the righteous is an abomination for the same two reasons, but in reverse. It exacts a loss of honor that does not enhance the honor of the law or society, and it takes from society the good influence of a person who is righteous.

So if a mother tried to take the place of her hardened criminal son, so that she would be executed and he would go free, this would be an abomination. It would not exalt the worth of the law, but rather would exalt the worth of her son at the law's expense. It would also release a dangerous criminal on society. Meanwhile, the mother's apparent goodness would be lost.

But God's putting Christ in our place on the cross is very different from this abomination. Christ's willingness to die in our place is not a desecration but an exaltation of the worth of the glory of God and his law: "For this purpose I have come to this hour. Father, glorify thy name" (John 12:27–28, RSV). The death of Christ is meant to demonstrate the righteousness of God in justifying the ungodly (Romans 3:25–26). Christ is not like a mother wanting to free her wayward son. He has a view to the honor and glory of God and his law. Thus the loss of honor that came to the law and to the name of God through our sin was, in fact, restored through the death of Jesus.

Not only that, the justification of the ungodly does not unleash any criminals onto the world. On the contrary, the death of Christ secures the reform of all his people: "[He] gave himself for us...to purify for himself a people...who are zealous for good deeds" (Titus 2:14, RSV). The death of

Christ did not take from society the influence of a good man. Jesus rose from the dead to continue his powerful, positive influence in the world.

The point is this: God's act in justifying the ungodly is so different from the human act of justifying the wicked that it is not an abomination. Much to the contrary, it is the apex of love and justice in one great event. ❧

Do All Things
without Grumbling

~~~

Meditation on Philippians 2:14–15

Do all things without grumbling or questioning; that you may be
blameless and innocent, children of God without blemish
in the midst of a crooked and perverse generation,
among whom you shine as lights in the world. (RSV)

One of the effects of my speaking at a pastors' conference in Alaska was conviction for my sin of grumbling. I spoke on the things that I love most. I spoke about the great and glorious God of Christian hedonism:

The God who "works for those who wait for him." (Isaiah 64:4, RSV)

The God who withholds no good thing "from those who walk uprightly."
(Psalm 84:11)

The God who pursues us with goodness and mercy all our days. (Psalm 23:6)

The God who "works for good with those who love him." (Romans 8:28, RSV)

The God who "did not spare his own Son but gave him up for us all, [and so will surely] give us all things with him." (Romans 8:32, RSV)

The God through whom we can do all things. (Philippians 4:14)

The God who supplies "every need of [ours] according to his riches in glory in Christ Jesus." (Philippians 4:19, RSV)

The God who will strengthen us, help us, and hold us up by the right hand of his righteousness. (Isaiah 41:10)

The God who "will never fail [us] nor forsake [us], hence we can confidently say, 'The Lord is my helper, I will not be afraid; what can man do to me?'" (Hebrews 13:5–6, RSV)

The God who will complete in me the work he began. (Philippians 1:6)

The God in whose "presence there is fullness of joy" and in whose right hand "are pleasures for evermore." (Psalm 16:11, RSV)

The God who has all authority in heaven and on earth and who will be with us to the end of the age. (Matthew 28:18, 20)

The God who "disciplines us for our good that we may share his holiness." (Hebrews 12:10, RSV)

The God whose eyes "run to and fro throughout the whole earth, to show his might in behalf of those whose heart is blameless toward him." (2 Chronicles 16:9, RSV)

The God who knows the hairs of our heads and without whom not a bird falls to the ground. (Matthew 10:29–30)

The God who rejoices to do us good with all his heart and soul. (Jeremiah 32:41)

The God who rejoices over us with gladness and exults over us with loud singing. (Zephaniah 3:17)

When I heard these things coming out of my own mouth, I was deeply convicted that my heart had grumbled in recent months. The Bible says,

"Do all things without grumbling." Grumbling is an evidence of little faith in the gracious providence of God in all the affairs of our lives. It is a kind of unbelief in these spectacular promises that I was describing to the pastors. And unbelief is a dishonor to God. It belittles his sovereignty and wisdom and goodness.

Do I believe these things? If my faith is strong, I will not grumble. O how we need to pray for each other that we would be glad in the Lord and receive willingly from his hand all he designs for our holiness—both painful and pleasant. As the great old Swedish hymn "Day by Day" says, He "gives unto each day what he deems best, lovingly its part of pain and pleasure, mingling toil with peace and rest."

If we really believe that—and all the promises that I was preaching that week in Alaska—then, as Paul says in Philippians 2:15, we will be "lights in the world." Grumbling only adds to the darkness because it obscures the light of God's gracious, all-controlling providence. But grumble-free, joyful, sacrificial love for others is the brightest reflection of God's glory in the world.

A passion for the supremacy of God is a passion to murmur no more. ❧

75

SAVING BABIES
AND SAVING SINNERS

—◆◆◆—

Thoughts on the Horrors of Abortion and Hell

I am frustrated that I have only one life to live for Christ. This morning after breakfast I was again distressed, very distressed, at the thought of the thousands of unborn children that are legally crushed to death by sterile medical instruments. I lay down on my bed and stared at the ceiling. The immensity of the horror of bloody little legs and arms and heads dismembered and piled on a clinic mat returned again and again.

For three years Noël and I lived a few miles from Dachau, the concentration camp outside Munich, Germany. Today it is open to the public. There are pictures. It is only because there are pictures that we believe it happened. Without the photographic record there would be no belief. We walked through the terrible chambers. We walked through the oven rooms. We walked between the stacked bunks. But that is not real. They are like props. It didn't really happen here in this very spot. Not really.

Then we saw the pictures. The pictures don't lie. Everything can lie but the pictures. We can escape anything but the pictures. Worldwide indignation came from the pictures. Without the pictures it is unimaginable; it couldn't have been like that. Or, yes, it could have, but I can't come close to feeling what I should feel—not without the pictures.

So it is with abortion. It is the pictures that stun me this morning—the incredible scenes from *Eclipse of Reason* and the photographs of legally mangled corpses. What shall I do? Would petitions and prayers really have sufficed in Nazi Germany?

Then I think of the immensity and horror of the sin of disbelieving God. I think of the offense against his immeasurable honor. I think of the reality of hell and the word pictures in the Bible: "And the smoke of their torment goes up for ever and ever, and they have no rest, day or night" (Revelation 14:11, RSV).

Suddenly, it hits me what an utter inconsistency it is to feel indignant as a Christian about the Holocaust of the Jews and the holocaust of abortion, but not about the holocaust of sinners perishing in unbelief. Killing babies is a horrendous evil and their destruction is hellish. But not trusting God is a more horrendous evil, and the destruction of unbelieving people is not hellish but hell.

Therefore I am frustrated that I have only one life to live for the glory of Christ. One life should surely be devoted to stopping the carnage (we must speak graphically or we lie) of abortion. Another life should surely be devoted to saving people from hell.

What shall I do? What is the solution to my frustration? The solution is the diversity of the members of the church of Jesus Christ. I cannot go to all the unreached peoples of the world with the good news of salvation from sin. I cannot spend all the time I would like writing, speaking, traveling, and agitating for the cause of threatened children. The only solution I know is you!

Which horror in the world today makes you ache most? Where will you pour yourself out in the few years you have before you give an account to the righteous Judge of all the earth? ⌖

76

THE PRESENT POWER OF HEAVEN AND HELL

Learning from Jesus to Hope and Fear

Jesus had a lively, daily awareness of heaven and hell. These awesome realities were always relevant for the way he lived and taught. He was radically reasonable about these things. If we will live forever in bliss or torment, then securing the one and escaping the other is more important than most of what we think about.

So he motivated loving actions with the hope of God's fellowship in heaven, and he motivated radical purity with the fear of separation and torment in hell. For Jesus a profound desire for heaven and a potent fear of hell were practical, daily parts of living a glad and holy life. For example:

Motivation for sacrificial generosity—

> *But when you give a reception, invite the poor, the crippled, the lame, the blind, and you will be blessed, since they do not have the means to repay you; for you will be repaid at the resurrection of the righteous.* (Luke 14:13–14)

Motivation for loving your enemies—

> *But love your enemies, and do good, and lend, expecting nothing in return; and your reward will be great, and you will be sons of the Most High.* (Luke 6:35)

Motivation for simplicity and charity—

> *Sell your possessions and give to charity; make yourselves money belts*
> *which do not wear out, an unfailing treasure in heaven, where no thief*
> *comes near nor moth destroys.* (Luke 12:33)

Motivation for evangelism and missions—

> *Make friends for yourselves by means of the wealth of unrighteousness, so that*
> *when it fails, they will receive you into the eternal dwellings.* (Luke 16:9)

Motivation for enduring persecution with joy—

> *Blessed are you when people insult you and persecute you, and falsely say*
> *all kinds of evil against you because of Me. Rejoice and be glad, for your*
> *reward in heaven is great.* (Matthew 5:11–12)

Motivation for avoiding lust—

> *I say to you that everyone who looks at a woman with lust for her has*
> *already committed adultery with her in his heart. If your right eye makes*
> *you stumble, tear it out and throw it from you; for it is better for you to lose*
> *one of the parts of your body, than for your whole body to be thrown into*
> *hell.* (Matthew 5:28–29)

Motivation not to fear death in the cause of the gospel—

> *And I say to you, My friends, do not be afraid of those who kill the body*
> *and after that have no more that they can do. But I will warn you whom to*
> *fear: fear the One who, after He has killed, has authority to cast into hell;*
> *yes, I tell you, fear Him!* (Luke 12:4–5)

Motivation to bear good fruit—

> *Every tree that does not bear good fruit is cut down and thrown into the*
> *fire.* (Luke 3:9)

Motivation to be doers and not just hearers of Jesus—

> *But the one who has heard and has not acted accordingly, is like a man who*
> *built a house upon the ground without any foundation; and the torrent*

burst against it and immediately it collapsed, and the ruin of that house
was great. (Luke 6:49)

Motivation to give our lives away for the gospel—

For whoever wishes to save his life shall lose it, but whoever loses his life for
My sake, he is the one who will save it. For what is a man profited if he
gains the whole world, and loses or forfeits himself? (Luke 9:24–25)

I never have understood the cynical attitude that treats heaven as an
irrelevant pie in the sky by and by nor the apparently pious claim that the
fear of hell is unworthy as Christian motivation. It seems to me that both
these misguided claims come from not really believing in the unspeakable
glory and horror of these two destinies.

We are playing games if we say we long for heaven more than this earth
and then live like earthbound people. "Everyone who has this hope fixed
on [Christ] purifies himself, just as He is pure" (1 John 3:3). You can't put
your hope in all that God promises to be for us in Christ and live like everyone else who depends on money, security, and prestige for contentment.
And you can't truly ponder the real possibility of endless centuries of torment and not be driven to the Calvary road that leads to life.

May God give us in perfect proportion the fruitful balance of loving
heaven and fearing hell. ❧

On Course in the Ever-Similar Storms of Change

The Values of Pondering the Past

T here is a gigantic statue outside the National Archives building in Washington, D.C. A noble Greek figure sits with spread knees and a huge book in his lap. On the front of the massive base are the words "Study the Past." That's good advice—and biblical too.

As you read this, there is probably some threatening crisis in the world. Perhaps in your own life. One way to have ballast in the boat of your life, so that you are not swamped by these things, is to know that it has happened before. For example, does it make you feel differently about our crises to learn that in 1893 the Philadelphia and Reading Railroads filed for bankruptcy, great financial trusts began to collapse, and 500 banks failed? The next year 142 more banks failed, one-quarter of all heavy industry was idle, in one seventeen-day period in January there was an eleven-million-dollar run on the gold of the federal treasury, and a forest fire near Hinkley, Minnesota, destroyed 160,000 acres and killed 400 Minnesotans.

The past is a record of setbacks and how people coped with them. It is a reservoir of folly to be avoided and wisdom to be loved, of lessons to be learned and warnings to be heeded, of heroes to be admired and villains to reject. It is full of the sovereign hand of God and the sinning hand of man.

It keeps us from exaggerating the present. It makes us mature and steady in the storms of change.

The Bible commends the great values of pondering the past. For example, it teaches us that studying the past:

Gives reassurance when we are discouraged—

I will call to mind the deeds of the LORD; yea, I will remember thy wonders of old. (Psalm 77:11, RSV)

I remember the days of old, I meditate on all that thou hast done; I muse on what thy hands have wrought. (Psalm 143:5, RSV)

Reminds us that God is God—

Remember the former things of old; for I am God, and there is no other; I am God, and there is none like me. (Isaiah 46:9, RSV)

Strengthens us for hard times—

But recall the former days when, after you were enlightened, you endured a hard struggle with sufferings. (Hebrews 10:32, RSV)

Enables us to build on good, old foundations—

Your ancient ruins shall be rebuilt; you shall raise up the foundations of many generations; you shall be called the repairer of the breach, the restorer of streets to dwell in. (Isaiah 58:12, RSV)

Lets us recover long-lost, precious truths—

Thus says the LORD: "Stand by the roads, and look, and ask for the ancient paths, where the good way is; and walk in it, and find rest for your souls." (Jeremiah 6:16, RSV)

Helps us stay humble under God's mighty hand—

You shall remember that you were a servant in the land of Egypt, and the LORD your God brought you out thence with a mighty hand and an out-stretched arm. (Deuteronomy 5:15, RSV)

> *And you shall remember all the way which the LORD your God has led you*
> *these forty years in the wilderness, that he might humble you.*
> (Deuteronomy 8:2, RSV)

Teaches us the lessons of God's great deeds—

> *Do you not yet perceive? Do you not remember the five loaves of the five thou-*
> *sand, and how many baskets you gathered?* (Matthew 16:9, RSV)

Warns us against the folly of the foolish—

> *Remember Lot's wife.* (Luke 17:32, RSV)

Stimulates repentance—

> *Remember then what you received and heard; keep that, and repent.*
> (Revelation 3:3, RSV)

Shows what is truly unique and marvelous—

> *Ask now of the days that are past, which were before you, since the day*
> *that God created man upon the earth, and ask from one end of heaven to*
> *the other, whether such a great thing as this has ever happened or was ever*
> *heard of.* (Deuteronomy 4:32, RSV)

Points to a glorious new and unprecedented future—

> *Remember not the former things, nor consider the things of old. Behold, I*
> *am doing a new thing.* (Isaiah 43:18–19, RSV)

I recently read a historical account of religion in America. It was like a rushing spring rain, washing away much fretting about the present times. It put God on the throne, paradoxically, by showing both the faith and the folly of God's saintly, sinful people. Let's put the necessary ballast in the ship of our lives so that we stay upright and on course in the ever-similar storms of change. ❧

78

How Not to Commit Idolatry in Giving Thanks

Jonathan Edwards on True Thanksgiving

Jonathan Edwards has a word for our time that could hardly be more pointed if he were living today. It has to do with the foundation of gratitude: "True gratitude or thankfulness to God for his kindness to us, arises from a foundation laid before, of love to God for what he is in himself; whereas a natural gratitude has no such antecedent foundation. The gracious stirrings of grateful affection to God, for kindness received, always are from a stock of love already in the heart, established in the first place on other grounds, viz. God's own excellency."[34]

In other words, gratitude that is pleasing to God is not first a delight in the benefits God gives (although that is part of it). True gratitude must be rooted in something else that comes first, namely, a delight in the beauty and excellency of God's character. If this is not the foundation of our gratitude, then it is not above what the "natural man"—apart from the Spirit and the new nature in Christ—experiences. In that case, gratitude to God is no more pleasing to God than all the other emotions that unbelievers have without delighting in him.

You would not be honored if I thanked you often for your gifts to me, but had no deep and spontaneous regard for you as a person. You would feel insulted no matter how much I thanked you for your gifts. If your character and personality do not attract me or give me joy in being around you, then you will just feel used, like a tool or a machine to produce the things I really love.

So it is with God. If we are not captured by his personality and character, then all our declarations of thanksgiving are like the gratitude of a wife to a husband for the money she gets from him to use in her affair with another man. This is exactly the picture in James 4:3–4. James criticizes the motives of prayer that treats God like a cuckold: "You ask and do not receive, because you ask with wrong motives, so that you may spend it on your pleasures. You adulteresses, do you not know that friendship with the world is hostility toward God?" Why does he call these praying people "adulteresses"? Because, even though praying, they are forsaking their husband (God) and going after a paramour (the world), and to make matters worse, they are asking their husband (in prayer) to fund the adultery.

Amazingly, this same flawed spiritual dynamic is sometimes true when people thank God for sending Christ to die for them. Perhaps you have heard people say how thankful we should be for the death of Christ because it shows how much value God puts upon us. What is the foundation of this gratitude?

Jonathan Edwards calls it the gratitude of hypocrites. Why? Because "they first rejoice, and are elevated with the fact that they are made much of by God; and then on that ground, he seems in a sort, lovely to them.... They are pleased in the highest degree, in hearing how much God and Christ make of them. So that their joy is really a joy in themselves, and not in God."[35] It is a shocking thing to learn that one of today's most common descriptions of how to respond to the cross may well be a description of natural self-love with no spiritual value.

We do well to listen to Jonathan Edwards. Does he not simply spell out for us the biblical truth that we should do all things—including giving thanks—to the glory of God (1 Corinthians 10:31)? God is not glorified if the foundation of our gratitude is the worth of the gift and not the excellency of the Giver. If gratitude is not rooted in the beauty of God before the gift, it is probably disguised idolatry. May God grant us a heart to delight in him for who he is so that all our gratitude for his gifts will be the echo of our joy in the excellency of the Giver! ❧

79

The Wonders of Pastoral "Polygamy"

Reflections on Twenty-Eight Years of Marriage

Being married and being a pastor is a bit like polygamy: It demands remarkable grace from wife and worshipers. I have been a doubly graced husband. About 60 percent of my married life with Noël has been spent in the double relationship with Bethlehem. Both have treated me with amazing grace during the sixteen years of our common life. It was December 7, 1979, that I first met with the search committee of Bethlehem Baptist Church. They even let my wife join me as the courtship began!

The tribute I owe to Noël and to Bethlehem is that neither has murmured against me with resentment for the other. In sixteen years I can recall only one critical word about Noël, and that person eventually left the church. I doubt that all our people think she is perfect. I know only that they care enough about her and me that what I hear is all positive.

On the other hand, Noël has never once—this is no exaggeration—not once has she ever come close to suggesting that Bethlehem and I are a bad partnership. To my recollection, she has never murmured that the church has done me wrong. Unlike most relationships of this sort, Noël constantly sticks up for my other partner when I am discouraged.

Similarly, Bethlehem has stuck up for her and my relationship to her. Noël has never been pressed to take a role she doesn't fit. She has never been made to feel as if the other partner were jealous if we take our day off or go on vacation. Bethlehem has always quietly carried in prayer the stresses and strains of our home without exploiting our imperfections.

Now this is something to wonder at. Two deep commitments of my life—each wanting more of my time, more of my love, more of my energy, and more of my creativity—but each sticking up for the other and pleading the cause of the other and caring about the other.

This is a wonder. How do we account for this? Here is my explanation. There is no true polygamy here. Bethlehem has only one husband—Jesus Christ. And Bethlehem's husband is Noël's first commitment, not I. Since they both have one common allegiance, namely Jesus, they are of one mind concerning me—grace. If there is any competition between Noël and Bethlehem, it is to see who can outdo the other in making sure that the other gets the attention from me that she needs.

Jesus is the key to peace in this three-way alliance. Jesus means peace. Twenty-eight years of marriage and sixteen years of pastoral relations make me stand in awe of the peacemaking power of Jesus. I love him, I love her, and I love Bethlehem.

But Jesus comes first for all three of us, and that has made all the difference. ❧

80

FOUR WAYS GOD LEADS
HIS PEOPLE

―――ᴕᴕᴥ―――

Thoughts on How to Know God's Will

I see at least four methods that God uses to lead us in his will. I put them in four D's to help me remember them.

1. *Decree.* God sovereignly decrees and designs circumstances so that we end up where he wants us to be even if we don't have any conscious part in getting there. For example, Paul and Silas found themselves in jail, and the result was the salvation of the jailer and his household (Acts 16:24–34). This was God's plan, not Paul's. God does this often—putting us in places we did not plan or decide to be. This is the leading of decree. It is unique above the other three leadings because it includes them (since God's decrees include all our decisions) and because it happens infallibly (since "no purpose of [God's] can be thwarted" [Job 42:2]). The other three leadings of God involve our being consciously led.

2. *Direction.* This is simply what God does for us by giving us the commands and teachings of the Bible. They direct us specifically what to do and what not to do. The Ten Commandments are one example. Don't steal. Don't kill. Don't lie. The Sermon on the Mount is another: Love your enemies. The Epistles are another: Be filled with the Holy Spirit. Put on humility. This is the leading of direction. God reveals his directions in the Bible.

3. *Discernment.* Most of the decisions we make are not spelled out specifically in the Bible. Discernment is how we follow God's leading through the process of spiritually sensitive application of biblical truth to the

specifics of our situation. Romans 12:2 describes this: "Do not be conformed to this world, but be transformed by the renewing of your mind, so
that you may prove what the will of God is, that which is good and acceptable and perfect." In this case, God does not declare a specific word about
what to do, but his Spirit shapes the mind and heart through the Word and
prayer so that we have inclinations toward what would be most glorifying
to him and helpful to others.

4. _Declaration_. This is the least-common means of God's leading. He
simply declares to us what we should do. For example, according to Acts
8:26, "An angel of the Lord spoke to Philip saying, 'Get up and go south to
the road that descends from Jerusalem to Gaza.'" And according to Acts
8:29, "The Spirit said to Philip, 'Go up and join this chariot.'"

Notice three implications. First, we should always rest in the decrees of
God. They will always be for our good if we love him and are called according to his purpose (Romans 8:28). This should remove worry from our lives
and put us at peace as we seek the _directed_, _discerned_, and _declared_ leading
of the Lord.

Second, there is the implication that God's leading of decree may bring
about acts that are contrary to his leading of direction, discernment, or declaration. In other words, he may direct, "Thou shalt not kill," but decree the
murderous death of his Son (Acts 4:28). There are mysteries here, but it is
manifest in dozens of places in the Bible that God wills that some things
come to pass which he forbids in his Word.[36]

Finally, our confidence that we are tracking accurately with God in each
of these leadings increases as we move from the bottom to the top of this
list. Subjectively perceived declarations from God are the least common and
most easily abused of all the ways God leads. Our confidence that we have
known the will of God in this method will not be as great as in the other
methods that relate directly to God's written Word. Discerning what to do
on the basis of biblical principle when we do not have a specific command
for our exact decision will yield less confidence than when we have an

explicit direction in the Bible. And the truth that God is sovereign and guides all things is the rock-bottom confidence under all others.

It is a good place to rest. ❧

81

CAN AN OMNISCIENT GOD BE SORRY FOR SOMETHING HE HAS DONE?

Reflections on Genesis 6:5–7

Then the LORD saw that the wickedness of man was great on the earth,
and that every intent of the thoughts of his heart was only evil continually.
The LORD was sorry that He had made man on the earth,
and He was grieved in His heart. The LORD said,
"I will blot out man whom I have created from the face of the land,
from man to animals to creeping things and to birds of the sky;
for I am sorry that I have made them."

C an God be sorry for an act he performed in the past if he knew when he did the act what consequences would take place? There are more and more people saying no, and thus using this and other texts to deny that God infallibly knows the future.[37] They say God simply could not regret doing something if he knew when he did it that it would prove regrettable. He would not have done it. So, they say, God does things without knowing many of their future consequences.

Genesis 6:6 says, "The LORD was sorry that He had made man on the earth, and He was grieved in His heart." In verse 7 God says: "I am sorry that I have made them."

Is it true that God could only talk like that if he had not known how creation would turn out? Here is the real question: Can God, in the moment of doing an act, feel sorrow and joy about the act at the same time? Can he regret the act in some measure and approve it in some measure at the same time?

To answer this, consider another instance of God's action that (like creation) resulted in great sin and pain. Acts 2:23 says that Jesus was delivered up to crucifixion "by the predetermined plan and foreknowledge of God." In other words, God knew ahead of time that he was sending Jesus to be killed. Yet the killing of the Son of God was more evil than all the evil in Noah's day that made God feel regret that he had made man. Thus if God regretted the creation of mankind when he saw the great misery and evil that it unleashed, may we not assume that he also felt a similar regret over the incarnation of his Son when he saw the undeserved, wicked, infinitely evil murder and suffering of his "only begotten" and "beloved" Son?

Yet we are told explicitly that God not only knew that this would happen, but planned it (Acts 2:23; Isaiah 53:10). So if he was capable of feeling genuine sorrow and revulsion at the wickedness of his Son's murderers and at the suffering of the Son himself, then it must be that he was capable of approving the sending of the Son and at the same time experiencing in advance the sorrow and regret over the sin and suffering involved in the Son's death. If this is conceivable in the incarnation of the Son, it is conceivable in the creation of man.

I conclude that God's foreknowledge of all things includes the foreknowledge of all the evil that will come, as Acts 2:23 implies. Therefore, his choosing to perform acts (like creation and incarnation) that will give rise to these evil things is a choosing done with the full awareness of all his future responses of wrath, regret, pity, and grace. Whatever sorrow or regret he experiences later, during the evil, he is aware of ahead of time. Thus, in some sense, God also experiences that sorrow and regret already in planning to bring about the circumstances where the sorrowful evil will happen.

Therefore the observation in Genesis 6:6–7 that God has such responses does not prove that he did not know the future responses.

It is a grief to me that theological teachers in evangelical schools in our day are departing from the historic biblical vision of God, including his knowledge of future human choices. Let us be thoughtful and rigorous in our biblical reflection before we throw over the great doctrine that "God executes his decrees in the works of creation and providence, according to his infallible foreknowledge, and the free and immutable counsel of his own will."[38] ❧

82

BETTER IS A LITTLE
WITH RIGHTEOUSNESS

Thoughts on Having and Happiness

Consider a few startling facts:

Fact #1: "During the 1980s the Irish had half the incomes and purchasing power of the West Germans. Yet year after year [according to national polls], the Irish were happier."

Fact #2: "People on Forbes's list of wealthiest Americans reported only slightly greater happiness than other Americans; 37% were less happy than the average American."

Fact #3: "[In 1992] compared to 1957, we have twice as many cars per person; we have microwave ovens, color TV's, VCR's, air conditioners, answering machines, and $12 billion a year worth of brand name athletic shoes.... [Nevertheless] in 1957, 35% of Americans told the National Opinion Research Center they were 'very happy.' In 1991, with doubled American affluence, 31% said the same. To judge by soaring rates of depression, the quintupling of the violent crime since 1960, the doubling of the divorce rate, the slight decline in marital happiness among the marital survivors, and the tripling of the teen suicide rate, we are richer and unhappier. How can we avoid the shocking conclusion: Economic growth in affluent countries gives little boost to human morale."[39]

These facts are less shocking when compared with the truly stunning stories about God's people who have learned that "a man's life does not consist in the abundance of his possessions" (Luke 12:15, RSV). For example, Richard Wurmbrand tells the story of a family among millions in Sudan where the Muslim majority want to impose Islam on the Christians. Some Christian parents said to their small child, "We will be deported for our faith and will die of starvation if we maintain it, but do not mind. We will be crowned martyrs in heaven." Then this child went to other children and gave them his "toys." (He had never had what we call a toy, but simply a ball of rags on a stick which he "rode" like a horse.) He said, "I do not need these anymore. In heaven I will have toys better than these."

Having is simply not the key to happiness. The biblical Proverbs make the point again and again. We must be wired to disbelieve this, or God would not insist on it so often.

Better is a dinner of herbs where love is than a fatted ox and hatred with it. (Proverbs 15:17, RSV)

Better is a little with righteousness than great revenues with injustice. (Proverbs 16:8, RSV)

It is better to be of a lowly spirit with the poor than to divide the spoil with the proud. (Proverbs 16:19, RSV)

Better is a dry morsel with quiet than a house full of feasting with strife. (Proverbs 17:1, RSV)

Better is a poor man who walks in his integrity than a rich man who is perverse in his ways. (Proverbs 28:6, RSV)

Happy is he who is kind to the poor. (Proverbs 14:21, RSV)

Happy is he who trusts in the LORD. (Proverbs 16:20, RSV)

It is a great mercy that having does not make us happy. If it did, we would be hopelessly deceived into thinking that things are God. As George

MacDonald said, "Happily for our blessedness, the joy of possession soon palls."[40] When it does, it may be that by grace we will follow the apostolic example and "look not to the things that are seen but to the things that are unseen; for the things that are seen are transient, but the things that are unseen are eternal" (2 Corinthians 4:18). ❧

83

WHEN RIGHTS CONFLICT

Why the Simple Right to Abortion Is Unjust

The most popular defense of abortion today seems to be that without it, women are forced to experience great misery and even death, especially in poor countries with limited access to contraceptives. In my conversations with people who make this defense, the bottom line does not seem to be that the unborn are not human beings or persons. Some admit that they are. The bottom line is a woman's right not to be pregnant and not to endanger herself with unsafe abortions.

There are at least three generally accepted principles of justice that stand in the way of this reasoning.

1. Justice proceeds on the assumption that if one person's legitimate right must be limited to protect another's legitimate right, the limitation that does the least harm will be the most just.

Injustice is not the denial of rights per se. Injustice is the denial of a greater right to preserve a lesser one. Denying rights that protect lesser values to maintain rights that protect greater values is what good laws are supposed to do. We deny the right to drive one hundred miles per hour because the value of life is greater than the value of being on time for an appointment. It is an act of justice to take away the right to speed.

Except in the rarest cases pregnancy does not threaten as much harm to the mother as abortion does to the child. The harm done to the child is almost always horrific, while the harm possible to the mother is almost always much less. Therefore it is just to deny the mother the right not to be pregnant at the cost of killing the child.

2. Justice proceeds on the assumption that when either of two people must be inconvenienced or hurt to alleviate their united predicament, the one who bore the greater responsibility for the predicament should bear more of the inconvenience or hurt to alleviate it.

If I take my fourteen-year-old son with me to rob a bank and both of us are arrested, I should bear a greater penalty than he because of my greater responsibility in the common predicament. Except in rare cases, the predicament of pregnancy is owing to free and conscious choices that the mother made in having sexual relations, while the child's predicament is owing to no choice of his or her own. Therefore in the great majority of cases, it is just to require the mother to bear the weight of her greater responsibility in the predicament and not require the ultimate price of the child who bore no responsibility for the predicament at all.

3. Justice proceeds on the assumption that persons may not coerce another into doing harm by threatening voluntary harm on themselves.

For example, you commit a grave injustice if you threaten to kill yourself to coerce someone to conspire with you to embezzle funds, kidnap, or kill. Similarly the threat of women to harm themselves with unsafe abortions, if society will not sanction the legal abortion of their children, is an unjust coercion of harm—ultimate harm—toward another person, the unborn child.

Conclusion: Since the right of an unborn human to live is greater than the right of a woman to use abortion as a means of birth control, and since the woman's right to be free from pregnancy is not as great as the unborn's right to be free from life-threatening violence, therefore, a law that reverses the order of these rights is unjust. ❧

84

An Amazing (Unused?) Means of Change

―⁂―

Considerations on the Power of Considering

One of the most remarkable capacities of the human mind is the capacity to direct its attention to something it chooses. We can pause and say to our minds, "Think about this and not that." We can focus our attention on an idea, a picture, a problem, or a hope.

It is an amazing power. I doubt that animals have it. They are probably not self-reflective, but rather governed by impulse and instinct. Humans have the amazing ability to think about thinking and to choose to dwell on an object of thought.

This is a gift from God, part of his image in us. It is an immensely powerful means of becoming what we ought to be. Have you been neglecting this great weapon in the arsenal of your war against sin? The Bible calls us again and again to use this remarkable gift. Let's take it out, polish it, and put it to use.

For example, Paul says in Romans 8:5–6, "Those who are according to the flesh set their minds on the things of the flesh, but those who are according to the Spirit, [set their minds on] the things of the Spirit. For the mind set on the flesh is death, but the mind set on the Spirit is life and peace."

This is stunning. What you set your mind on determines whether the issue is life or death!

We have become far too passive in our pursuit of change, wholeness, and peace. In our therapeutic age we have fallen into the passive mind-set of simply "talking through our problems" or "dealing with our issues" or "discovering the roots of our brokenness in our family of origin." As helpful as these may be from time to time, I think we tend to slip into a passive way of thinking about change—that change may simply happen to me one of these days as I talk through my problems.

I see a much more aggressive, nonpassive approach to change in the New Testament. Namely, "Set your mind..." "Set your mind on the things above, not on the things that are on earth" (Colossians 3:2). "Enemies of the cross," Paul says, "set their minds on earthly things" (Philippians 3:18–19). "Those who are according to the flesh set their minds on the things of the flesh" (Romans 8:5).

Our emotions are governed in large measure by what we "consider"— what we dwell on with our minds. For example, Jesus told us to overcome the emotion of anxiety by what we consider: "Do not be anxious.... Consider the ravens.... Consider the lilies" (Luke 12:22, 24, 27, RSV).

The mind is the window of the heart. If we let our minds constantly dwell on the dark, the heart will feel dark. If we open the window of our mind to the light, the heart will feel the light.

This is what Paul meant in Philippians 4:8, "Whatever is true, whatever is honorable, whatever is right, whatever is pure, whatever is lovely, whatever is of good repute, if there is any excellence and if anything worthy of praise, dwell on these things."

Above all, this great capacity of our minds to focus and consider is meant for considering Jesus: "Holy brethren, partakers of a heavenly calling, consider Jesus.... Consider Him who has endured such hostility by sinners against Himself, so that you may not grow weary and lose heart" (Hebrews 3:1; 12:3).

This is the path toward change. We are called to take it and not wait passively while our minds are drawn away with all kinds of passions that wage war against our souls (1 Peter 2:11). It is when we focus our minds on the glory of Christ that we are transformed from one degree of glory to another (2 Corinthians 3:18). Take this moment to resolve that you will be intentional about what your mind considers. It will dwell on something, and what it dwells on, it becomes like. ❧

85

STRONG MEAT FOR THE
MUSCLE OF MISSIONS

Thoughts on the Ministry of Adoniram Judson

More and more I am persuaded that a deep and lasting missions movement will need a deeply rooted doctrine of salvation. On vacation I read some of the memoirs of Adoniram Judson. You recall he was a Congregationalist-turned-Baptist who went to Burma in 1812 and didn't come home for thirty-three years.

Courtney Anderson tells the thrilling and romantic story in *To The Golden Shore*, but like so many missionary biographers, Anderson seems not to know what made Judson tick. It's the memoirs that let you see the theological roots. We are so theologically superficial today we can't even imagine how passionately doctrinal these early missionaries were.

What made Judson tick, very simply, was a white-hot evangelical commitment to the sovereignty of grace (a burning, humble, worshipful, missionary love called "Calvinism"). He wrote a Burmese liturgy and creed that included the following statements: "God, originally knowing that mankind would fall and be ruined, did, of his mercy, select some of the race, and give them to his Son, to save from sin and hell.... The God...who sends the Holy Spirit to enable those to become disciples who were chosen before the world was, and given to the Son, we worship."[41]

The Westminster Shorter Catechism, Question Twenty, goes right to the heart of Judson's faith and ignites the fuse of missions.

Question: Did God leave all mankind to perish in the condemnation of sin and misery?

Answer: God, out of his mere good pleasure, from all eternity, having chosen a people to everlasting life, did enter into a covenant of grace, to deliver them out of the condition of sin and misery, and to bring them into a condition of salvation by a Redeemer. (Ephesians 1:3–4; 2 Thessalonians 2:13; Romans 8:29–30; 5:21; 9:11–12; 11:5–7; Acts 13:48; Jeremiah 31:33)

The term "covenant of grace" is filled with sweet and precious hope. It refers to the free decision and oath of God to employ all his omnipotence, wisdom, and love to rescue his people from sin and misery. It is wholly initiated and carried through by God. It cannot fail. "I will make an everlasting covenant with them that I will not turn away from them, to do them good; and I will put the fear of Me in their hearts so that they will not turn away from Me" (Jeremiah 32:40).

The covenant of grace is valid for all who believe. Whosoever will may come and enjoy this salvation. And, since this "willing" is a work of God's sovereign grace (Ephesians 2:5–8), those who believe and come are the elect—"chosen in Christ before the foundation of the world" (Ephesians 1:4). The covenant was sealed in the heart of God before the world was (2 Timothy 1:9).

This covenant of grace is the cry of victory over all the battle strife in missions. The grace of God will triumph. He is covenant-bound, oath-bound to save all those who are foreordained to eternal life from every tongue, tribe, people, and nation (Acts 13:48; Revelation 5:9). "Jesus [died] for the nation [of Jews], and not for the nation only, but [to] gather together into one the children of God who are scattered abroad" (John 11:51–52). The battle cry of missions is, "[The Lord has] other sheep, which are not of this fold; [He] must [covenant-bound!] bring them also, and they will [sovereign grace!] hear [his] voice" (John 10:16).

Adoniram Judson preached one sermon in English while in Burma. His text was John 10:1–18. What was his point? "Though enclosed in the Saviour's electing love, [his sheep] may still be wandering on the dark mountains of sin." So the missionary must cry out to all with the message of salvation in order that, as Judson says, the "invitation of mercy and love, which will penetrate the ears and hearts of the elect only," may be made effectual.[42]

If we desire to see the likes of Adoniram Judson, William Carey, John Paton, Henry Martyn, and Alexander Duff rise up among us again, let us drink from the same strong doctrine that mastered them for the cause of missions. ❧

86

O Lord, Give Us Children of Promise, Not Children of the Flesh!

Meditation on Romans 9:8

It is not the children of the flesh who are the children of God,
but the children of the promise are regarded as descendants.

This is Paul's comment on the story of the birth of Ishmael and Isaac (Genesis 16; 17:15–21; 18:9–15; 21:1–7). The whole story fills me with longing not to build a "successful" church with multiplied "children of the flesh."

Here's what I mean. God promised Abraham, "your own son shall be your heir" (Genesis 15:5, RSV). As the stars "so shall your descendants be" (Genesis 15:6, RSV). But Sara, his wife, was barren (Genesis 11:30). She "bore him no children" (Genesis 16:1).

Picture Abraham as a pastor. The Lord says, "I will bless you and prosper your ministry." But after a time there is little fruit. The church is barren and bears no children.

What does Abraham do? He begins to despair of supernatural intervention. He is getting old. His wife remains barren. So he decides to bring about God's promised son without supernatural intervention. He has sex with Hagar, his wife's handmaid (Genesis 16:4). The result, however, is not a "child of promise" but a "child of the flesh," Ishmael.

God stuns Abraham by saying, "I will give you a son by [Sarah]" (Genesis 17:16, RSV). So Abraham cries out to God, "O that Ishmael might live in your sight" (Genesis 17:18, RSV). He wants the work of his own flesh to be the fulfillment of God's promise. But God says, "No, but Sarah your wife shall bear you a son" (Genesis 17:19, RSV).

Sarah is now ninety years old. She has been barren all her life, and now she no longer menstruates (Genesis 18:11). Abraham is one hundred. God has put off the promise so long it is now humanly impossible. The only hope for a child of promise is supernatural intervention.

That is what it means to be a child of promise—to be born "not [by] the will of the flesh nor of the will of man, but of God" (John 1:13). The only children that count for children of God in this world are supernaturally begotten children of promise. That's the point of this Old Testament text. In Galatians 4:28 Paul says, "You [Christians], like Isaac, are children of promise." You are born according to the Spirit, not according to the flesh (Galatians 4:29).

Think of Abraham as a pastor again. His church is not growing the way he believes God promised. He is weary of waiting for the supernatural intervention. What does he do? He turns to the "Hagar" of mere human devices and decides he can attract people without the supernatural work of the Holy Spirit.

And he can. However, it will not be a church of Isaacs, but Ishmaels— children of the flesh, not children of God.

God save us from this kind of success. O how subtle is the temptation to "succeed" in the eyes of man. But God looks on the heart and knows the difference between the lifted sails of prayer and the outboard motor of human method. ❧

87

Fireworks and a Full Moon—A Parable

Meditations from the Eleventh Avenue Curb

t 10 P.M. on July 4, Noël, Barnabas, and I walked out onto the Eleventh Avenue bridge and sat down on the curb. Looking north, over the Metrodome, we could see the fireworks from the Mississippi River. Looking south we could see the fireworks over Powderhorn Park. We were sandwiched in the sky glitz of Independence Night.

A small crowd shared our oohs and aahs at the spectacular explosions. For fifteen minutes we were impressed and delighted by the bigness, beauty, and power of man-made light. It got us out of our houses. It gave us a sense of wonder.

About ten minutes into the display, as I turned my head from north to south, I suddenly noticed a white light behind the trees to the southwest. *What's that?* I thought. A second later I could tell it was the moon. It was very large and looked full. It was politely waiting its turn.

The moon was in no hurry to be noticed. It had been there before (Adam, Abraham, and Jesus looked on this same moon); and it would be there again when all the glitz was gone. It was quietly rising at its own pace, irresistibly and without any human help. Yet hardly anyone was noticing.

So it is with the glory of God and the glitz of sin. We are more amazed at sin, and we ignore the glory of God. This is truly amazing.

The moon rises about 240,000 miles above the earth, which means it soars about 500,000 times higher than the highest fireworks. The moon travels at 2,300 miles per hour in its outward serenity around the earth, which is probably five times faster than the fireworks. The moon is 2,160 miles in diameter (from San Francisco to Cleveland). It weighs 81 quintillion tons (3 more zeros than a trillion). It has mountain ranges with peaks almost as high as Mount Everest. It has empty seas 750 miles across and craters 146 miles wide and 20,000 feet deep.

The power of the moon is unimaginable. Nothing on earth that man has ever made can compare. Every day the moon takes the oceans of the earth and lifts them quietly—millions upon millions upon millions of tons of water quietly and irresistibly lifted into the air. In Boston the tide recedes ten feet. In Eastport, Maine, it recedes nineteen feet. In Nova Scotia, in the Bay of Fundy, the tides vary up to forty-three feet.

The moon is an awesome thing. If you stood in the sunlight on the moon, the fluids in your body would boil, but if you walked into the shadow of a large rock, you would quickly freeze solid.

But who sees the moon? Who stands in awe of the moon? Who looks at the moon on Independence Night when there are man-made fireworks to watch? Who notices the really great things in life? No wonder we are oblivious to the glory of God when there are such clear parables of our blindness built into everyday experience.

Then call this to mind, that the moon is but a reflection of the sun, which quietly keeps its ninety-three-million-mile distance lest we be consumed. Then think that the sun is but a medium-size star. Then think that God created them all and leads them out by number and calls them by name. "Because of the greatness of His might and the strength of His power, not one of them is missing" (Isaiah 40:26).

Read your emotional barometer. Do the amazements and delights of your life correspond to God's reality? Or do they rise and fall on the passing waves of human glitz? ❧

88

CONSEQUENCES OF
FORGIVEN SIN

When Pain Is Not a Penalty

I was again overcome by the story of David's sin against Uriah (murder) and Bathsheba (adultery) and God's response in 2 Samuel 11–12. David acknowledges that the one who has done such a thing deserves to die (2 Samuel 12:5), but in the end Nathan says, "The LORD also has taken away your sin; you shall not die" (12:13). This is amazing grace. God passes over the sin and takes away the penalty of death.

Although the sin is forgiven and the death sentence removed, Nathan says, "Nevertheless, because by this deed you have utterly scorned the LORD, the child that is born to you shall die" (12:14, RSV). In spite of forgiveness, some "penalty" for the sin remains. I put *penalty* in quotes because I think we must distinguish the consequences of forgiven sin (verse 13) from the consequences of unforgiven sin. The latter are properly called penalties; the former we should probably call "disciplinary consequences." That is, they are related to the sin, and they reflect the displeasure of God for the sin, but their aim is not retributive justice. They are not part of condemnation. The aim of the consequences of forgiven sin is not to settle the accounts demanded by a just penalty.

That's what hell is for. There is a judgment whose purpose is to vindicate the right by paying back the wrong, and thus establishing equity in God's kingdom of righteousness. This is done on the cross for those who are in Christ, and it is done in hell for those who are not. The curse that we deserve came down on Christ at the cross if we trust in him (Galatians 3:13), but it comes down on our own heads in hell if we don't (Matthew 25:41). "'Vengeance is mine, I will repay,' says the Lord" (Romans 12:19, RSV). If he passes over sins and treats them, as he did with David, as though they are not worthy of punishment, that is only a merciful delay in the retribution. Either it will be made right in the cross, as Paul says so plainly in Romans 3:25, or it will be settled in "the day of wrath and revelation of the righteous judgment of God" (Romans 2:5).

But the aim of God-sent consequences of forgiven sin is not to settle accounts demanded by the penalty of justice. The aims of the God-sent consequences of forgiven sin are: (1) to demonstrate the exceeding evil of sin, (2) to show that God does not take sin lightly even when he lays aside his punishment, and (3) to humble and sanctify the forgiven sinner.

Thus Hebrews 12:6 teaches that "the Lord disciplines him whom he loves, and chastises every son whom he receives." The purpose is not to penalize, but to purify. "He disciplines us for our good, so that we may share His holiness. All discipline for the moment seems not to be joyful, but sorrowful; yet to those who have been trained by it, afterwards it yields the peaceful fruit of righteousness" (Hebrews 12:10–11, RSV).

Not all of the disciplinary pain ordained by God is directly owing to some sin we have committed, but all of it is ordered for our good as forgiven sinners. This is immensely important to teach in a day when there is an imbalance of emphasis on the Father's forgiving tenderness to the exclusion of the Father's forgiving toughness. Thus many people have no categories to handle the consequences of the sins in their lives except to underestimate the preciousness of forgiveness or to accuse God of double jeopardy in punishing what he has already forgiven.

By the power of truth and the Spirit, we must learn to revel in the grace of God, the forgiveness of sins, the hope of glory, and the joy of the Lord at the very same time that we are suffering from the consequences of forgiven sin. We must not equate forgiveness with the absence of painful impact. David's life is a vivid illustration of this truth. ❧

89

LEGAL KILLING, ILLEGAL MAIMING

———

Abominating Abortion

bortion is a horrendous assault on the unique person-forming rights of our Creator. "For You formed my inward parts; You wove me in my mother's womb" (Psalm 139:13). I have sat with an abortionist over lunch and tried to understand what makes him tick. Once when I was serving a couple days in jail for my part in a "rescue," the pro-choice nurse who walked by to keep an eye on us let me engage him in a long conversation. In the end he said, "We know that they are children and that it is killing. It is simply the lesser of two evils." The abortionist said basically the same thing. For him it was a crusade for the reproductive rights of women, which means that women, like men, should be able to have sex at will without suffering the consequences of pregnancy. It's the only way that men and women can have equality in sexual license.

I abominate this way of thinking, and I believe that the day will come when our culture as a whole will share this abomination and consider abortion as unthinkable as it does racial discrimination. This is why I ponder the tortured pro-choice logic from time to time and include some of my reflections in these readings. For example, in 1993 I wrote to my people the following thoughts. The ugly bluntness of the language is inevitable if we are to speak the horror of the reality.

If you start by cutting off arms and legs, you might get interrupted and have to leave a maimed child alive. So it's better to start by sucking out the brains. Then if you get interrupted, at least the child will be dead. This is certainly a shrewd choice when killing is legal and maiming is not.

Abortionist Abu Hayat found that out too late. So did the baby who lost her right arm when Hayat cut it off in her mother's womb in October 1991. Hayat got in trouble because he failed to kill the child.

This is definitely bad press for abortion defenders. One solution is improved methods of killing late-term babies. I am sure most of our pro-choice leaders do not like any abortions, especially late-term abortions. They simply insist that they must be legal. They support laws that would protect the legality of abortion even in the late months if a "health" reason can be found, including psychological health. The assumption is that the unborn child does not have the right to life, morally or constitutionally.

So the newer late-term abortion procedures and day-after pills will help make abortion more tolerable for Americans by making sure that babies get killed instead of maimed. Maimed babies make us uneasy with abortion; killed babies don't.

As far as I can tell, our pro-choice leaders who quote Scripture have been taught that "life" (the eternal soul) is given to a child the moment the child first breathes, not before. This is based partly on Genesis 2:7, (RSV): "The LORD God formed man of dust from the ground, and breathed into his nostrils the breath of life; and man became a living being."

This is a very risky interpretation. The text does not say or imply that because a child lacks one thing (air), it also lacks life, soul, and personhood. Moreover, there are also texts that say the life is in the blood, not the breath (Genesis 9:4; Leviticus 17:11, 14; Deuteronomy 12:23). And babies bleed even before women know they are pregnant. We are hard put to get the Bible onto the side of abortion.

We do well not to kill unborn human beings created in the image of God when they only lack time or air. ❧

90

How Does God Grade
at the Judgment?

———✦———

Thoughts on Our Imperfect Obedience

What about the New Covenant promise that God will not remember the sins of his people? Will they be remembered at the judgment day? Hebrews 10:16–17 says, "This is the covenant that I will make with them,…their sins and their lawless deeds I will remember no more." What does it mean for an infinite, all-knowing God to choose not to remember something?

Philippians 3:13–14 points to an answer. Paul says, "Forgetting what lies behind…I press toward the goal." Paul chose not to remember his past. But what about Ephesians 2:12? Here Paul says that Christians should remember the terrible past: "Remember that you were at that time separate from Christ,…having no hope and without God in the world."

I think what Paul means is that the sins and the lostness of the past should be forgotten in the sense that we should never bring them to mind in a way that hinders our growth and obedience. If remembering can cause a deeper dependence on grace, a deeper love for Christ, and a greater trust in his power, then let there be periodic remembering of the hopeless past. But the norm is forgetting the past, lest it drag us down.

Similarly, God promises to forget our sins. That is, he will never bring them up before us or others if that would diminish our love for him, our delight in his grace, or our zeal for the glory of God. But if there is an occasion when he knows it would be good for us and for the glory of his grace, then he will bring our sins before us for a season.

So what about the last judgment? Will our sins be remembered? Will they be revealed? Anthony Hoekema puts it wisely like this: "The failures and shortcomings of...believers...will enter into the picture on the Day of Judgment. But—and this is the important point—the sins and shortcomings of believers will be revealed in the judgment as forgiven sins, whose guilt has been totally covered by the blood of Jesus Christ."[43]

Picture it like this. God has a file on every person (the books of Revelation 20:12). All you've ever done or said (Matthew 12:36) is recorded there with a grade from A to F. When you stand before the judgment seat of Christ (2 Corinthians 5:1) to be judged according to what you have done, whether good or bad, God will open the file and lay out the tests with their grades. He will pull out all the F's and put them in a pile. Then he will take all the D's and C's and pull the good parts of the test out and place them with the A's, and put the bad parts with the F's. Then he will take all the B's and A's and pull the bad parts out of them and put them in the F pile, and put all the good parts in the A pile.

Then he will open another file (the book of life [Philippians 4:3]) and find your name. Behind your name will be a wood-stick match made from the cross of Jesus. He will take the match, light it, and set the F pile, with all your failures, imperfections, and deficiencies, on fire and burn them up. They will not condemn you, and they will not reward you.

Then he will take from your book-of-life file a sealed envelope marked "free and gracious bonus" and put it on the A pile (see Mark 4:24 and Luke 6:38). Then he will hold up the entire pile and declare: "By this your life bears witness to the grace of my Father, the worth of my blood, and the fruit of my Spirit. Enter into the joy of your Master." ❧

91

WHY DID GOD CREATE FAMILIES?

—◈—

Pondering the Unveiling of God

Why did God create families? One obvious answer to this question is that families are for the sake of multiplying and filling the earth. That's what God said to Adam and Eve in the beginning: "Be fruitful and multiply, and fill the earth" (Genesis 1:28).

But that's not enough of an answer, because God could have created humans to reproduce like earthworms. He could have skipped childhood and avoided the whole idea of a lifetime of marriage and years of childhood and parenting. So why did he create and ordain that a man and woman marry, that they have tiny, helpless children, and that they spend years and years rearing these children in a family relationship? (I am assuming that single-parent homes are families, as bodies are still bodies even if they have lost a limb.)

Here are six biblical reasons for why God did it the way he did it.

1. God created men and women so that their enjoyment of him comes to fullness by sharing the gift of life, not by being isolated. "It is not good that man should be alone" (Genesis 2:18, RSV).

Marriage is the most basic means of extending and expanding the enjoyment of God in the good of another, but single people experience this, too, in precious friendships and the life of the body of Christ. Our need of this is so profound that little children without families become autistic.

2. God created marriage as an advertisement for the relationship

between Christ and the church. "A man leaves his father and his mother and cleaves to his wife, and they become one flesh.... This mystery is a profound one, and I am saying that it refers to Christ and the church" (Genesis 2:24; Ephesians 5:32, RSV).

This is the most profound reason why God hates divorce (Malachi 2:16). Broken marriage vows deface the portrait of Christ's unbreakable covenant love for his bride, the church (Ephesians 5:25).

3. God created parenting, especially fatherhood, to reveal to children and to all of us the Fatherhood of God and his strong and tender care. "It is for discipline that you have to endure. God is treating you as sons; for what son is there whom his father does not discipline?" (Hebrews 12:7, RSV).

God is mainly revealed as Father, and to a lesser degree as Mother, I think, because he intends to highlight his protecting, providing, guiding strength and authority. In a family with a father and a mother, God calls fathers to this special responsibility. Mothers balance and complement this in many ways, especially with their unique feminine warmth, tenderness, and nurture which are their own deep strength. Families exist to reveal God to children.

4. God created families with parents and little babies who have to grow up so that parents and all of us could learn the childlikeness of faith. "Truly, I say to you, unless you turn and become like children, you will never enter the kingdom of heaven. Whoever humbles himself like this child, he is the greatest in the kingdom of heaven" (Matthew 18:3–4, RSV).

Families reveal not only how God relates to us in the loving authority, strength, provision, and guidance of the parents, but also how we are to relate to him in the helpless, happy dependence that little children have toward their parents.

5. God ordained families for the transmitting of his truth and our faith from one generation to the other. "Fathers, do not provoke your children to anger, but bring them up in the discipline and instruction of the Lord" (Ephesians 6:4, RSV). "He commanded our fathers to teach to their children;

that the next generation might know them, the children yet unborn, and arise and tell them to their children, so that they should set their hope in God" (Psalm 78:5–7, RSV).

6. God created families to reveal the way that members in the church are to relate to each other, namely, as a family of brothers, sisters, mothers, and fathers. "Do not rebuke an older man but exhort him as you would a father; treat younger men like brothers, older women like mothers, younger women like sisters, in all purity" (1 Timothy 5:1–2, RSV).

Paul constantly calls fellow Christians "brothers" or "sisters." In the coming kingdom there will be no marriage and no bearing children. "For in the resurrection they neither marry nor are given in marriage, but are like angels in heaven" (Matthew 22:30, RSV). The family as we know it will be changed, but in the present time it is meant to reveal God to the world and to elucidate relationships in the body of Christ that will endure forever. ❧

92

Do You Delight
to Be Afraid?

Meditation on Some Wonderful Words of Fear

Rather than try to define the "fear of the Lord," I would like to motivate you to pursue it. If you want to experience the fear of the Lord badly enough, you will probably do the necessary reading and meditation to discover what it means. But for most of us, fear is something we want to get rid of, not get more of. If that's true of the fear of God then there is something wrong with our hearts or something wrong with our understanding of this fear.

Have you ever gathered the spectacular promises made to those who fear God? They are so wonderful that you would think fearing God must be the most thrilling thing in the world—which it is. So I hope you will be moved now to pursue it with all your might.

The friendship of the Lord—

> *The friendship of the LORD is for those who fear him, and he makes known to them his covenant.* (Psalm 25:14, RSV)

The watch care of the Lord—

> *The eye of the LORD is on those who fear him.* (Psalm 33:18, RSV)

The deliverance of the Lord's angels—

> *The angel of the LORD encamps around those who fear him, and delivers them.* (Psalm 34:7, RSV)

*You shall fear the LORD your God, and he will deliver you out of the hand
of all your enemies.* (2 Kings 17:39, RSV)

Freedom from craving—
Those who fear [God] have no want! (Psalm 34:9, RSV)

The Lord's fatherly pity—
As a father pities his children, so the LORD pities those who fear him.
(Psalm 103:13, RSV)

The permanent love of God—
*The steadfast love of the LORD is from everlasting to everlasting upon those
who fear him.* (Psalm 103:17, RSV)

Being enjoyed by the Lord—
The LORD takes pleasure in those who fear him. (Psalm 147:11, RSV)

Having the beginning and the essence of wisdom—
The fear of the LORD, that is wisdom. (Job 28:28, RSV)

The fear of the LORD is the beginning of wisdom. (Psalm 111:10;
Proverbs 9:10, RSV)

Drinking at the fountain of life—
*The fear of the LORD is a fountain of life, that one may avoid the snares of
death.* (Proverbs 14:27, RSV)

Being satisfied—
The fear of the LORD leads to life; and he who has it rests satisfied.
(Proverbs 19:23, RSV)

This is so good, we might well ask whether sinners like us have any hope
to do something so wonderful that God responds with such spectacular goodness, but that would be a backward way of thinking. It is not that we sinners
wonderfully overcome our sin so that God responds with blessing; it's the

other way around. "There is forgiveness with You [O God] that You may be feared" (Psalm 130:4). God calls forth fear by forgiving our sin, not by condemning it. I know that sounds strange, but it is also very comforting. If benefits hang on our fearing God, remember that our fearing God hangs on the utterly undeserved forgiveness of God. Is it any wonder Isaiah says of the servant of the Lord, "His delight shall be in the fear of the LORD" (Isaiah 11:3, RSV)? I hope you will feel so much delight in this that you pursue it with all your might. ❧

93

HOW DO YOU OBEY
THE COMMAND TO BE BORN?

Reflections on Waking Up from the Dead

H ow do you obey the command to be born? Ask another question first: When Jesus commanded Lazarus to rise from the dead, how did he obey that command? John 11:43 says, "[Jesus] cried out with a loud voice, 'Lazarus, come forth.'" That was a command to a dead man. The next verse says, "The man who had died came forth, bound hand and foot with wrappings."

How did Lazarus do that? How does a dead man obey a command to live again? The answer seems to be: The command carries the power to create new life. Obedience to the command means doing what living people do. This is extremely important. The command of God, "Rise from the dead!" carries in it the power we need to obey it. We do not obey it by creating that life. We obey it by doing what living people do—Lazarus came forth. He rose. He walked out to Jesus. The call of God creates life. We respond in the power of what the call created.

In Ephesians 5:14, Paul says, "Awake, O sleeper, and arise from the dead, and Christ will shine on you" (RSV). How do you obey a command to wake up from sleep? If your house has carbon monoxide in it, and someone cries out, "Wake up! Save yourself! Get out!" you don't obey by waking yourself up. The loud, powerful command itself wakes you up. You obey by doing what wakeful people do in the face of danger. You get up and leave the house. The call creates the waking. You respond in the power of what the call created.

I believe this explains why the Bible says paradoxical things about new birth: namely, that we must get ourselves new hearts, but that it is God who creates the new heart. For example:

- Deuteronomy 10:16: *"Circumcise your heart!"*
  Deuteronomy 30:6: *"The LORD your God will circumcise your heart."*

- Ezekiel 18:31: *"Make yourselves a new heart and a new spirit!"*
  Ezekiel 36:26: *"I will give you a new heart and put a new spirit within you."*

- John 3:7: *"You must be born again."*
  1 Peter 1:3: *"[God] caused us to be born again."*

"Circumcise your heart" means do what people do who have circumcised hearts. Be tender toward God and forsake all that is evil. Set your life apart for God and be different from the world. All this is possible only because of the promise, "The LORD your God will circumcise your heart." As Philippians 2:12–13 says, "Work out your salvation…for it is God who is at work in you, both to will and to work for his good pleasure." "Work out your salvation" corresponds to "Circumcise your heart." "God who is at work in you" corresponds to "The LORD your God will circumcise your heart." The connection is that our doing it depends on God's doing it first. He initiates and enables.

Similarly, "Make yourselves a new heart" means we should act in the newness of a new heart and take steps into newness. The promise "I will give you a new heart" means that God is the decisive creator of the new heart. He gives it and we act in the power of it.

In the same way, the way to obey the command to be born is first to experience the divine gift of spiritual life and breath and then to do what living, breathing people do—cry out to God in faith, gratitude, and love. When the command of God comes with the creating, converting power of the Holy Spirit, it gives life. The evidence that it has come in this life-creating way is that we respond in life, faith, hope, and joy. If that response is in us, we are born of God, and we have obeyed the command.

Have you been born again? Do you have a new heart? Are you raised spiritually from the dead? This is God's work in and under your response of faith. So respond in humble trust and know in that very act the sovereign touch of God. ❧

94

INSPIRED BY THE
INCREDIBLE EARLY CHURCH

Lord, Give Us a Holy Imitation

I t is an overwhelming thing to be caught up in the spirit of those early centuries when Christianity spread far and wide by countless, nameless saints in totally pagan cultures. By A.D. 300 there was no part of the Roman Empire that had not been to some extent penetrated by the gospel. What human factors did God ordain to bring about this amazing spread of the Christian movement? In his *History of Christian Missions*, Stephen Neill suggests six (pages 39–43).

1. First and foremost was the burning conviction that possessed a great number of the early Christians. The church historian Eusebius of Caesarea (A.D. 260–340) described the way the gospel spread:

At that time [about the beginning of the second century] many Christians felt their souls inspired by the holy word with a passionate desire for perfection. Their action, in obedience to the instructions of the Savior, was to sell their goods and to distribute them to the poor. Then, leaving their homes, they set out to fulfill the work of an evangelist, making it their ambition to preach the word of the faith to those who as yet had heard nothing of it, and to commit to them the books of the divine Gospels. They were content simply to lay the foundations of the faith among these foreign peoples: they then appointed other pastors, and committed to them the responsibility for building up those whom they had merely brought to the faith. Then they

passed on to other countries and nations with the grace and help of God.
(Ecclesiastical History, 3.37.2–3)

2. The solid historical message that Christians brought was indeed good news and a welcome alternative to the mystery religions of the day. It was not a philosophy, but news of something that had happened. "Now I make known to you, brethren, the gospel...that Christ died for our sins according to the Scriptures, and that He was buried, and that He was raised on the third day according to the Scriptures" (1 Corinthians 15:1–5).

3. The new Christian communities commended themselves by the purity of their lives. "[Christ] gave Himself for us to redeem us...and to purify for Himself a people for His own possession, zealous for good deeds" (Titus 2:14).

4. The Christian communities were marked by mutual loyalty and an overcoming of antagonisms between alienated classes. "There is no...Greek and Jew, circumcised and uncircumcised, barbarian, Scythian, slave and freeman, but Christ is all, and in all" (Colossians 3:11).

5. The Christians were known for an elaborate development of charitable service, especially to those within the fellowship. "Let us do good to all men, and especially to those who are of the household of the faith" (Galatians 6:10). The Roman Emperor Julian, writing in the early fourth century, regretted the progress of Christianity because it pulled people away from the Roman gods. He said, "Atheism [i.e., Christian faith!] has been specially advanced through the loving service rendered to strangers, and through their care for the burial of the dead. It is a scandal that there is not a single Jew who is a beggar, and that the godless Galilaeans care not only for their own poor but for ours as well; while those who belong to us look in vain for the help that we should render them."[44]

6. The persecution of Christians and their readiness to suffer made a dramatic impact on unbelievers. "Keep your behavior excellent among the Gentiles, so that in the thing in which they slander you as evildoers, they

may because of your good deeds, as they observe them, glorify God in the day of visitation" (1 Peter 2:12). Stephen Neill observes, "Under the Roman Empire Christians had no legal right to exist.... Every Christian knew that sooner or later he might have to testify to his faith at the cost of his life."[45]

Here we are at the turn of the millennium. May God raise up hundreds of thousands of superordinary Christians and Christian communities with this kind of passion. With this kind of heritage I am inspired again to hear and obey the word from Hebrews 6:12: "[Do] not be sluggish, but imitators of those who through faith and patience inherit the promises." Lord, give us this holy imitation of those mighty days. ❧

95

MATTHEW'S AMAZING WARNINGS NOT TO BE A FALSE DISCIPLE

Thoughts on the
Necessity for Practical Righteousness

Matthew seems unusually burdened to alert us about the danger of thinking we are saved when we are not. This seems to be the opposite concern of many today who seem much more eager to give feelings of assurance where there may not be any authentic spiritual life. We need to hear the warnings of Jesus as Matthew reports them. Assurance of salvation is a precious thing, so precious and so necessary (Hebrews 3:14) that we dare not dilute it with feelings of safety apart from transformed lives.

Matthew 5:20: "I tell you, unless your righteousness exceeds that of the scribes and Pharisees, you will never enter the kingdom of heaven" (RSV). The righteousness called for here is not the imputed righteousness of Christ, as utterly crucial as that is at the bottom of the Christian life. The rest of Matthew 5 illustrates the practical heart-righteousness Jesus is calling for. It contrasts commands of Jesus with the commands (and the Pharisees' misuse) of the Old Testament. The righteousness that exceeds the Pharisees' and leads to the kingdom is spelled out in Matthew 5:21–48.

Matthew 7:21–23: "Not every one who says to me, 'Lord, Lord,' shall enter the kingdom of heaven, but he who does the will of my Father who is in heaven. On that day many will say to me, 'Lord, Lord, did we not prophesy in your name, and cast out demons in your name, and do many mighty works in your name?' And then will I declare to them, 'I never knew you; depart from me, you evildoers'" (RSV). Prophesying, casting out demons, and doing mighty works in the name of Jesus do not prove that Jesus has known us. The evidence of being savingly known by Jesus is to be an evildoer no longer, that is, to have righteousness that surpasses that of the scribes and Pharisees. Religious zeal and even miracle working do not prove a new heart of love.

Matthew 13:20–21: "As for what was sown on rocky ground, this is he who hears the word and immediately receives it with joy; yet he has no root in himself, but endures for a while, and when tribulation or persecution arises on account of the word, immediately he falls away" (RSV). Joy that evaporates in the heat of affliction was not joy in God, but in comfort. Paul said that he knew God had chosen the Thessalonians because, "You received the word in much affliction, with joy inspired by the Holy Spirit" (1 Thessalonians 1:6, RSV). Joy in tribulation is the evidence of joy in God, not ease.

Matthew 13:47–50: "The kingdom of heaven is like a net which was thrown into the sea and gathered fish of every kind; when it was full, men drew it ashore and sat down and sorted the good into vessels but threw away the bad. So it will be at the close of the age. The angels will come out and separate the evil from the righteous, and throw them into the furnace of fire; there men will weep and gnash their teeth" (RSV). Notice carefully that the fish thrown into the furnace are not the ones missed by the net of the kingdom. They are the ones caught by the kingdom and yet unfit for eternal life. It is possible to taste the powers of the kingdom and not be of the kingdom—just like the miracle workers of Matthew 7:22 (see Hebrews 6:5).

Matthew 22:2, 10–14: "The kingdom of heaven may be compared to a king who gave a marriage feast for his son…. [His] servants went out into the streets and gathered all whom they found, both bad and good; so the wedding hall was filled with guests. But when the king came in to look at the guests, he saw there a man who had no wedding garment; and he said to him, 'Friend, how did you get in here without a wedding garment?' And he was speechless. Then the king said to the attendants, 'Bind him hand and foot, and cast him into the outer darkness; there men will weep and gnash their teeth.' For many are called, but few are chosen" (RSV). This situation is similar to the bad fish drawn into the net of the kingdom. The lack of a wedding garment probably represents the lack of the righteousness that surpasses the scribes' and Pharisees'. The ill-clad man was drawn with kingdom power from the world into the banquet hall, like the fish into the net, but he was not fit for the kingdom and so was cast out.

Besides all these warnings, consider the penalty of the unforgiving servant (18:23–35), the five foolish virgins who lived with the faithful but were careless about their oil (25:1–13), the fate of the man who received an investment from the Lord but made nothing of it (25:14–30), the doom of the servant (in the church!) who is unfaithful (24:45–51), the people who look like disciple-sheep in many ways but are in fact wolves (7:15), the professing Christian prophets who do signs and wonders but are false (24:24), and the (three-year!) disciple named Judas Iscariot, who betrayed Jesus (10:4).

O how serious is this matter of authenticity in the Christian life! A decision for Christ is not nearly so crucial as a life for Christ. Only reality counts with God. So let us learn three lessons: (1) "Test yourselves to see if you are in the faith; examine yourselves" (2 Corinthians 13:5), (2) "Enter by the narrow gate.... For the gate is narrow and the way is hard, that leads to life, and those who find it are few" (Matthew 7:13–14, RSV), and (3) "You will know them by their fruits!" (Matthew 7:16), which is not justification by works but the indispensable evidence of justification by faith. ❧

96

THE PROBLEM OF PREEMIES

An Open Letter to the Star Tribune

Dear Editor,

Are you aware that the same day the Senate Health and Human Services Committee approved the unconditional permission to terminate the life of twenty-four-week-old fetuses, the neonatology unit at Abbott Northwestern was caring for a twenty-two-and-a-half-week-old (500-gram) preemie with good chances of healthy life?

Now that is news and calls for profound reflection. Instead, your lead editorial the morning after glossed over this critical issue and endorsed abortion because it is "one of the most personal decisions a woman can make" and because "the abortion decision is undeniably sensitive." This level of reflection is unworthy of major editorials in good newspapers.

I assume that by "personal decision" you do not mean "having deep personal implications," but you do mean "having deep personal implications for only one person, the mother."

Abortion is emphatically not a "personal" decision in that limited sense. There is another person, namely, the unborn child. If you deny this, you must give an account of what that little preemie is at Abbott Northwestern. Abortion is a decision about competing human rights: the right not to be pregnant and the right not to be killed.

I assume you approve of the committee's action. But I also assume you would not approve of the mother's right to strangle the preemie at Abbott hospital before its twenty-fifth week of life since conception. If so, you owe your readers an explanation of your simple endorsement of abortion because it is "personal" and "sensitive."

In fact, I challenge you to publish two photographs side by side: one of this "child" outside the womb and another of a "fetus" inside the womb both at twenty-three or twenty-four weeks, with a caption that says something like: "We at the *Star Tribune* regard the termination of the preemie as manslaughter and the termination of the fetus as the personal choice of the mother."

I have read in your pages how you disdain the use of pictures because abortion is too complex for simplistic solutions, but I also remember how you approved the possible televising of an execution as one of the most effective ways of turning the heart of America against capital punishment (a similarly complex issue).

We both know that if America watched repeated terminations of twenty-three-week-old fetuses on television (or saw the procedure truthfully documented in your paper), the sentiment of our society would profoundly change. There are thousands of such terminations each year. (The Alan Guttmacher Institute, for example, estimated that more than nine thousand abortions after twenty-one weeks were performed in 1987.)

Words fail to describe the barbarity of an unconditional right to take the life of a human being as fully developed as twenty-three weeks. You could never successfully defend it in the public presence of the act itself.

You can do so only in the moral fog of phrases like abortion must be left to the woman because it is "undeniably sensitive." This is not compelling. There are many sensitive situations where the state prescribes limits for how we express our feelings where others are concerned. And there is another person concerned. If you are willing, you may meet this "other person" face to face in dozens of hospitals around the country.

Sincerely yours,
John Piper ❧

97

HOW EXILES
SERVE THE CITY

―∾∾―

Living Well When God and Satan
Claim the Earth

S uppose I visit a friend's house and, on my way out the door, I throw an empty Coke can in the yard. You see me do it and say, "You're not going to leave that are you?" I say, "Why not? It's not my yard." Would you be impressed?

There is a similar attitude we must avoid when we think of ourselves as refugees on the earth. The apostle Peter called Christians "aliens and exiles" (1 Peter 2:11), and Paul said, "Our citizenship is in heaven" (Philippians 3:20). So we may find ourselves carelessly saying, about the way we treat our city, "Why not? It's not my world?"

It's true that Maltbie Babcock's hymn proclaims, "This Is My Father's World." That's right. "The earth is the Lord's and the fullness of it" (Exodus 9:29; Psalm 24:1; 1 Corinthians 10:26). It is also true that man was put here to fill the earth, subdue it, and rule over it (Genesis 1:28). Moreover, God promised Abraham and his heirs that he would be "heir of the world" (Romans 4:13). Jesus said, "Blessed are the meek, for they shall inherit the earth" (Matthew 5:5, RSV).

Nevertheless, Paul speaks of Satan as the "god of this age" (2 Corinthians 4:4), and John says that "the whole world is in the power of the evil one" (1 John 5:19). In the wilderness the devil makes the claim to have "all the kingdoms of the world" at his disposal to give to Christ, if he would worship him (Matthew 4:8). Even though Paul says that "there is no authority except from God, and those which exist are established by God," nevertheless he also speaks of "principalities and powers and world rulers of this present darkness" (Ephesians 6:12). Evidently this world is under a siege that God allows for his own wise and holy purposes. Jesus is sent to invade and conquer the foreign powers that now, under God, lay claim to this world. Thus Jesus says, "Now judgment is upon this world; now the ruler of this world will be cast out" (John 12:31). Satan is a ruler of this world, but not by Creator rights, nor by inheritance, nor by might. His rule is subordinate and temporary.

Therefore, even though, as the children of God, we will inherit the earth when it is made new in the kingdom (Revelation 21:1), nevertheless in a profound sense this world is not our home. When we are away from our bodies we will be "at home with the Lord" (2 Corinthians 5:8). Since our true homeland is with God in heaven, we are not to be "conformed to this age" (Romans 12:2). Our lives "are hid with Christ in God" (Colossians 3:3). We have been "rescued...from the domain of darkness and transferred...to the kingdom of his beloved Son" (Colossians 1:13). We have "passed out of death and into life" (1 John 3:14). We are exiles and strangers here.

How then are we to act in this foreign place? Should we be involved at all with the way this world works? Should we care about what happens here?

One answer comes simply from the Christian courtesy of not trashing another's yard. Doing unto others as we would have them do to us (Matthew 7:12) goes a long way in settling this matter. We would surely like exiles in our country to pitch in and do their part to make things work.

But there is more. God has a word for his exiles and how they behave in foreign places. The word is found in Jeremiah 29:4–7: "Thus says the LORD of hosts, the God of Israel, to all the exiles whom I have sent into exile from Jerusalem to Babylon, 'Build houses and live in them; and plant gardens and eat their produce.... Seek the welfare of the city where I have sent you into exile, and pray to the LORD on its behalf; for in its welfare you will have welfare.'"

If that was true for God's exiles in Babylon, it would seem to be even more true for Christian exiles in this very "Babylonian" world. What then shall we do?

We should do the ordinary things that need to be done: build houses, live in them, plant gardens. This does not contaminate you if you do it all for the real King and not just for eye service as men-pleasers.

Seek the welfare of the city where God has sent you—Minneapolis, Los Angeles, Atlanta, Detroit, Bangkok, London, Almata, Manila, Kankan, Grand Rapids. Think of yourself as sent to your town by God, because you are.

Pray to the Lord on behalf of your city. Pray metro prayers. Ask for great and good things to happen for the city. Evidently God is not indifferent to the welfare of your "foreign" town. One reason he is interested is that in the welfare of the city his people find welfare.

This does not mean that we give up our exile orientation. In fact, we will do most good for this world by keeping a steadfast freedom from its beguiling attractions. We will serve our city best by getting our values from the "city which is to come" (Hebrews 13:14). We will do our city most good by calling as many of its citizens as we can to be citizens of the "Jerusalem above" (Galatians 4:26). May the Lord of heaven and earth give us the grace and wisdom to live so that the natives will want to meet our King. Let us be helpfully out of step for the good of the city. ❧

MOUNTAINS ARE NOT MEANT TO ENVY

Awed Thoughts on Charles Spurgeon

Mountains are not meant to envy. In fact they are not meant even to be possessed by anyone on earth. They are, as David says, "the mountains of God" (Psalm 36:6).

If you try to make your Minnesota hill imitate a mountain, you will make a fool of your hill. Hills have their place. So do the plains of Nebraska. If the whole world were mountains, where would we grow bread? Every time you eat bread say, "Praise God for Nebraska!"

I'm talking about Charles Haddon Spurgeon. I am warning my wavering self that he is not to be imitated. Spurgeon preached as a Baptist pastor in London from 1854 until 1891—thirty-eight years of ministry in one place. He died January 31, 1892, at the age of fifty-seven.

His collected sermons fill sixty-three volumes equivalent to the twenty-seven-volume ninth edition of the *Encyclopedia Britannica* and stand as the largest set of books by a single author in the history of Christianity. He read six serious books a week and could remember what was in them and where. He read *Pilgrim's Progress* more than one hundred times.

He added 14,460 people to his church membership and did almost all the membership interviews himself. He could look out on a congregation of 5,000 and name the members. He founded a pastors' college and trained almost 900 men during his pastorate.

Spurgeon once said he had counted as many as eight sets of thoughts that passed through his mind at the same time while he was preaching. He often prayed for his people during the very sermon he was preaching to them. He would preach for forty minutes at 140 words a minute from a small sheet of notes that he had worked up the night before. The result? More than twenty-five thousand copies of his sermons were sold each week in twenty languages, and someone was converted every week through the written sermons.

Spurgeon was married and had two sons who became pastors. His wife was an invalid most of her life and rarely heard him preach. He founded an orphanage, edited a magazine, produced more than 140 books, responded to 500 letters a week, and often preached ten times a week in various churches as well as his own.

He suffered from gout, rheumatism, and Bright's disease, and in the last twenty years of his ministry he was so sick that he missed a third of the Sundays at the Metropolitan Tabernacle.

He was a politically liberal, conservative Calvinistic Baptist who smoked cigars, spoke his mind, believed in hell, and wept over the perishing, tens of thousands of whom were saved through his soul-winning passion. He was a Christian hedonist, coming closer than anyone I know to my favorite sentence: "God is most glorified in us when we are most satisfied in him." Spurgeon said, "One thing is past all question; we shall bring our Lord most glory if we get from Him much grace."

What shall we make of such a man? Neither a god nor a goal. He should not be worshiped or envied. He is too small for the one and too big for the other. If we worship such men, we are idolaters. If we envy them, we are fools. Mountains are not meant to be envied. They are meant to be marveled at for the sake of their Maker. They are the mountains of God.

More than that, without envy, we are meant to climb into their minds and hearts and revel in what they saw so clearly and what they felt so deeply. We are to benefit from them without craving to be like them. When we learn this, we can relax and enjoy them. Until we learn it, they may make us miserable, because they highlight our weaknesses. Well, we are weak, and to be reminded of it is good. But we also need to be reminded that, compared with our inferiority to God, the distance between us and Spurgeon is as nothing. We are all utterly dependent on our Father's grace.

Spurgeon had his sins. That may comfort us in our weak moments. But let us rather be comforted that his greatness was a free gift of God—to us as well as him. Let us be, by the grace of God, all that we can be for the glory of God (1 Corinthians 15:10). In our smallness, let us not become smaller by envy, but rather larger by humble admiration and gratitude for the gifts of others.

Do not envy the mountain; glory in its Creator. You'll find the air up there cool, fresh, and invigorating and the view stunning beyond description. So don't envy. Enjoy! ❧

99

WOULD YOU
ACCEPT EXECUTION FOR
BEING A CHRISTIAN?

Martyrdom Is Modern Too

When we have time for an extended family devotion in the evening, my younger children have wanted to read the stories of Christians who suffered for their faith. For example, we read the story of John Bunyan, the author of *Pilgrim's Progress*. For more than twelve years he was imprisoned while his second wife, Elizabeth, cared for their six children. His crime? Preaching the gospel without state sanction. The authorities would have let him go if he had promised not to preach. He said he would remain in prison until the moss grew on his eyelids rather than fail to do what God had commanded him to do. He said that parting from his wife and children "has often been to me in this place as the pulling of the flesh from my bones."[46] This was especially true with regard to his eldest daughter, who was blind.

On another evening we read about the Anabaptists. What a heart-wrenching story they offer. Hans Brett was executed January 4, 1577, after eight painful months of imprisonment in the Netherlands. On the morning of his being burned at the stake, the executioner clamped his tongue with a metal screw device and seared it with a hot iron to make it swell. All this to keep him from testifying as he burned!

Women were not safe either. On March 10, 1528, Balthasar Hubmaier was burned at the stake in Vienna for Anabaptist beliefs, and three days later his wife was forcibly drowned in the Danube. The same death came to Margaretha Sattler, eight days after the burning of her husband, Michael. She was drowned in the Neckar River that flowed past Rottenburg.

Then we began to realize as a family that martyrdom was also happening in our own day. On December 3, 1990, after being tortured during a month of imprisonment, Hossein Soodmand, a fifty-five-year-old ordained minister of the Assemblies of God, was hanged in Iran. He was one of a handful of Iranian pastors who had left Islam for the Christian faith.

In March 1991, Lynda Bethea, a forty-two-year-old Southern Baptist missionary, was killed in Kenya when she came to assist her husband near Nairobi, Kenya. They were on their way to get their two children from Rift Valley Academy.

David Barrett in his 1996 "Status of Global Mission" reported in the *International Bulletin of Missionary Research* (January, pages 24–25) that there were about 159,000 Christian martyrs that year around the world, people who died from causes relating to their profession of faith as a Christian.

When I read these things, it makes me want to live more and more simply. It makes me want to have little to hold me here. It makes me want to be utterly enthralled with Jesus so that "to live is Christ and to die is gain" (Philippians 1:21).

Can you say with these Christians, "Your lovingkindness is better than life" (Psalm 63:3)? Better than life! To live in the love of God is better than life with wife and children and significant ministry. O that God would come and ravish us to such a single-hearted devotion! ∼

100

WHEN THOUSANDS DIE IN BANGLADESH

———

Pondering Pain and the Power of God

I n 1991 storms and flooding caused a huge loss of life in Bangladesh. Hundreds of thousands died. It was like thousands of other catastrophes in history, but it caused me, more than usual, to search the Scriptures for help in dealing with it.

The Bible reveals to us that life is given freely to us by God (Acts 17:25; Job 1:21). Life is not something we possess by virtue of our merit. We do not "own" our life in relation to God. It is a "loan," as is implied in Luke 12:20 where the soul (life) is required "back" by the Lord. Life is God's and is on loan to us freely so that we might enjoy glorifying God with it. It is always and totally at his disposal, never rightfully at our disposal. Life belongs to God.

The Bible reveals that God is the one who takes life as he is the one who gives it (Job 1:21; 1 Samuel 2:6; Deuteronomy 32:39; 2 Kings 5:7). As God's rightful possession, life is God's to take when he pleases. He does not need to consult with anyone else because his authority as Creator, Sustainer, and Owner of life puts it totally at his disposal. He is not doing any evil when he takes back the life he gave whenever he chooses.

In some sense the devil is the one "who has the power of death" (Hebrews 2:14, RSV). And in Job 1:12 God seems to give the life of Job's family into the hand of Satan, even though Job rightly says, "The LORD [not just Satan] has taken away" (1:21). So there is a sense in which God's sovereignty overrules but also uses the death-dealing work of Satan in the tragedies of the world. We must come to terms with both the sovereignty of God and the truth that Satan, on God's leash, is involved in the miseries of pain and death.

When Jesus was asked about a tragedy in which a tower in Siloam fell on eighteen people and killed them, he answered, "Do you think that they were worse offenders than all the others who dwelt in Jerusalem? I tell you, No; but unless you repent you will all likewise perish" (Luke 13:4–5, RSV). This means that God's purpose in suddenly taking life is not necessarily to show a group's greater sinfulness. Rather, in dealing with them in a just way according to his authority and ownership of life and his right to rule the world as Lord of all things, one of his purposes is to warn the rest of us that our lives are in his hands and that we should repent of sin and be ready at any time to die.

The Book of Revelation reveals that in the last days God will release terrible devastation on the earth and many millions will die. For example, Revelation 9:13–21 describes the death of one-third of the world's population by the "four angels" (verse 15). Verse 20 says, "The rest of mankind, who were not killed by these plagues, did not repent of the works of their hands." In other words the catastrophic loss of life was meant to bring the world to its senses so that it would reckon with the one true and living God and repent.

Ezekiel 18:32 reveals that God does not have pleasure in the death of anyone. Jesus weeps over the Jerusalem that does not recognize the time of its visitation (Luke 19:41–44). The heart of God is large and complex. He is able to be grieved over the pain of his creatures, while at the same time ordaining that this very pain and death take place for a higher and greater purpose that brings him more joy than if he had run the world in another way.[47]

Our response therefore should be to weep with those who weep (Romans 12:15) and not to delight callously in the destruction of anyone in this age, but to extend the love of Christ and the hope of salvation as long as we can to those who live. When confronted with the question why, we must look to the God who has absolute rights over us and take heed to ourselves knowing that our time will be very soon.

Let us repent and live utterly for the glory of the one who made us for the joy of knowing him and showing his glory. Let us gather as many of the perishing as we can into his spacious banquet hall while there is time. ᵔᵔ

BECAUSE HE IS OUR FATHER?
OR,
THAT WE MAY BE SONS?

Meditation on Luke 6:35–36
and the Conditionality of Our Salvation

Love your enemies, and do good, and lend, expecting nothing in return;
and your reward will be great, and you will be sons of the Most High;
for he is kind to the ungrateful and the selfish.
Be merciful, even as your Father is merciful. (RSV)

Two phrases in these words of Jesus point to a deep truth in the Christian life. "Be merciful as your Father is merciful" implies clearly that Jesus is treating his disciples as children of God. God is their Father. They are his children. So they should be merciful because they have a Father who has and who will treat them (and others) mercifully.

But what about the words, "Love your enemies…and you will be sons of the Most High"? This sounds like loving your enemies is the condition for being the sons of God rather than the result. It's as if Jesus says, on the one hand: "Love your enemies because God is your Father," and on the other: "Love your enemies in order that God might be your Father."

There is a similar perplexity in John 15:8: "By this my Father is glorified, that you bear much fruit, and become my disciples" (author's translation). He says this even though he has just said that he is the vine and they are the branches (verse 5) and, "You are already made clean by the word which I have spoken to you" (verse 3). So the point is not that we become disciples for the first time by bearing fruit, but that we "become" disciples in the sense of living out what we really are. We become in action and practice what we are by our calling and by our faith.

That is what I think Jesus means in Luke 6:35. "Love your enemies...and you will be sons of the Most High" means "When you act this way, you prove to be chips off the Old Block." That is the way your Father is. So you show that you are born of God. You have his nature. You prove to be his children. What you are by calling and adoption (verse 36) is the ground of what you are becoming in action (verse 35), namely, people who love their enemies.

What then if we don't love our enemies? There is a very sober implication. In that case we do not prove to be "sons of the Most High." This is very serious. Jesus reckons with the real possibility that some of those who hear his commandment to love will not do it and will be like the man who built his house on sand and lost everything in the flood of judgment (Luke 6:49). His professing disciple Judas, for example, traded love for silver.

This does not mean that loving our enemies is what makes God our Father. Having the facial features of your earthly father does not make you his child, but it shows you are his child. So it is with love. It does not make us children of God. Love is the way people act who are born of God (1 John 3:14). Be merciful as your Father is merciful.

So let us be children of God. How? (1) Trust God as your Father to take care of you in all the risks of love; "Your Father knows what you need before you ask him" (Matthew 6:8). (2) Love your enemies and be merciful the way your Father is. ❧

102

TEENAGE RESOLUTIONS IN HONOR OF MOM AND DAD

What I Pray Our Teens Will Say

As I write this, two of my children are through their teen years (twenty-four and twenty-one), two are in them (seventeen and fourteen), and one is twelve years away (one). I prepared these resolutions and presented them to the junior high and senior high groups at our church several years ago. This is my vision of what is possible in the power of Christ's Spirit under the influence of God's Word.

1. *Resolved:* I will obey your instructions and do what I know you expect of me, even when it is not mentioned. I will not force you into repeated reminders, which I sometimes call nagging.

2. *Resolved:* I will not grumble or complain when I do my chores but remember what a great thing it is to have a family, a home, clothes, food, running water, electric lights, and central heating in a world where millions of teenagers have none of these.

3. *Resolved:* When I think your demands are unfair, I will move to do them first, and after showing an obedient attitude, I will ask if we can talk. Then I will explain my side and try to understand yours.

4. *Resolved:* I will not stonewall you and give you the silent treatment, which I dislike when my friends do it to me. If I am depressed and want to be left alone, I will say, "I'm sorry, I don't feel like talking now. Can we talk later? I'm not mad. I just need to be alone."

5. *Resolved*: When I do something wrong and let you down, I will apologize sincerely with words that you can hear. Something like, "Mom, I'm sorry I didn't pick up the pile of clothes."

6. *Resolved*: I will call you by affectionate family titles like "Mommy," "Daddy," "Mom," or "Dad." I won't let other kids pressure me into calling you nothing or calling you something disrespectful as though true affection were embarrassing or childish.

7. *Resolved*: I will say thank you again and again for the ordinary things you do for me. I will not take them for granted as though you were my slave.

8. *Resolved*: I will talk about my feelings. Both the positive ones (like happiness, pity, excitement, and sympathy) and the negative ones (like anger, fear, grief, loneliness, and discouragement). I will remember that unshared feelings lead to estrangement, coldness, and even more loneliness and discouragement.

9. *Resolved*: I will laugh with the family and not at the family. I will especially laugh when my little brother or sister tells a simple joke with expectant excitement.

10. *Resolved*: I will give two compliments for every criticism. And every criticism will aim to help someone improve, not just belittle or cut down.

11. *Resolved*: I will enter into family devotions and treat Bible reading and prayer with respect and do my part to help others in the family enjoy them. When I don't feel spiritually strong, I will pray about this as a personal need rather than pouring it on others as a glass of cold water. I will remember that confessed weakness knits hearts together.

12. *Resolved*: I will not return evil for evil or try to justify my meanness because somebody treated me meanly first.

13. *Resolved*: I will read my Bible and pray every day, even if it is only a verse and a brief call for help. I know that teens cannot live by bread alone but by every word that comes out of the mouth of God.

14. *Resolved*: I will come home at the time we agreed on. If something happens to stop me, I will call and explain and ask your guidance.

15. *Resolved*: I will greet our guests with courtesy and respect and try to make them glad they came.

16. *Resolved*: I will always tell the truth so that you can trust me and give me more and more freedom as I get older.

17. *Resolved*: I will pray for you as long as I live, that we will be united in faith and love, not only now in this world, but for all of eternity in the kingdom of God. ❧

103

DOING WELL
AND DOING BETTER

⟐

Thoughts on the Space of Grace
inside Perfection

O ne way to undergird our efforts to love is to recognize moral gradations inside the bounds of good and evil. In other words, the Bible teaches that there is evil and there is worse evil. The Bible also teaches that there is good and there is better. Sometimes we lose this perspective because we believe that falling short of perfection is sin. How can sin be called good?

Perhaps we define perfection differently than God does. Jesus said, "Be perfect as your heavenly Father is perfect" (Matthew 5:48), but Paul said, "He who marries his betrothed does well; and he who refrains from marriage will do better.... Let him do what he wishes, he does not sin; let her marry" (1 Corinthians 7:38, 36). So you can fall short of doing "better" and still "do well." So is less than "better" sin in this case? No. Paul explicitly says that doing less than better in this case is "not sin."

Is less than "better" a falling short of perfection? Probably, if you define "perfection" in absolute terms, but evidently Paul did not think this way. It seems that "perfection" had some room in it for good and better. It seems that at least sometimes there are several options that may not be sin, even though one may be better than the other. So we must be careful not to overstate the demands of perfection. Even inside perfection, there is good, better, and best.

The same is true of evil. Inside evil there is bad, worse, and worst. This is why Jesus ended one of his parables about the end of the age by saying, "That slave who knew his master's will and did not get ready or act in accord with his will, shall receive many lashes, but the one who did not know it, and committed deeds worthy of a flogging, will receive but few" (Luke 12:47–48). In other words, hell is not a place of invariable suffering. There are gradations of evil and gradations of torment.

That's not my main concern here. My concern here is to caution us about overabsolutizing perfection. Most Christians realize that none of us will attain sinless perfection in this life (Philippians 3:12; 1 John 1:8, 10). That is true. It is also comforting that there is always forgiveness for sinners who bank on Jesus (1 John 1:9). Moreover, most of us also know that there are many gray areas in life where we do not know the ideal course of action and must choose what we hope will do the greatest good when we are quite unsure. It is both frustrating and comforting. We must live with ambiguity, and we are relieved of the burden of omniscience.

But perhaps we are less aware of what I am saying here, which is different but not contradictory. That is, not only will we fall short of the sinlessness demanded in this life, and not only are there gray areas of ambiguity in the choices we make, but also (this is the new thing), even when we don't sin, we may be doing well, better, or best. In other words, not only are there gray areas between good and evil, but there are shades of white inside of the good, and the darker shades of white are not sin (1 Corinthians 7:36).

Knowing this, I say, will help us love as we ought. Why is this? Two reasons. One regards how we think about our own behavior and the other regards how we think about the behavior of others.

With regard to ourselves, we will be spared the paralyzing torture of choosing between total perfection and total failure. There will be space for us to move forward by grace without the presumption of perfection or the despair of utter failure. This will free us from the loveless paralysis of pride and gloom.

With regard to the behavior of others, we will be less given to condemn the lower gradations of good and will be more hopeful that people are on the way, rather than pigeonholing their behavior in inflexible categories of bad or good. "Love hopes all things" (1 Corinthians 13:7). The space of grace inside perfection is a great encouragement to this hope. ❧

104

ONE-ISSUE POLITICS, ONE-ISSUE MARRIAGE, AND THE HUMANE SOCIETY

*Pondering One-Issue Politics and
Cruelty to Animals*

Investigating dog life in Minnesota has solidified my decision to vote against those who endorse the right to abortion. So then, what is my response to the charge of being a one-issue voter?

No endorsement of any single issue qualifies a person to hold public office. Being pro-life does not make a person a good governor, mayor, or president, but there are numerous single issues that disqualify a person from public office. For example, any candidate who endorsed bribery as a form of government efficiency would be disqualified, regardless of his party or platform. Or a person who endorsed corporate fraud (say under fifty million dollars) would be disqualified no matter what else he endorsed. Or a person who said that no black people could hold office—on that single issue alone he would be unfit for office. Or a person who said that rape is only a misdemeanor—that single issue would end his political career. These examples could go on and on. Everybody knows a single issue that for them would disqualify a candidate for office.

It's the same with marriage. No one quality makes a good wife or husband, but some qualities would make a person unacceptable. For example, back when I was thinking about getting married, not liking cats would not disqualify a woman as my wife, but not liking people would. Drinking coffee would not, but drinking whiskey would. Kissing dogs wouldn't, but kissing the mailman would. And so on. Being a single-issue fiancé does not mean that only one issue matters. It means that some issues may matter enough to break off a relationship.

So it is with politics. You have to decide what those issues are for you. What do you think disqualifies a person from holding public office? I believe that the endorsement of the right to kill unborn children disqualifies a person from any position of public office. It's simply the same as saying that the endorsement of racism, fraud, or bribery would disqualify him—except that child killing is more serious than those.

We were buying a dog a few years ago. At the humane society I picked up a brochure on the laws of Minnesota concerning animals. Statute 343.2, subdivision 1, says, "No person shall...unjustifiably injure, maim, mutilate or kill any animal." Subdivision 7 says, "No person shall willfully instigate or in any way further any act of cruelty to any animal." The penalty: "A person who fails to comply with any provision of this section is guilty of a misdemeanor."

This set me to pondering the rights of the unborn. An eight-week-old human fetus has a beating heart, an EKG, brain waves, thumb sucking, pain sensitivity, finger grasping, and genetic humanity, but under our present laws is not a human person with rights under the Fourteenth Amendment, which says that "no state shall deprive any person of life...without due process of law." I wondered, if the unborn do not qualify as persons, it seems that they could at least qualify as animals, say a dog, or at least a cat. Could we not at least charge abortion clinics with cruelty to animals under Statute 343.2, subdivision 7? Why is it legal to "maim, mutilate and kill" a pain-sensitive unborn human being but not an animal?

These reflections have confirmed my conviction never to vote for a person who endorses such an evil—even if he could balance the budget tomorrow and end all taxation. ❧

105

LEARNING FROM A GREAT MAN TO ENJOY FELLOWSHIP WITH GOD

Thoughts on Relating to the Trinity Personally

Not many books have taken me deeper into fellowship with God than John Owen's *Communion with God*. It was written in 1657 by the greatest Puritan pastor-theologian of the seventeenth century.[48] J. I. Packer says, "For solidity, profundity, massiveness and majesty in exhibiting from Scripture God's ways with sinful mankind there is no one to touch him."[49] It is true that Owen is not easy to read, but Packer is right. "The reward to be reaped from studying Owen is worth all the labour involved."[50]

Owen defines communion with God like this: "Our communion, then, with God consisteth in his communication of himself unto us, with our [return] unto him of that which he requireth and accepteth, flowing from that union which in Jesus Christ we have with him" (*Works,* 2.8).

One unique and remarkable thing about this book is Owen's careful illustration of how Christians may have communion with each of the three divine Persons in the Trinity individually as well as with all of them corporately. He says, "There being such a distinct communication of grace from the several persons of the Deity, the saints must needs have distinct communion with them" (page 16).

First he takes us into the pleasures of communion with the Father: "I come now to declare what it is wherein peculiarly and eminently the saints have communion with the Father; and this is love, free, undeserved, and eternal love" (page 19). "Indeed our fellowship is with the Father" (1 John 1:3).

In summary he explains how we enjoy this communion with the Father: "Communion consists in giving and receiving. Until the love of the Father be received, we have no communion with him therein. How, then, is this love of the Father to be received, so as to hold fellowship with him? I answer, By faith. The receiving of it is the believing of it" (page 22). "We have come to know and have believed the love which God has for us" (1 John 4:16). What is this faith? It is "a comfortable persuasion and spiritual perception and sense of his love" (page 23) by which the soul reposes and rests itself in God. This is what I have tried to express in the phrase, faith is "being satisfied with all that God is for us in Jesus."[51]

Then Owen takes us into the communion with the Son. "God is faithful, by whom you were called into the fellowship of his Son, Jesus Christ our Lord" (1 Corinthians 1:9, RSV). The most delectable verse on this fellowship with Jesus is Revelation 3:20: "Behold, I stand at the door and knock; if anyone hears my voice and opens the door, I will come in to him, and will eat with him, and he with me" (RSV).

Owen takes very seriously Jesus' table fellowship with us. What does each of us eat at the table of our hearts? We feed on the spiritual truth and beauty and power of all that Jesus is for us. What does Jesus himself eat at the table of our heart? Owen says, "He refreshes himself with his own graces in [the saints], by his Spirit bestowed on them. The Lord Christ is exceedingly delighted in tasting of the sweet fruits of the Spirit in the saints" (page 40).

Finally Owen takes up our communion with the Holy Spirit, the great Comforter (John 16:7). He says that "the life and soul of all our comforts lie treasured up in the promises of Christ," but he admits that these promises of Christ are "powerless...in the bare letter, even when improved to the uttermost by our considerations of them." However, "sometimes [they] break upon the soul with a conquering, endearing life and vigour," and just at this point "faith deals peculiarly with the Holy Ghost. It considers the promises themselves; looks up to him, waits for him, considers his appearances in the word depended on, owns him in his work and efficacy. No sooner doth the soul begin to feel the life of a promise warming his heart, relieving, cherishing, supporting, delivering from fear, entanglements, or troubles, but it may, it ought, to know that the Holy Ghost is there; which will add to his joy, and lead him into fellowship with him" (page 239, all quotes this paragraph).

O how we need to learn what it is to commune with God—to fellowship with him, Father, Son, and Holy Spirit. It is clear from Owen's insights that the Word of God is the place of communion. God stands forth from his Word. What we long for is God himself. Where shall we meet him? Where does he reveal himself? The answer is given in 1 Samuel 3:21: "The LORD revealed Himself to Samuel at Shiloh by the word of the LORD." The Lord himself is met, and known, and loved, and enjoyed "by the word of the Lord."

For your own soul, come to the fountain of the Word and drink. You will not be alone. ❧

106

THE POWER OF
A FATHER'S DISCIPLINE

———❧———

Memories of John G. Paton's Father

John Paton was a Scottish missionary to the New Hebrides, islands which are today called Vanuatu, located one thousand miles north of New Zealand and four hundred miles west of Fiji. Paton arrived November 5, 1858, on the island of Tanna at the age of thirty-four, with his wife, Mary Ann. A son was born February 12, 1859. "Our island exile filled with joy," Paton wrote in his autobiography[52] (page 79), but "the greatest of sorrows was treading hard upon the heels of that joy!" First came the fever, then diarrhea, then pneumonia and delirium. On March 3 Mary died. "To crown my sorrows, and complete my loneliness, the dear baby boy, whom we had named after her father, Peter Robert Robson, was taken from me after one week's sickness, on the 20th of March" (page 79).

Paton buried both of them with his own hands and "with ceaseless prayers and tears...claimed that land for God." He confessed, "But for Jesus, and the fellowship He vouchsafed me there, I must have gone mad and died beside that lonely grave!" (page 80). What kind of father prepared John G. Paton for that kind of perseverance—another fifty years of rugged, faithful missionary labor?

Paton's father, James, was converted at seventeen and immediately convinced his mother and father that the family should have morning and evening prayer together. Paton writes about his father:

And so began in his seventeenth year that blessed custom of Family Prayer, morning and evening which my father practiced probably without one single avoidable omission till he lay on his deathbed at seventy-seven years of age.... None of us can remember that any day ever passed unhallowed thus; no hurry for market, no rush to business, no arrival of friends or guests, no trouble or sorrow, no joy or excitement, ever prevented at least our kneeling around the family altar, while the High Priest led our prayers to God, and offered himself and his children there. (page 14)

The place of the Lord's Day was just as crucial in shaping the children in their relation to God and the joy of his fellowship. Paton writes:

Our place of worship was the Reformed Presbyterian Church at Dumfries...four miles from our Torthorwald home; but the tradition is that during all these forty years my father was only three times prevented from attending the worship of God.... Each of us, from very early days, considered it no penalty, but a great joy, to go with our father to the church; the four miles were a treat to our young spirits, the company by the way was a fresh incitement.... A few other pious men and women, of the best Evangelical type, went from the same parish...and when these God-fearing peasants 'foregathered' on the way to or from the House of God, we youngsters had sometimes rare glimpses of what Christian talk may be and ought to be. They went to church, full of beautiful expectancy of spirit—their souls were on the outlook for God, and they returned from church, ready and even anxious to exchange ideas as to what they had heard and received of the things of life. (pages 15–16)

There were eleven of us brought up in a home like that; and never one of the eleven, boy or girl, man or woman, has been heard, or ever will be heard, saying that Sabbath was dull or wearisome for us. (page 17)

Such was the father and the family that fit John G. Paton to suffer, survive, and rejoice in the glorious work of the gospel among the cannibalistic tribes of the New Hebrides.

So I ask myself and you, (1) Is my family altar established? Is there a place and a time for family focus on the Word and prayer that takes priority over less important things? (2) Do I come to worship with a beautiful expectancy of spirit on the lookout for God?

One secret of rearing children who endure for fifty years in the New Hebrides is to be a disciplined, Bible-saturated, worshiping, and joyful parent. ❧

107

BEGIN BY BLOWING OUT ALL HIS LAMPS

———

The Light in Samuel Rutherford's Prison

I have never heard anyone say, "The really deep lessons of my life have come through times of ease and comfort." But I have heard strong saints say, "Every significant advance I have ever made in grasping the depths of God's love and growing deep with him has come through suffering."

This is a sobering biblical truth. For example: "For [Christ's] sake I have suffered the loss of all things, and count them as refuse, in order that I may gain Christ" (Philippians 3:8, RSV). Note the words "in order that." Suffering loss is a means to the end of gaining Christ.

Here's another example: "Although he was a Son, Jesus learned obedience through what he suffered" (Hebrews 5:8, RSV). The same book said he never sinned (Hebrews 4:15). So learning obedience does not mean switching from disobedience to obedience. It means growing deeper and deeper with God in the experience of obedience. It means experiencing depths of yieldedness to God that would not have been otherwise demanded. This is what came through suffering.

Do you not love your beloved more when you feel some strange pain that makes you think you have cancer? We are strange creatures indeed. If we have health and peace and time to love, it is a thin and hasty thing. But if we are dying, love is a deep, slow river of inexpressible joy, and we can scarcely endure to give it up.

Samuel Rutherford was a Scottish minister who was born about 1600. After teaching humanities at the University of Edinburgh for a season, he took a theology degree and became the pastor at Anworth in 1627. When the Episcopalians gained power over the Scottish Church, Rutherford was imprisoned two years in Aberdeen for nonconformity. He survived to preach again and to serve on the council that wrote the famous Westminster Confession.

In 1661 he was arraigned again, this time for high treason. He was given the death penalty—all because of his Presbyterian persuasions— but the summons came too late. He received it with a diseased hand and undiminished faith: "Tell them," he said, "that I have a summons already from a superior Judge and judicatory, and I behoove to answer my first summons; and, ere your day arrives, I will be where few kings and great folks come."[53]

When Rutherford was in prison, he was not silent. About 220 letters are preserved from the two years in Aberdeen, and they are perhaps, of all his writings, the most enduring. The spirit conveyed through them is radiant with the glory and all-sufficiency of Christ. On his way to prison he had said, "I go to my King's palace at Aberdeen; tongue, pen, and wit cannot express my joy."[54] This joy overflowed. Taylor Innes said that Rutherford was "impatient of earth, intolerant of sin, rapt into the continual contemplation of one unseen Face, finding his...happiness in its returning smile."[55] His glory was his absorption in Christ. "He went to sleep with Christ as his pillow; he awoke in Christ."[56]

There in prison he made a great discovery about the source of enduring happiness. He expressed it in these stunning words:

> If God had told me some time ago that He was about to make me as happy as I could be in this world, and then had told me that He should begin by crippling me in all my limbs, and removing me from all my usual sources of enjoyment, I should have thought it a very strange mode of accomplishing

His purpose. And yet, how is His wisdom manifest even in this! For if you should see a man shut up in a close room, idolizing a set of lamps and rejoicing in their light, and you wished to make him truly happy, you would begin by blowing out all his lamps; and then throw open the shutters to let in the light of heaven.[57]

O how I pray that when God, in his mercy, begins to blow out my lamps, I will not curse the wind. ☙

108

A Mother's Day
without Noël

On Obeying Proverbs 31:28

Her children rise up and call her blessed;
her husband also, and he praises her.

On Mother's Day, Noël was in Wheaton, Illinois, at her class reunion. I stayed home to preach and play single parent for two and a half days. Since she wasn't around to hear me say nice things about her on Sunday, I thought I would go public with my praises.

Where shall I begin? I missed her at the door after the morning services. One of the people said, "That's a pretty big hole there beside you." That's true. Bigger than anybody knows. Noël's standing beside me on Sunday morning is symbolic of an unwavering support in the ministry.

For example, she guards me again and again. She knows how to make a sandwich for a street person who rings the doorbell. She teaches our children when they may interrupt and when not. She absorbs phone calls and ministers as well as I could to who knows how many needs.

She eases my mind about the four boys and Talitha, caring for them on every hand. There she goes hauling one to a soccer practice. There she is guiding the hand of another to make his Y's frontward and not backward. There she is reading a missionary biography to all of them. I watch with a heart full of thanks to God that Noël is willing to pour so much of her life into the making of four young men and a woman of God.

She virtually never complains. Not about my schedule, about the demands of the ministry—in season and out of season—about my disappearance on Friday and Saturday as I work on the sermon, about late night council meetings, or about "fried" Sunday afternoons or moody Mondays. She is not a complainer. Never once have I felt the least whiff of desire from her that I not be a pastor, even in the darkest times of conflict.

Instead she is an adventurer. She went to Africa and the Philippines with me (and would have stayed too, if the Lord had said, Stay!). Then she went off without me to Guatemala, Japan, China, Hong Kong, and Bangkok—mainly to pray over the cities and strengthen the missionaries. I love this about her.

She puts on no airs. When we have college presidents and the like over for Sunday dinner (which isn't very often), she serves them on paper plates. If necessary, we inform them that this is a sign of friendship and a way of keeping the Sabbath holy after dinner.

She has no hidden agenda. What she says is what she is. I know this now after more than thirty years of being together. She holds no grudges and has an amazing gift for forgetting offenses. Even before the sun goes down, which may be why she goes to sleep in about two minutes. Her mind expends no energy bemoaning mistakes or fretting about tomorrow. "Sufficient unto the day..."

I missed her on Mother's Day. The covenant between us is very deep. One of the boys was writing something for her. He came to me and asked, "Is there a verse about moms?" I said, "Yes. Why don't you use this one: 'Her children rise up and call her blessed; her husband also, and he praises her.'" ❧

109

HAPPINESS IN BEING LOVED AND LOVING BY BEING HAPPY

Thoughts on Leading with Joy and Praying for the Joy of Leaders

There is profound joy in being loved. This feeling is not a superficial zing or fleeting "high." It is rooted in the heart God fashioned and in the truth of Ephesians 2:7. This verse says that the aim of God in saving us is "that in the coming ages he might show the immeasurable riches of his grace in kindness toward us in Christ Jesus" (RSV).

Stay with this for a minute; it's overwhelming. Consider these things. (1) God is graciously disposed to us and intends to show us lavish kindness. He has planned the coming ages for the purpose of showing the immeasurable riches of his grace in kindness toward us. (2) The amount of this grace and kindness is described in terms of "riches" or "wealth," and the degree of the wealth is called "immeasurable." (3) But the "immeasurable wealth of grace" is not like a trust account out of reach in a bank; it is something God intends to "demonstrate" or "show" us. The whole account will be withdrawn and spent on us. (4) The scope and variety of God's kindness toward us is so great that it will not take one age but multiple "coming ages" to accomplish.

This simply means that his kindness will never be exhausted. God will never run out of fresh ways for us to revel in the profound joy of being loved! The wealth of his grace is immeasurable. It will take eternity for him to show us all the kindness he has to show. That is what it means to be God. In him there is always more to know, more to marvel at, and more to enjoy.

This makes me very happy. And it is very important that not only I, but all church leaders, be happy in their work. Or as the Bible says, that we "serve the LORD with gladness" (Psalm 100:2). Why is it so important for us to be happy in the love of God as we do our ministry?

Because the Bible says that a church experiences love through the happiness of its leaders. Consider Hebrews 13:17: "[Your leaders] are keeping watch over your souls, as men who will have to give account. Let them do this joyfully, and not sadly, for that would be of no advantage to you" (RSV).

It is no advantage to a church when the leaders are joyless in their ministry, and for a leader to be of no advantage to a church is an unloving thing. So when elders go about their work sadly, as if the ministry were an oppressive thing, the church experiences less advantage. Therefore it isn't loving for leaders to minister in a gloomy way, because it is no advantage to the church. The church gets its greatest spiritual advantage when its leaders are serving with joy.

So if you love the church of Christ, "which He purchased with His own blood" (Acts 20:28), then I urge you to pray for the happiness of your leaders. And since you know that the deepest and most lasting happiness comes from being loved by God, pray that they would be overwhelmed by the reality of Ephesians 2:7: that God's irrevocable purpose is to spend countless "coming ages...[to] show the immeasurable riches of his grace in kindness toward us in Christ Jesus" (RSV).

Then it will come true that they will be happy in being loved, and you will be loved in their happiness. All this will be from God whose happiness overflows in love to all who hope in him, as it says in Psalm 147:11: "The LORD takes pleasure in those who...hope in his steadfast love" (RSV). ❧

110

YOU ARE NOT ENSLAVED
TO YOUR PAST

—◆◆◆—

Meditation on the Possibility of Change

Christianity means change is possible. Deep, fundamental change. It is possible to become tender-hearted when once you were callous and insensitive. It is possible to stop being dominated by bitterness and anger. It is possible to become a loving person no matter what your background has been.

The Bible assumes that God is the decisive factor in making us what we should be. With wonderful bluntness the Bible says, "Put away malice and be tender-hearted." It does not say, "If you can…" or, "If your parents were tender-hearted to you…" or, "If you weren't terribly wronged or abused…" It says simply, "Be tender-hearted."

This is wonderfully freeing. It frees us from the terrible fatalism that says change is impossible. It frees from mechanistic views that make our backgrounds our destinies.

If I were in prison and Jesus walked into my cell and said, "Leave this place tonight," I might be stunned, but if I trusted his goodness and power, I would feel a rush of hope that freedom is possible. If he commands it, he can accomplish it.

If it is night and the storm is raging and the waves are breaking high over the pier, and the Lord comes and says, "Set sail tomorrow morning," there is a burst of hope in the dark. He is God. He knows what he is doing. His commands are not throw-away words.

His commands always come with freeing, life-changing truth to believe. For example: "Be kind to one another, tender-hearted, forgiving each other [that's the command], just as God in Christ also has forgiven you [that's the life-changing truth]. Therefore be imitators of God [command], as beloved children [life-changing truth]; and walk in love [command], just as Christ also loved you and gave Himself up for us, an offering and a sacrifice to God as a fragrant aroma [life-changing truth]" (Ephesians 4:32–5:2).

There is life-changing power in the truths of this text. Ponder them with me as you pray for that power to change you.

1. God adopted us as his children. We have a new Father and a new family. This breaks the fatalistic forces of our "family of origin." "Do not call anyone on earth your father; for One is your Father, He who is in heaven" (Matthew 23:9). I once heard a young man quote Hebrews 12:10–11 with tears of deep conviction and great joy because they assured him that he was not doomed to think of God in the terms of his abusive earthly father: "They [our earthly fathers] disciplined us for a short time as seemed best to them, but He disciplines us for our good, so that we may share His holiness. All discipline for the moment seems not to be joyful, but sorrowful; yet to those who have been trained by it, afterwards it yields the peaceful fruit of righteousness."

They did this...but he does that. This is a life-changing truth. We can know it, believe it, and be changed by it, no matter what kind of earthly fathers we have. God reveals himself in his word to revolutionize our thinking about his fatherhood. We are not cursed to think in the old categories if our upbringing was defective.

2. God loves us as his children. We are "loved children." The command to imitate the love of God does not hang in the air; it comes with power: "Be imitators of God as loved children." "Love!" is the command. "Being loved" is the power.

3. God has forgiven us in Christ. Be tender-hearted and forgiving just

as God in Christ forgave you. What God did for us becomes the power to change. He forgave us. That opens a relationship of love and a future of hope. And does not tender-heartedness flow from a heart overwhelmed with being loved undeservedly and being secured eternally? The command to be tender-hearted has more to do with what God has done for you than what your mother or father did to you. You are not enslaved to your past.

4. Christ loved you and gave himself up for you. "Walk in love just as Christ loved you." The command to walk in love comes with the life-changing truth that we are loved. At the moment when there is a chance to love, and some voice says, "You are not a loving person," you can say, "Christ's love for me makes me a new kind of person. His command to love is just as surely possible for me as his promise of love is true for me."

My plea is that you resist fatalism with all your might. No, with all God's might. Change is possible. Pursue it until you are perfected at the coming of Christ. ∽

III

REARING CHILDREN
FOR THE WORLD'S END

How Amy Carmichael Got That Way

Amy Carmichael was born December 16, 1867, in the village of Millisle on the north coast of Ireland. After a lifetime of service in India she died, the beloved Amma, with a family of thousands. She was eighty-three years old. They covered her bed with flowers. The boys sang for an hour and a half. It was January 18, 1952.

She had suffered and she had endured to the end. What kind of home had made this remarkable woman? How do you rear a child in a way that makes her free from self-indulgence, rugged in the face of suffering, and ever-confident in the goodness of a chastising Heavenly Father?

Elisabeth Elliot, in her biography of Amy Carmichael, *A Chance to Die*, gives us a glimpse of that remarkable Irish home—"the toughness of Irish Presbyterians, the ruggedness bred by winters on that cold sea, the no-nonsense principles of child rearing."

There was no question in the minds of the Carmichael children as to what was expected of them. Black was black. White was white. Their parents' word could be trusted absolutely, and when it was not obeyed there were consequences. Five kinds of punishment were used: being stood in a corner with one's face to the wall, forbidden to go out to play, slapped, "pandied," and (worst of all) given Gregory powder.[58]

Read the biography to find out about the Gregory powder; I'm interested in the "pandying." A pandy was a stroke with a thin, flat ebony ruler.

The child was required to stand still, to hold out his hand at once and not pull it away, to make no fuss, and finally to say politely, "Thank you, Mother."

There is a great biblical principle behind this punishment of disobedience. Even Ted Koppel of ABC's *Nightline* can see it. Speaking to the graduates at Duke University he said that the reason "Honor thy father and thy mother" was included in the first five commandments (which deal with our relation to God) is that parents stand in the place of God for their children. We are charged by God to show our children what God is like.

"Behold then the kindness and severity of God!" (Romans 11:22). "The Lord disciplines him whom he loves.... It is for discipline that you have to endure" (Hebrews 12:6–7).

Where did Amy Carmichael learn that the blasts and buffetings of her laborious life were at the hand of a no-nonsense God of holiness and love? Where did she learn to say, "Thank you, Father" for the affliction of her hands? Where did she learn to pray like this: "Not relief from pain, not relief from the weariness that follows, not anything of that sort at all, is my chief need. Thou, O Lord my God, art my need—Thy courage, Thy patience, Thy fortitude. And very much I need a quickened gratitude for the countless helps given every day."[59]

Elisabeth Elliot is right: "As the sternness of an Irish winter, with its gloom and wetness and icy winds, puts apple cheeks on both old and young, so the sternness of Christian discipline put red blood—spiritual health—into the girl who could not have imagined then the buffetings she would be called on to endure."[60]

What was Amy's own estimation of this awesome, God-like home? Long afterward she wrote, "I don't think there could have been a happier child than I was."[61] ❧

112

WORDS OF HOPE
FOR A BABY BORN BLIND

———∽∾∽———

A Letter to the Parents

Dear John and Diane,

Last night as I prayed with Noël, you were heavy on my mind. I said, "O Lord, please let me be a pastor who preaches and leads and loves in a way that makes the impossibilities of life possible for your people by a miracle of sustaining grace. Help me to know the weight and pain of this life and not to be breezy when the mountains have fallen into the sea. Help me to have the aroma of Christ's sufferings about me. Prevent shallowness and callousness to pain. O Lord, make me and my people a burden-bearing people."

O John and Diane, I am so heavy with your child's sightlessness! God is visiting Bethlehem with such pain these days in the birth of broken children. Randy and Ann Erickson with their baby's broken heart; Jan and Rob Barrett with their baby's all-too-short one-day life; and your precious little one! Is the Lord saying, "I have a gift for your community"? This is not one or two or three couples' burden. This is a gift and call to the whole church. This is a word concerning the brokenness of this fallen age of futility. This is an invitation for all of us to believe that "here we have no lasting city" (Hebrews 13:14, RSV). This is an invitation for us to count every gain "as loss for the sake of Christ" (Philippians 3:7, RSV). This is a shocking test to see if we will lose heart when, in fact, God's purpose is to show that his grace is sufficient to renew our inner person every day to deal with the "slight momentary affliction [which] is preparing for us an eternal weight of glory beyond all comparison, because we look not to the things that are seen but to the things that are unseen; for the things that are seen are transient, but the things that are unseen are eternal" (2 Corinthians 4:17–18, RSV).

O Lord, open our eyes to your love in this pain. Open our eyes. "Then Elisha prayed, and said, 'O LORD, I pray thee, open his eyes that he may see.' So the LORD opened the eyes of the young man, and he saw; and behold, the mountain was full of horses and chariots of fire round about Elisha" (2 Kings 6:17). John and Diane, the mountains surrounding your lives are filled with the horses and chariots of God. Only to the eyes of unbelief does the devil have the upper hand here. God is at work in ways and for years and generations and millions of people that we cannot now imagine. This is ours to believe and to bear, no matter the cost. This is ours for this short life.

It seems to me that this life is a proving ground for the kingdom to come. Some are asked to devote forty or fifty years to caring for a handicapped child instead of breezing through life without pain. Others are asked to be blind all their lives.

But only in this life—only in this life. I want to be the kind of person who makes that "only" what it really is—very short. Prelude to the infinity of joy, joy, joy—but not yet, not entirely.

How will we ever cope with the burdens of this life if we believe this is all there is, or even that this is the main act in the drama of reality? O Lord, give us your view of things.

May God fill you with anticipated joy!

"I consider that the sufferings of this present time are not worth comparing with the glory that is to be revealed to us" (Romans 8:18, RSV).

I love you,
Pastor John ❧

113

RENDER TO CAESAR THE THINGS THAT ARE CAESAR'S

The Tension of Being Aliens and Heirs

When Jesus said, "Render to Caesar the things that are Caesar's," Tiberius was the Caesar of Rome. He was a good administrator, but of course, not a Christian. He knew no Christian influence at all, since Christianity was born during his reign. So Jesus was calling the Jews to render to a pagan Caesar some kind of honor.

The whole saying goes like this: "Render to Caesar the things that are Caesar's; and to God the things that are God's" (Matthew 22:21). What is God's? Answer: Everything is God's. So the point seems to be: When you realize that all of life, including all of Caesar's rights and power and possessions, are God's, then you will be in a proper frame of mind to render to Caesar what is Caesar's.

When you know that all is God's, then anything you render to Caesar you will render for God's sake. Any authority you ascribe to Caesar you will ascribe to him for the sake of God's greater authority. Any obedience you render to Caesar you will render for the sake of the obedience you owe first and foremost to God. Any claim Caesar makes on you, you test by the infinitely higher claim God has on you.

Rendering to Caesar is limited and defined by rendering to God. What is Caesar's is determined by the fact that everything is God's first and only becomes Caesar's by God's permission and design. Only God decides what is a rightful, limited rendering to Caesar. The only reason God ordains the rights of a Caesar is for the sake of God.

Thus Peter says, "Be subject for the Lord's sake to every human institution, whether it be to the emperor as supreme, or to governors as sent by him" (1 Peter 2:13–14). "For the Lord's sake" is Peter's way of saying, "Everything is God's, and this limits what is Caesar's and how you render it to him." That is, render to Caesar nothing that you cannot render for the Lord's sake.

Peter and Jesus are calling for Christians to have the mind-set of aliens and heirs at the same time. "Live as free people, not using your freedom as a cloak of evil, but being servants of God" (1 Peter 2:16, author's translation). We are God's servants, not the servants of any government. We are free from all governments and human institutions because we belong to the owner of the universe and share, as his children, in that inheritance ("fellow heirs with Christ" [Romans 8:17]). We are aliens in this world, and we are heirs of the owner of the world.

God has made us and bought us for himself (1 Corinthians 6:20). We are slaves of no man and no government (1 Corinthians 7:22–23). Our citizenship is in heaven (Philippians 3:20). We are aliens and exiles on the earth (1 Peter 2:11). We are not "at home" here but await our Lord from heaven.

In this freedom from the world and from Caesar, God sends us for a season back into the "foreign" structures and institutions of society to bear witness that they are not ultimate, but God is. We are to live out the alien ideas of another kingdom in the midst of our earthly homeland. There will always be tension as we live in these two kingdoms, but God sends us into the world and not out.

Beware of rendering too much to Caesar the way Pilate did (John 19:12). When you render to Caesar, do it only "for the Lord's sake." If you cannot, do not. May the Lord give us grace and wisdom to be the salt and light of God in an alien land. ༈

114

BE INSPIRED BY ARISTEIDES

How the Early Christians Loved

About A.D. 133 Aristeides, a teacher of philosophy, presented a defense of Christianity to Emperor Hadrian. From it we get a glimpse of what the early Christians were like and why the church grew the way it did—like wildfire—in those early centuries. Surely this is a fulfillment of the words of Jesus that we should let our lights so shine that men may see our good deeds and give glory to our Father in heaven (Matthew 5:16). O Lord, give us the mantle of these early Christians!

Christ died and was buried; and they say that after three days He rose and ascended to heaven; and then these twelve disciples went forth into all the kingdoms of the world, telling of his greatness with all humility and sobriety; whence they who still serve the righteousness of his preaching are called Christians, who are well known....

Now the Christians, O King...have the commandments of the Lord Jesus Christ himself engraven on their hearts, and they observe, looking for the resurrection of the dead and the life of the world to come. They commit neither adultery nor fornication; nor do they bear false witness. They do not deny a deposit, nor covet other men's goods; they honor father and mother, and love their neighbors; they give right judgment; and they do not worship idols in the form of man. They do not unto others that which they would not have done unto themselves. They comfort such as wrong them, and make friends of them. They labor to do good to their enemies (they are meek and gentle).... As for their servants or handmaids, or their children if any of them has any, they persuade them to become Christians for the love that they have towards them; and when they have become so, they call them without distinction "brethren."

They despise not the widow, and grieve not the orphan. He that hath distributeth liberally to him that hath not. If they see a stranger, they bring him under their roof and rejoice over him, as if it were their own brother; for they call themselves brethren, not after the flesh, but after the spirit and in God.... And if they hear that any of their number is imprisoned or oppressed for the name of their Messiah, all of them provide for his needs, and if it is possible that he may be delivered, they deliver him.

And if there is among them a man that is poor and needy, and they have not an abundance of necessities, they fast two or three days that they may supply the needy with their necessary food. For Christ's sake they are ready to lay down their lives.[62]

So it was spread abroad, "Behold how they love one another." What shall we be known for? Let it be that we are willing to die for Christ and, even more, that we are willing to live for him in loving his people—and his enemies. The early Christians fasted so that they would have more to give to the needy, which means they did not have a lot stored up. O Lord, help us see Christ, be satisfied with Christ, and to show Christ as they did. ❧

THE POWER OF GOD
AND PRO-CHOICE REASONING

———⟐———

Thoughts on a Prison Conversation

For about an hour through the bars of my jail cell (after a rescue in 1989) I talked about abortion with the prison nurse. He had left the Catholic church over birth control and become Presbyterian. He was not willing to talk about getting right with God, but he was willing to talk about my "ludicrous" ideas on abortion.

He knew some of the evil and misery of our society well. He spoke of cocaine babies and AIDS babies. He spoke of the women in prison who were pregnant again and again, and usually on drugs. He spoke of the twenty-three children per month at St. Joseph's Home, pulled from abusive or drug homes, but not up for adoption because you have to have the parents' authorization for adoption. Abortion, he said, at least relieves some of this misery. To which I responded, "Killing innocent people is not a good way to relieve misery."

At first he said, "You people always use emotional language like 'killing,'" but before the hour was over he had conceded almost everything. He was willing to say, yes, the unborn are human persons; abortion is killing a child; abortion diminishes the value of life; abortion leads to euthanasia and fetal tissue experimentation; abortion is wrong; and "I wouldn't get one for my wife." Yet he insisted that the right of a woman to abort must be protected at virtually all costs.

What could I say? No arguments could touch him. He had conceded all the facts that I thought would lead to a pro-life position. The unborn are human persons. Aborting them is killing. It is even wrong. But none of this carried any weight against one overriding article of faith in his mind: The right of women to choose abortion functions in his mind as an absolute—it is not debatable. It is an article of faith. He even said, "This is my belief" in a very solemn way.

I was mystified. I asked, "Is there any other area of life in which you admit the human personhood of someone but give other persons the absolute right to treat that person any way they please, even to the point of killing?" He said, "No. Only here." "But why?" I marveled. "It's my belief," he said. The woman's "right to choose" (to have her child killed) is the supreme and ultimate value. It cannot be touched by any reasoning or any facts. It is god.

When he walked away I lay there stunned at the power and irrationality of evil. There was no getting through. Child killing (he allowed the phrase!) is permissible if the child is in the womb. He justified that position with the absolute, unassailable, supreme right of a woman to do as she wishes with her "pregnancy," that is, the child.

What this encounter has caused me to think about again and again is the need for divine power in evangelism and social engagement. Paul said, "The weapons of our warfare are not fleshly but are powerful in God for the tearing down of strongholds. We tear down arguments and every proud obstacle to the knowledge of God, and take every thought captive to obey Christ" (2 Corinthians 10:3–5, author's translation).

What sort of power might break through and wake up this nurse and win his obedience to Christ? Romans 15:18–19: "I will not venture to speak of anything except what Christ has wrought through me to win obedience from the Gentiles, by word and deed, by the power of signs and wonders, by the power of the Holy Spirit" (RSV). ❧

When Does
God Answer Prayer?

Meditation on 1 John 3:22–23

*We receive from him whatever we ask,
because we keep his commandments and do what pleases him.
And this is his commandment, that we should believe in the name of
his Son Jesus Christ and love one another,
just as he has commanded us.* (RSV)

John says that God answers prayers for people who keep his commandments. Then he sums up the commandments in one commandment (singular) which he defines as two (they are so interwoven he treats them as one):

1. Believe in the name of God's Son, Jesus Christ
2. Love one another

So God answers the prayers of people who believe in his Son and who love each other. People might take this to mean two very different things. For example, some might take it to mean that believing Jesus and loving people are ways to earn answers to prayer. This would be wrong for two reasons.

It would be wrong because I cannot earn anything by believing. Earning is a way of showing my worth and putting God in debt to me. That cannot be done. God already owns everything; any worth I have is a gift from him. I can't earn from a God like that. If I want his gifts, I must believe they are better than any other gifts and then trust him to give them freely to those who look to him and not to the world for help.

Second, loving people cannot earn God's blessing, because love is the fruit of trusting God (Galatians 5:6) and the result of God's work in us, not our self-reliant work for him. John plainly teaches that love is the evidence of the gift of life, not the earning of the wage of life: "We know that we have passed out of death into life, because we love the brethren" (1 John 3:14, RSV).

What then does John mean when he says that God answers prayers for people who believe in his Son and who love each other?

I think he means something like this: Prayer has a specific purpose. God designed it in wisdom to fit his perfect way of working in the world. If you misuse it, it malfunctions. What then is the design of prayer? I think these verses show that prayer is designed by God to be the effect of faith and the cause of love.

Therefore if we try to pray when we really do not believe in the name of God's Son, or if we try to pray when our aim is not love, prayer malfunctions.

"We receive from him whatever we ask, because we keep his commandments." This does not mean that keeping his commandments earns answers to prayer; it means prayer is designed to give power in the path of obedience. That is what it is for. Prayer is God's way of making himself available for us when we are pouring ourselves out in love for others. Prayer is the power to love. Therefore if we do not aim to love, we pray in vain. Prayer is not designed to compound hoarded pleasures.

Not only that, prayer is meant to be the effect of faith. Believing in the name of Jesus means that we are satisfied with the way he is and what he offers. We receive, admire, and delight in what we see in his life and word. We stake our lives on his promises. Prayer comes from this faith. We see the promise that God will be for us all we need in Jesus, and we are moved to call on him for joy and peace and power to do his gracious will. So prayer comes from being satisfied with all that God promises to be for us in Jesus. Which means prayer is the effect of faith. Where there is no faith in the name of Jesus, prayer is driven by an alien power and will malfunction.

The link between faith and love explains why these two are a single condition for answered prayer. "This is his commandment [singular!], [1] that we should believe in the name of his Son Jesus Christ and [2] love one another." Believing in Jesus is being satisfied with all that God is for us in him, and the power to love is one of the glorious things that God is for us in Jesus. So when faith drives prayer, it drives it in the path of love. If prayer turns out of the path of love, we know that faith is no longer driving, and we know why prayer malfunctions.

Another way to say this is that prayer is a way of calling God alongside us to enable us to do what Jesus came to do, namely, love others at the cost of his life. "By this we know love, that he laid down his life for us; and we ought to lay down our lives for the brethren" (1 John 3:16, RSV). This is why believing in the name of Jesus and loving others are linked as the pathway to answered prayers. Being satisfied with such a Savior and loving as he loved are almost one thing.

Since God was entirely behind Jesus with all his power and gave him all the help he needed, he will be behind us, too, when we believe in Jesus and love like Jesus. So the reason God answers the prayers of those who believe in the name of Jesus and love others like Jesus is that God loves to magnify Jesus. ❧

117

THE POWER OF BOOKS AND
HOW TO USE THEM

~~~

Thoughts on Reading to Each Other Out Loud

The Bible is a book. It has changed the world. Some uninspired books have also done tremendous good for the cause of God and truth. Some classic biographies, for example, have fueled the fire of missions for hundreds of years, like Jonathan Edwards's *Life of David Brainerd*.

Let me suggest something to do with books and friends that you may never have done before. Evidently it was the custom of the pastors of the Northamptonshire Baptist Association in England in the late 1700s to meet periodically for prayer, fasting, and reading to each other.

For example, John Ryland's diary from January 21, 1788, says, "Brethren Fuller, Sutcliffe, Carey and I, kept this day as a private fast, in my study; read the Epistles to Timothy and Titus, Booth's *Charge* to Hopkins, Blackerby's *Life* in Gillies' *Historical Collections* and Rogers of Dedham's *Sixty Memorials for a Godly Life*, and each prayed twice. Carey with singular enlargement and pungency. Our chief design was to implore a revival in the power of godliness in our own souls, in the Churches, and in the Church at large."

Their aim was not recreation, but spiritual warfare and strategy. Reading to each other was part of the tactics.

On another occasion, another member of this fellowship of mission-minded Baptists, Andrew Fuller, wrote in his diary, "Read to our friends this evening a part of Mr. Edwards's *Attempt to Promote Prayer for the Revival of*

Religion to excite them to the like practice. Felt my heart profited, and much solemnized by what I read."

We have done this as a pastoral staff at our church. I photocopied a chapter from David Brainerd's diary and a chapter from a biography of Ann Judson (Adoniram's wife). We went on an overnight retreat and for two hours together that evening we read these to each other, one page each, around the circle until we were done.

It was a powerful experience. Brainerd's chapter led us into one of the most intense times of prayer we have ever had together. We heartily recommend the practice to other groups.

It is crucial that you read rich, God-centered material, not just anything under the name Christian. Let me mention some examples. Matthew Henry, who died in 1714, wrote a commentary on the whole Bible in six large volumes. George Whitefield used to read from this commentary on his knees along with the Greek New Testament. It is a rich and perceptive devotional commentary, as good for your heart as for your head.

I'm tempted to start listing my favorite books, but that would be too lopsided and narrow. It is not my point to promote a particular group of books, but to commend public reading in groups. If you have a small group and you are trying to read a good book together and discuss it, but you are all having trouble finding the time to read the chapter for the week, why not plan to spend the first hour just reading to each other?

Really good writing is a benefit to hear as well as read. God gave us his Word in a book, the Bible, but he also appointed preaching and teaching. There is something about the living voice that quickens the truth and brings it home to us. You may find more power in your mouth than you dreamed, and your ears may open in ways that will change your life. ❧

118

DOES THE ANCHOR
OF MY SOUL DANGLE OUT
OF HEAVEN?

Meditation on Hebrews 6:18–20

We who have fled for refuge
have strong encouragement to take hold of the hope set before us.
This hope we have as an anchor of the soul,...
both sure and steadfast and one which enters within the veil,
where Jesus has entered as a forerunner for us,
having become a high priest forever according to
the order of Melchizedek.

God means for our souls to be anchored to heaven. He does not want us to bob and drift on the sea of opinion, culture, trend, and passion. He wants us to know our position on the coast and be safe from dashing on the rocks. So he has given us an "anchor of the soul" (Hebrews 6:19). It is "sure and steadfast." Strangely, it enters within the veil, where Christ has entered as a high priest.

What does that mean? The veil was the divider between the outer sanctuary of the Old Testament tabernacle and the inner holy of holies, where God met once a year with the high priest who took the blood of animals to make atonement for the people. The writer of Hebrews saw this as an earthly picture of a heavenly reality. Now, in reality, Christ has entered once for all into the heavenly holy of holies as our high priest, not with the blood of animals, but with his own blood and with the power of an indestructible life. There he lays claim, by his blood and righteousness, to the eternal joy promised to all God's people.

So the anchor of our soul is the absolutely certain hope of eternal joy with God which Jesus has secured by his priestly work in the holy of holies. Or to see it another way, the anchor of our souls is hooked and tied around the ark of the covenant and held there firmly by God's omnipotent hand as a reward of his Son's sacrifice for us. So we are as secure as the blood of Christ is precious.

Now the question: Does the other end of the anchor rope dangle out of heaven and lay limp and unfastened across the deck of our souls? Or did Christ's blood purchase security at both ends of the anchor? Is the anchor of our souls bound as firmly to us as it is to heaven? Does the death of Christ secure salvation at the top and not at the bottom? Is there security on God's side and none on ours?

The answer of the Book of Hebrews is that the anchor is secure at both ends. Yes, we must hold fast to the anchor, but the good news is that our holding fast was secured by the blood of Jesus. We know this because the blood of Jesus is the blood of the new covenant, and what the new covenant promised was that God would secure our salvation at the top and the bottom. The new covenant promised that God would not only forgive and accept those who love him (Jeremiah 31:34), but also that he would see to it that we love him (Deuteronomy 30:6), walk in his statutes (Ezekiel 36:27), and fear him and not turn away from him (Jeremiah 32:40).

When Jesus died he purchased by his blood the promises of the new covenant. "This cup," he said at the last supper, "is the new covenant in [or by] my blood" (Luke 22:20, RSV). Hebrews 13:20 calls it the "blood of the eternal covenant." Then, as a fulfillment of the new covenant, the next verse says that God will "work in us that which is pleasing in his sight through Jesus Christ." In other words, our "holding fast to our hope" is something that God "works in us through Jesus Christ." The words "through Jesus Christ" mean that Jesus Christ bought this blessing for us. This is part of our salvation purchased at Calvary. Jesus obtained our security at the top and the bottom.

The anchor is bound in heaven and secured in my soul. The rope does not dangle in my face and lie limp across the deck of my soul. God, by his Holy Spirit, takes up the rope and ties it to the little ship of my weak and vulnerable soul with unbreakable, sovereign covenant love. This was promised in the new covenant and purchased by the blood of Jesus.

But now someone asks, Why then does the writer of Hebrews exhort us to "hold fast to our hope" (6:18)? If our holding fast was obtained and irrevocably secured by the blood of Jesus, then why does God tell us to hold fast?

The answer is this: What Christ bought for us when he died was not the freedom from having to hold fast, but the enabling power to hold fast. What he bought was not the nullification of our wills (as though we didn't have to hold fast), but the empowering of our wills because we want to hold fast. What he bought was not the canceling of the commandment to hold fast, but the fulfillment of the commandment to hold fast. What he bought was not the end of exhortation, but the triumph of exhortation. It is not foolishness, it is the gospel, to exhort dead and helpless sinners to do what only grace can enable them to do: lay hold on hope in God. ❧

119

THE GREAT "THEREFORE" OF
THE RESURRECTION

---*∾*---

Pondering the Consequences of Ideas

Victor Frankl was imprisoned in the Nazi concentration camps of
Auschwitz and Dachau during the Second World War. As a Jewish
professor of neurology and psychiatry he became world
renowned for his book, *Man's Search for Meaning*, which sold more than
eight million copies. In it he unfolds the essence of his philosophy that came
to be called Logotherapy—namely, that the most fundamental human
motive is to find meaning in life. He observed in the horrors of the camps
that man can endure almost any "how" of life if he has a "why," but there is
a less well-known quote that may be just as profound: "I am absolutely convinced that the gas chambers of Auschwitz, Treblinka, and Maidanek were
ultimately prepared not in some ministry or other in Berlin, but rather at the
desks and in the lecture halls of nihilistic scientists and philosophers."[63]

In other words, ideas have consequences that bless or destroy. People's
behavior—good and bad—does not come from nowhere. It comes from
prevailing views of reality that take root in the mind and bring forth good
or evil. This is why some of us put such a high premium on teaching. It is
why we preach the way we do and care so deeply about issues of truth.

One of the ways that the Bible makes plain the truth that ideas have
practical consequences is by saying things like, "Whatever was written in
earlier times was written…that…we might have hope" (Romans 15:4). The
ideas presented in the Scriptures produce the practical consequence of

hope. Again, Paul says, "The goal of our instruction is love" (1 Timothy 1:5). The imparting of ideas by "instruction" is meant to produce love. Hope and love do not come from nowhere. They grow out of ideas—views of reality—revealed in the Scriptures and applied in the power of God's Spirit.

Another way the Scriptures show us that ideas have consequences is by using the word "therefore" (1,039 times in the NASB). For example, "Therefore, having been justified by faith, we have peace with God through our Lord Jesus Christ" (Romans 5:1). "Therefore, there is now no condemnation for those who are in Christ Jesus" (Romans 8:1). "Therefore, do not be anxious for tomorrow" (Matthew 6:34). "Therefore, do not fear; you are of more value than many sparrows" (Matthew 10:31). "Therefore, treat people the same way you want them to treat you" (Matthew 7:12). "Therefore let us not judge one another anymore" (Romans 14:13). "Therefore do not let sin reign in your mortal body" (Romans 6:12). "Therefore glorify God in your body" (1 Corinthians 6:20). "Therefore whether we live or die, we are the Lord's" (Romans 14:8).

Every one of these great "therefores" flows from a view of reality. If we want to live in the power of these great practical "therefores," we must be gripped by the ideas—the views of reality—that go before them and support them.

One of the most important ideas in the universe is found in 1 Corinthians 15:51–58—the resurrection and a precious "therefore" that flows from it: "Behold, I tell you a mystery, we will not all sleep, but we will all be changed, in a moment, in the twinkling of an eye, at the last trumpet.... 'O death, where is your victory? O death, where is your sting?' The sting of death is sin, and the power of sin is the law; but thanks be to God, who gives us the victory through our Lord Jesus Christ. Therefore, my beloved brethren, be steadfast, immovable, always abounding in the work of the Lord, knowing that your toil is not in vain in the Lord."

The greatest vision of reality—the greatest idea—is Christ triumphant over sin, guilt, death, and hell. O to be utterly gripped and guided by this great ground of steadfastness! ᴗ

120

ALL THE ANGELS
ARE COMING WITH HIM

⟨∿∿⟩

Meditation on Matthew 25:31–46

I t has been thrilling to me to read again in Matthew the sequence of events and sayings in Jesus' final days on earth. Two back-to-back sayings of the Lord stunned me a few days ago. Sometimes familiar things become fresh and powerful by being seen in a new relationship.

At the end of Matthew 25 there is the parable of the sheep and the goats. Picture Jesus, who looked as ordinary as any other man, beginning this parable with these astonishing words, "When the Son of man comes in his glory, and all the angels with him, then he will sit on his glorious throne. Before him will be gathered all the nations, and he will separate them one from another as a shepherd separates the sheep from the goats, and he will place the sheep at his right hand, but the goats at the left. Then the King will say…" (verses 31–34, RSV).

Let these words sink in. First let's nail down who the Son of Man is. There is no doubt. In Matthew 16:13 Jesus had said, "Who do men say that the Son of man is?" and then two verses later he said, "But who do you say that I am?" There it is. Jesus is the Son of Man. It was one of his favorite titles for himself. There was hidden in it the mystery of his humanness and his heavenly dignity, because in Daniel 7:13–14 "one like a son of man" in heaven was to receive an eternal kingdom from God.

Now let it sink in what Jesus said about himself in Matthew 25:31–33:

"He will come someday in glory." This glory is not the mere glory of a sunset or the Grand Canyon or a great comet or the universe. This is the glory of God—as Matthew 16:27 says, "the glory of his Father." If the creation has glory that stops our mouths with its waterfalls, ravines, snow-capped Rockies, and star-sheeted night skies, then the glory of the One who conceived and created it all will put all that in the shade. The Son of Man is coming with that glory.

"And all the angels with him." All of them. Did you get that? Heaven will be left empty of its armies. All the angels will be with him! This means that the triumph is so sure that one doesn't have to cover his rear guard. No one will threaten heaven. All the armies of God will be on the front line with the Son of Man. Jesus could handle the conquest of earth alone—he is God—but the angels come to magnify him and do his bidding. What is that bidding? Just this: "He will send out his angels with a loud trumpet call, and they will gather his elect from the four winds." They are going to gather you and me to meet the Son of Man.

"Then, he will sit on his glorious throne." He is on a throne because he is King. "Then the King will say…" Jesus is king of the universe now. He rules all and upholds all (Matthew 28:18; Colossians 1:17). But when he comes, this kingship will be plain to everyone in Minneapolis and Moscow and Madras.

"Before him will be gathered all the nations." Jesus, the Son of Man, the King of the universe, will sit on his throne, and every people and every president and chief and prime minister and premier and king on earth will gather and say, "Jesus is Lord," to the glory of God the Father. When the elect are gathered, and the king sits in glorious judgment, then will be fulfilled the words of the prophet, "Nations shall come to your light, and kings to the brightness of your rising" (Isaiah 60:3, RSV).

Then suddenly after this parable I read in the very next verses: "When Jesus had finished all these sayings, he said to his disciples, 'You know that after two days the Passover is coming, and the Son of man will be delivered up to be crucified.'" Same Son of Man. Delivered up and crucified. Did you ever wonder what joy and hope sustained Jesus in those horrific hours of suffering?

He is risen and he is coming. In the meantime, "Let us go forth to him outside the camp and bear the abuse he endured" (Hebrews 13:13, RSV). ❧

NOTE ON RESOURCES
DESIRING GOD MINISTRIES

The reader who wants to ponder further the vision of God and life presented in this curriculum may be interested in the resources provided by Desiring God Ministries (DGM)—an extension of Bethlehem Baptist Church in Minneapolis, Minnesota. DGM exists to spread a passion for the supremacy of God in all things for the joy of all peoples by:

1. producing and distributing resources for the wider Christian church that promote the vision that *God is most glorified in us when we are most satisfied in him;* and

2. appealing to non-Christians to hope in God and be satisfied with all that he is for them in Jesus.

We make all of John Piper's books available at a significant discount, and we are continually producing new audio tape, article, and manuscript collections from our archives, containing over twenty years of Dr. Piper's preaching and writing ministry. At your request we would be happy to send you a free resource catalog. We are equipped to accept VISA, MasterCard, and Discover if you would like to place your order over the phone.

Whatever You Can Afford!

Our goal at DGM is not to make money. Our goal is to make the treasure of the gospel as accessible to you as possible. The suggested prices in our catalog help to cover our costs, but we offer all of our resource on a whatever-you-can-afford basis. We won't allow money to be a barrier to those who wish to receive biblical teaching for their personal use. Don't be afraid to use this policy!

FOR MORE INFORMATION:

TOLL FREE	1-888-346-4700
ON THE WEB	www.DesiringGod.org
E-MAIL	DGMinistry@aol.com
WRITE	Desiring God Ministries
	Bethlehem Baptist Church
	720 13th Avenue South
	Minneapolis, Minnesota 55415-1793
	1-612-338-7653

NOTES

PREFACE

1. C. S. Lewis, *The Weight of Glory* (Grand Rapids: Wm. B. Eerdmans Publishing Co., 1965), 1–2.

2. Quoted from Augustine's *Confessions,* Book VIII, in Peter Brown, *Augustine of Hippo: A Biography* (Berkeley, Calif.: University of California Press, 1967), 108–9.

INTRODUCTION

1. Quoted in Daniel Fuller, "I Was Just Thinking," in *Today's Christian,* September 1977.

2. Calvin says this (quoting Augustine's *Letters* 143.2) in the introduction to the *Institutes of the Christian Religion,* vol. 1 (Philadelphia: Westminster Press, 1960), 5.

3. Quoted from his *Autobiography* in Iain Murray, *The Forgotten Spurgeon* (Edinburgh: Banner of Truth Trust, 1973), 34.

4. Jonathan Edwards, *Personal Narrative,* in *Jonathan Edwards, Selections* (New York: Hill and Wang, 1962), 59, 67.

5. Augustine, quoted from the *Confessions,* in *Documents of the Christian Church,* ed. Henry Bettenson (London: Oxford University Press, 1967), 54.

READINGS

1. All the quotes in this reading are taken from Mark Noll, "The Struggle for Lincoln's Soul," in *Books and Culture,* vol. 1, no. 1, September/October 1995, 3–6.

2. For a fuller development of the concept of future grace, see John Piper, *The Purifying Power of Living by Faith in Future Grace* (Sisters, Ore.: Multnomah Press, 1995).

3. For more information on street children, write Action International Ministries, P.O. Box 490, Bothell, WA 98041–0490.

4. Ernest Reisinger, "Every Christian a Publisher," *Free Grace Broadcaster,* no. 51 (winter 1995): 17.

5. Ibid., 18.

6. Charles Hodge, *Commentary on the Second Epistle to the Corinthians* (Grand Rapids: Wm. B. Eerdmans Publishing Co., n.d.), 133.

7. Ibid., 136.

8. Ibid., 133.

9. One powerful Christian voice and action for these children is Action International Ministries, from whom I took the statistics. See note 3.

10. C. S. Lewis, *Beyond Personality* (New York: Macmillan Co., 1948), 21–2.

11. Quoted in C. S. Lewis, ed., *George MacDonald: An Anthology* (London: Geoffrey Bles and Centenary Press, 1946), 36.

12. The observations and quotations are adapted from J. Edwin Orr, *The Flaming Tongue: The Impact of 20th Century Revivals* (Chicago: Moody Press, 1973), 70–81.

13. This quote and the others preceding it are taken from Iain Murray, *Australian Christian Life: An Introduction and an Anthology* (Edinburgh: Banner of Truth Trust, 1988), 259, 255.

14. "California redwoods make me think of England's Puritans, another breed of giants." J. I. Packer, *A Quest for Godliness: The Puritan Vision of the Christian Life* (Wheaton, Ill.: Crossway Books, 1990), 11.

15. Quoted in Peter Toon, *God's Statesman: The Life and Work of John Owen* (Exeter, Devon: Paternoster Press, 1971), 55.

16. A. Thomson, *Life of Dr. Owen,* in *The Works of John Owen,* vol. 1 (Edinburgh: The Banner of Truth Trust, 1965), lxiv–lxv.

17. John Owen, *The Glory of Christ,* in ibid., 275.

18. Robert Coleman, *The Master Plan of Discipleship* (Old Tappan, N.J.: Fleming H. Revell Co., 1987), 55.

19. Ibid., 57.

20. Ibid., 56.

21. Daniel Yankelovich, *New Rules: Searching for Self-Fulfillment in a World Turned Upside Down* (New York: Random House, 1981), 237.

22. Charles Spurgeon, "God's Providence," Sermon on Ezekiel 1:15–19 in *Spurgeon's Sermons,* 2d series (New York: Robert Carter and Brothers, 1883), 201.

23. H. C. G. Moule, *Charles Simeon* (1892; reprint, London: InterVarsity Fellowship, 1942), 65f.

24. The reading "prayer and fasting" is not in the best manuscripts and was probably added by a scribe.

25. This is an appendix in John Piper, *Desiring God* (Sisters, Ore.: Multnomah Press, 1996), 267–76.

26. Lewis Smedes, *Love within Limits* (Grand Rapids: Wm. B. Eerdmans Publishing Co., 1978).

27. Paul Johnson, *Intellectuals* (New York: Harper and Row, 1988), 52.

28. Mark Noll, *The Princeton Theology* (Grand Rapids: Baker Book House, 1983), 18.

29. Martin Lloyd-Jones, *Revival* (Westchester, Ill.: Crossway Books, 1987), 93.

30. Ibid., 99–100.

31. Ibid., 100.

32. Ibid., 101.

33. Ibid., 101–3.

34. Jonathan Edwards, *Religious Affections*, in *The Works of Jonathan Edwards*, vol. 2 (1746; reprint, New Haven: Yale University Press, 1959), 247.

35. Ibid., 250–1.

36. For many examples of this, with extended reflection, see John Piper, "Are There Two Wills in God? Divine Election and God's Desire for All to Be Saved," in *The Grace of God, The Bondage of the Will,* ed. Thomas Schreiner and Bruce Ware (Grand Rapids: Baker Book House, 1995), 107–32.

37. For example, Gregory Boyd says, "So God can't foreknow the good or bad decisions of people He creates until He creates these people and they, in turn, create their decisions" (*Letters to a Skeptic* [Grand Rapids: Victor Books, 1994], 30). Another example is: "All that God does not know is the content of future free decisions, and this is because decisions are not there to know until they occur" (Richard Rice, "Divine Foreknowledge and Free Will," in *The Grace of God, the Will of Man: A Case for Arminianism,* ed. Clark Pinnock [Grand Rapids: Zondervan Publishing House, 1989], 134). Clark Pinnock argues for this viewpoint as well: "Decisions not yet made do not exist anywhere to be known even by God.... God can predict a great deal of what we will choose to do, but not all of it, because some of it remains hidden in the mystery of human freedom" (idem, 25). See my response to Pinnock, Rice, and Boyd in *The Pleasures of God* (Sisters, Ore.: Multnomah Press, 1991), 70–4, note 6.

38. Westminster Larger Catechism, Question 14.

39. These three quotes are from *Christianity Today,* 23 November 1992, 24.

40. Quoted in Lewis, ed., *George MacDonald,* 107.

41. Quoted in Thomas J. Nettles, *By His Grace and for His Glory: A Historical, Theological, and Practical Study of the Doctrines of Grace in Baptist Life* (Grand Rapids: Baker Book House, 1986), 153.

42. Ibid., 149.

43. Anthony Hoekema, *The Bible and the Future* (Grand Rapids: Wm. B. Eerdmans Publishing Co., 1979), 259.

44. Quoted in Stephen Neill, *A History of Christian Missions* (Harmondsworth, England: Penguin Books, 1964), 42.

45. Ibid., 43.

46. Quoted from John Bunyan's *Grace Abounding,* in Rebecca Beal, "Pulling Flesh from My Bones," *Christian History* 5 no. 3:14.

47. I have tried to deal with this in greater detail in *The Pleasures of God* (Sisters, Ore.: Multnomah Press, 1991), 63–9.

48. If you would like to listen to a biographical lecture I gave on the life and ministry of John Owen, you may order it from Desiring God Ministries (for information, see the back of this book). If you would like to read *Communion with God*, it is available in *The Works of John Owen*, vol. 2 (Edinburgh: Banner of Truth Trust, 1965), as well as in a Puritan Paperback from the same publisher.

49. Packer, *A Quest for Godliness*, 81.

50. Ibid., 147.

51. See especially, Piper, *Future Grace*, 209ff.

52. John G. Paton, *The Autobiography of John G. Paton* (Edinburgh: Banner of Truth, 1965).

53. Quoted in Alexander Smellie, *Men of the Covenant* (London: Andrew Melrose, 1905), 50.

54. Ibid., 53.

55. Ibid., 56.

56. Ibid.

57. Quoted in E. M. Bounds, *Heaven: A Place, a City, a Home* (Grand Rapids: Baker Book House, 1975), 13.

58. Elisabeth Elliot, *A Chance to Die: The Life and Legacy of Amy Carmichael* (Old Tappan, N. J.: Fleming H. Revell Co., 1987), 21.

59. Ibid., 365.

60. Ibid., 26.

61. Ibid.

62. Quoted in J. Stevenson, *A New Eusebius* (London: SPCK, 1968), 56–7.

63. "Victor Frankl at Ninety: An Interview," in *First Things*, April 1995, 41.

SUBJECT INDEX

Abortion
    abominating, 239-240
    and saving sinners, 205-206
    as anarchy, 184-186
    horrors of hell and, 205-206
    one-issue politics, 279-280
    problem of preemies, 258-259
    pro-choice reasoning, 305-306
    why the right to is unjust, 226-227

Advertising with sex, 117-119

Affections, see Emotions

Affliction, see Pain

Aging
    resolutions on, 134-136

Assurance
    anchor of my soul, 312-314
    for tomorrow's trouble, 25
    necessity of practical righteousness,
        255-257

Astronomy and God, 53, 235-236

Atheism
    making room for, 62-64

Bangladesh, 268-270

Bethlehem Baptist Church mission statement, 18, 62

Bible
    Bunyan bleeds Bible, 17
    calls for human teachers, 16
    importance of learning to read, 81-83
    man of one book, 16
    wielding it as weapon, 56-57

Blindness and hope, 299-300

Books, how to use them, 310-311

Calvinism, in ministry of Adoniram Judson,
    230-232

Change
    in history ever-similar, 210-212
    is possible in your life, 294-296

Children
    baby born blind, 299-300
    caring about, 65-67
    how Amy Carmichael got that way,
        297-298
    nursery work, 140-141
    of promise, not flesh, 233-234
    rearing them for world's end, 297-298

    receiving Jesus in children, 140-141
    street kids, 40-41

Christ
    born to die for our freedom, 157-159
    death of, for us, 20-21
    his cross, my power, 153-154
    playing the lottery, 169-170
    power over all things, 86-88
    second coming, 317-319
    why believe in his resurrection, 166-168
    works for us, 29

Christian hedonism and defense of doctrine, 47-49

Christian, what is one, 60-61

Church growth
    why early church grew, 252-254

Communion with God, 281-283

Conditionality of salvation, 271-272

Condom ads, 162-163

Contracts, see Oaths

Conversion
    how to obey the command to be born,
        249-251
    to Christianity, 60-61
    St. Augustine's, 13

Covenant of works, 171-173

Covenants, see Oaths

Cross
    my liberty and power, 153-154
    taking it up with Christ, 147-149

Death
    already on earth, 147-149
    freedom from fear of, 157-159
    great gain, 50-52

Debtor's ethic, 36-37

Depression, 89-90

Desire
    as thirst for God, 84-85
    on the stretch for God, 128-130

Devotions, discipline and spontaneity, 56-57

Discipline
    a father's, 284-286
    demanded and given, 38-39
    of children, 297-298
    and spontaneity, 56-57

Doctrine, see Truth

PERSON INDEX

SCRIPTURE INDEX